Lennon
THE NEW YORK YEARS

Become our fan on Facebook **facebook.com/idwpublishing**
Follow us on Twitter **@idwpublishing**
Subscribe to us on YouTube **youtube.com/idwpublishing**
See what's new on Tumblr **tumblr.idwpublishing.com**
Check us out on Instagram **instagram.com/idwpublishing**

COVER ART BY
HORNE

ISBN: 978-1-63140-879-3
20 19 18 17   1 2 3 4

PRODUCTION & DESIGN BY
ROBBIE ROBBINS

EDITORIAL ASSISTANCE BY
ALONZO SIMON AND
SARAH J. DUFFY

PUBLISHED BY
TED ADAMS

LENNON: THE NEW YORK YEARS. FIRST PRINTING.
MAY 2017. Translation and Lettering © 2017 Idea and
Design Works, LLC. Artwork and Adaptation ©
Hachette Livre (Marabout), Paris, 2015. "Lennon"
Story © David Foenkinos, 2010. All Rights Reserved.
The IDW logo is registered in the U.S. Patent and
Trademark Office. IDW Publishing, a division of Idea
and Design Works, LLC. Editorial offices: 2765
Truxtun Road, San Diego, CA 92106. Any similarities
to persons living or dead are purely coincidental.
With the exception of artwork used for review
purposes, none of the contents of this publication
may be reprinted without the permission of Idea and
Design Works, LLC. Printed in Korea.
IDW Publishing does not read or accept unsolicited
submissions of ideas, stories, or artwork.

Ted Adams, CEO & Publisher
Greg Goldstein, President & COO
Robbie Robbins, EVP/Sr. Graphic Artist
Chris Ryall, Chief Creative Officer/Editor-in-Chief
Laurie Windrow, Senior Vice President of Sales & Marketing
Matthew Ruzicka, CPA, Chief Financial Officer
Lorelei Bunjes, VP of Digital Services
Jerry Bennington, VP of New Product Development

STORY BY
FOENKINOS

ADAPTATION BY
CORBEYRAN

ILLUSTRATION BY
HORNE

TRANSLATED BY
IVANKA HAHNENBERGER

LETTERED BY
TROY LITTLE

EDITED BY
JUSTIN EISINGER

first session

I WANTED A CLEAN SLATE

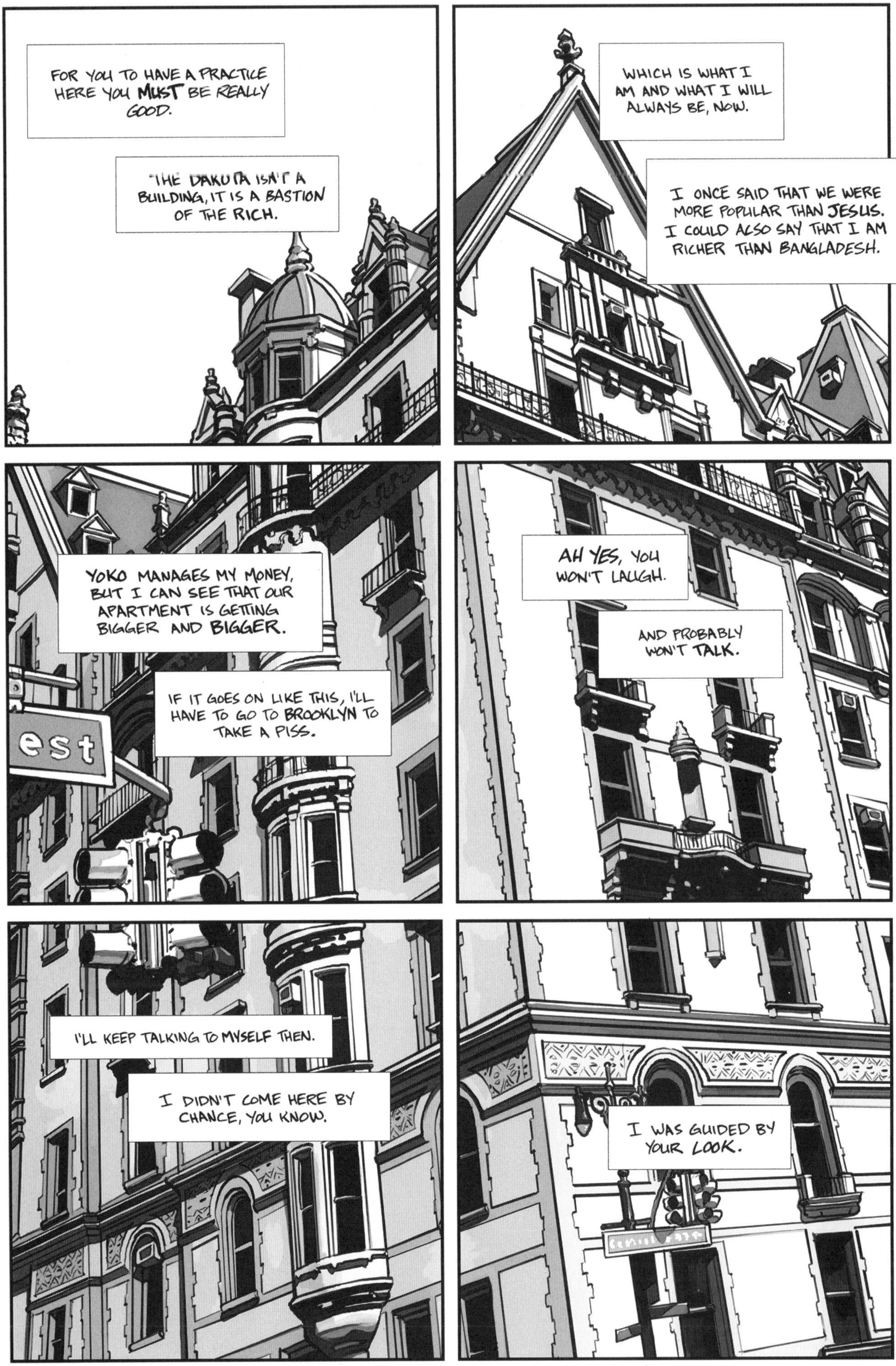
FOR YOU TO HAVE A PRACTICE HERE YOU MUST BE REALLY GOOD.
THE DAKOTA ISN'T A BUILDING, IT IS A BASTION OF THE RICH.
WHICH IS WHAT I AM AND WHAT I WILL ALWAYS BE, NOW.
I ONCE SAID THAT WE WERE MORE POPULAR THAN JESUS. I COULD ALSO SAY THAT I AM RICHER THAN BANGLADESH.
YOKO MANAGES MY MONEY, BUT I CAN SEE THAT OUR APARTMENT IS GETTING BIGGER AND BIGGER.
IF IT GOES ON LIKE THIS, I'LL HAVE TO GO TO BROOKLYN TO TAKE A PISS.
est
AH YES, YOU WON'T LAUGH.
AND PROBABLY WON'T TALK.
I'LL KEEP TALKING TO MYSELF THEN.
I DIDN'T COME HERE BY CHANCE, YOU KNOW.
I WAS GUIDED BY YOUR LOOK.

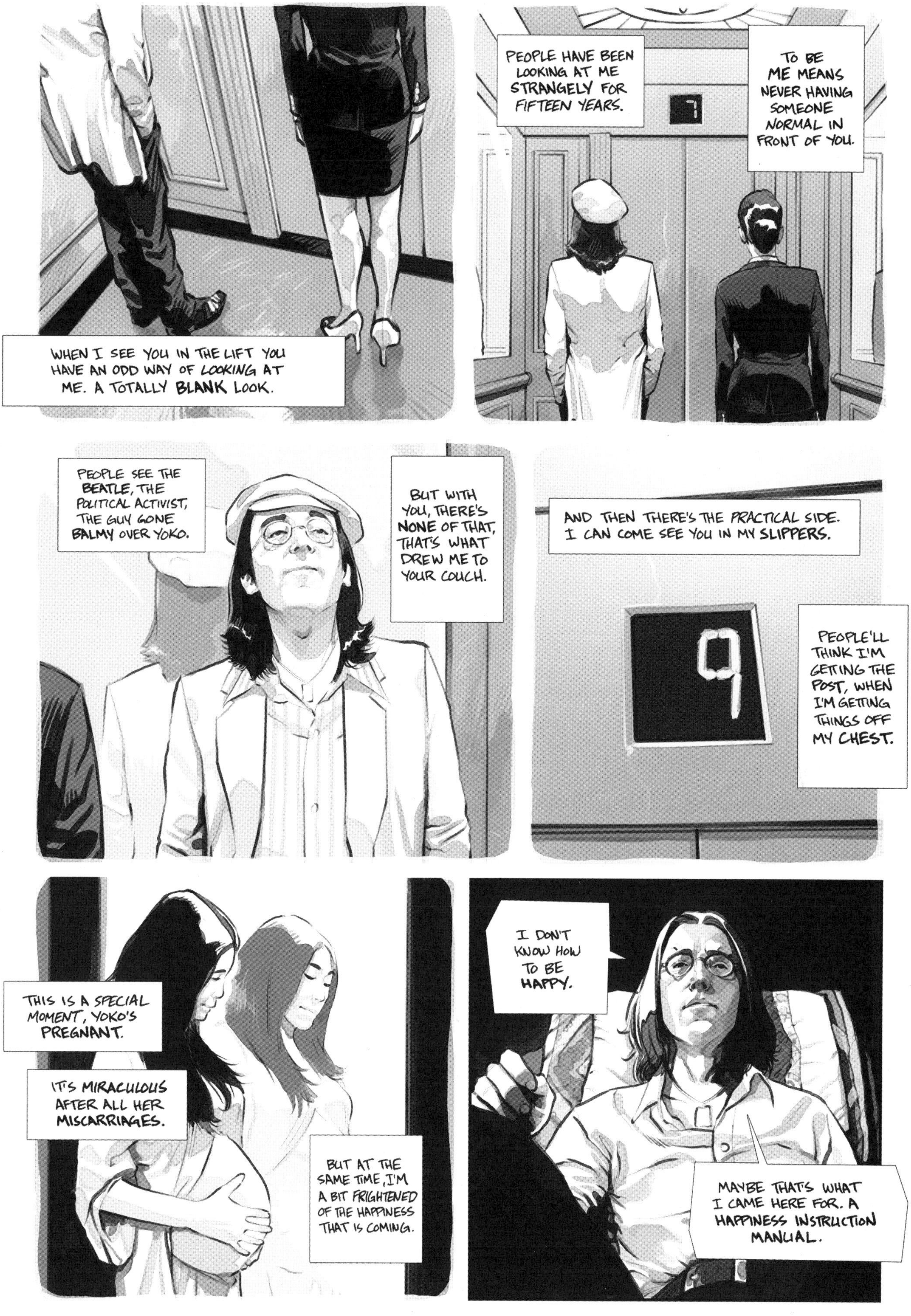

WHEN I SEE YOU IN THE LIFT YOU HAVE AN ODD WAY OF LOOKING AT ME. A TOTALLY BLANK LOOK.
PEOPLE HAVE BEEN LOOKING AT ME STRANGELY FOR FIFTEEN YEARS.
7
TO BE ME MEANS NEVER HAVING SOMEONE NORMAL IN FRONT OF YOU.
PEOPLE SEE THE BEATLE, THE POLITICAL ACTIVIST, THE GUY GONE BALMY OVER YOKO.
BUT WITH YOU, THERE'S NONE OF THAT, THAT'S WHAT DREW ME TO YOUR COUCH.
AND THEN THERE'S THE PRACTICAL SIDE. I CAN COME SEE YOU IN MY SLIPPERS.
9
PEOPLE'LL THINK I'M GETTING THE POST, WHEN I'M GETTING THINGS OFF MY CHEST.
THIS IS A SPECIAL MOMENT, YOKO'S PREGNANT.
IT'S MIRACULOUS AFTER ALL HER MISCARRIAGES.
BUT AT THE SAME TIME, I'M A BIT FRIGHTENED OF THE HAPPINESS THAT IS COMING.
I DON'T KNOW HOW TO BE HAPPY.
MAYBE THAT'S WHAT I CAME HERE FOR. A HAPPINESS INSTRUCTION MANUAL.

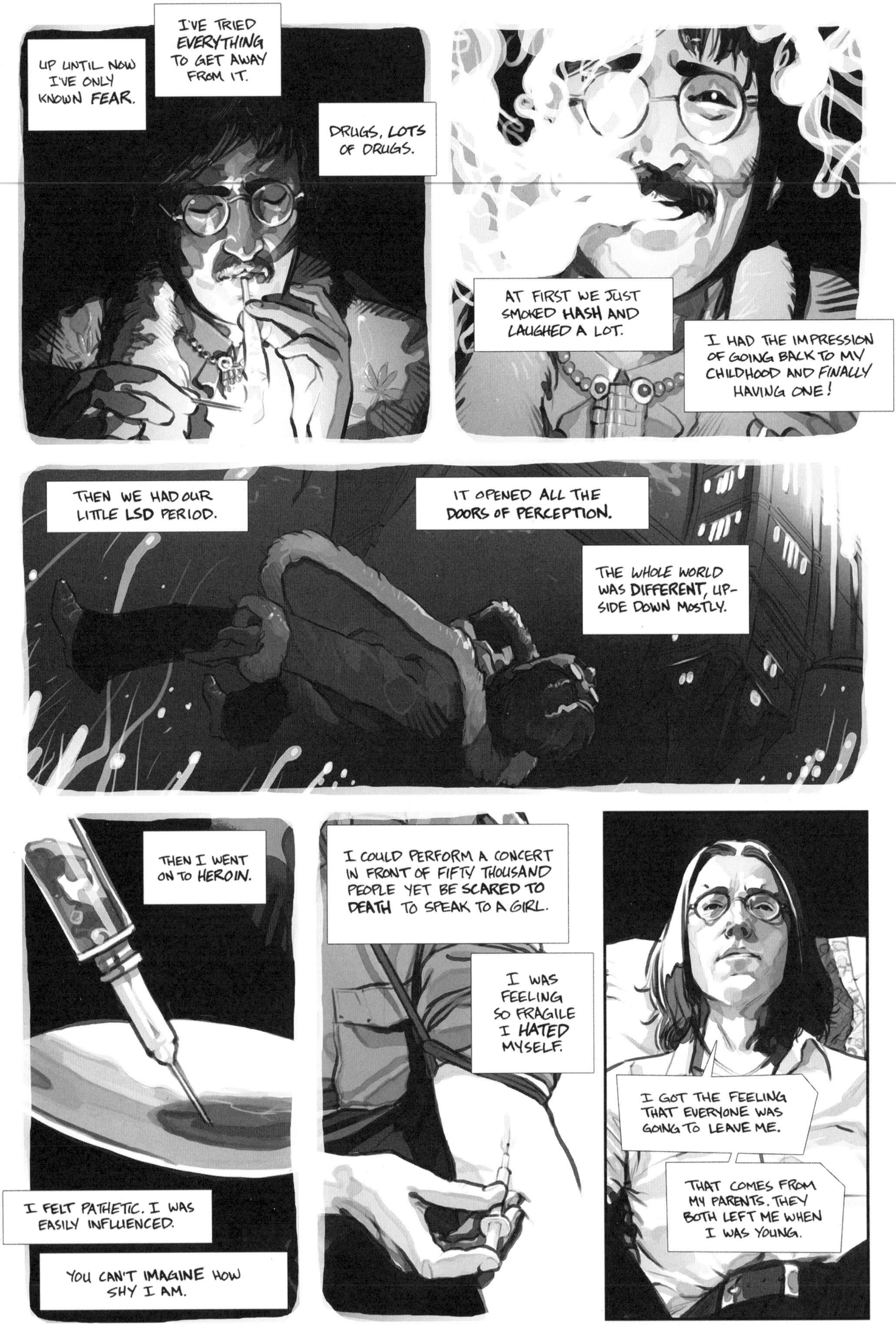
UP UNTIL NOW I'VE ONLY KNOWN FEAR.
I'VE TRIED EVERYTHING TO GET AWAY FROM IT.
DRUGS, LOTS OF DRUGS.
AT FIRST WE JUST SMOKED HASH AND LAUGHED A LOT.
I HAD THE IMPRESSION OF GOING BACK TO MY CHILDHOOD AND FINALLY HAVING ONE!
THEN WE HAD OUR LITTLE LSD PERIOD.
IT OPENED ALL THE DOORS OF PERCEPTION.
THE WHOLE WORLD WAS DIFFERENT, UP-SIDE DOWN MOSTLY.
THEN I WENT ON TO HEROIN.
I FELT PATHETIC. I WAS EASILY INFLUENCED.
YOU CAN'T IMAGINE HOW SHY I AM.
I COULD PERFORM A CONCERT IN FRONT OF FIFTY THOUSAND PEOPLE YET BE SCARED TO DEATH TO SPEAK TO A GIRL.
I WAS FEELING SO FRAGILE I HATED MYSELF.
I GOT THE FEELING THAT EVERYONE WAS GOING TO LEAVE ME.
THAT COMES FROM MY PARENTS. THEY BOTH LEFT ME WHEN I WAS YOUNG.

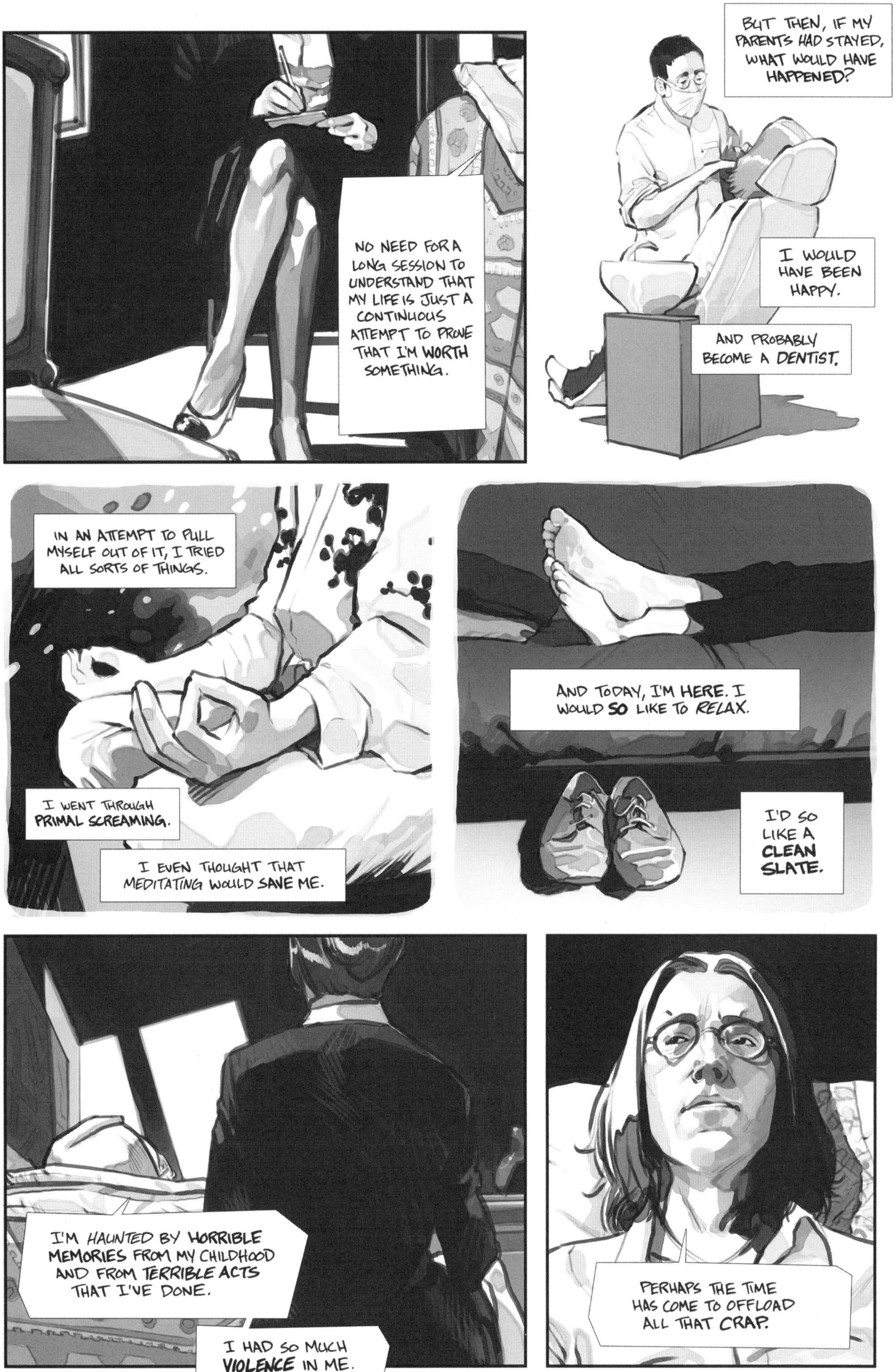
NO NEED FOR A LONG SESSION TO UNDERSTAND THAT MY LIFE IS JUST A CONTINUOUS ATTEMPT TO PROVE THAT I'M WORTH SOMETHING.
BUT THEN, IF MY PARENTS HAD STAYED, WHAT WOULD HAVE HAPPENED?
I WOULD HAVE BEEN HAPPY.
AND PROBABLY BECOME A DENTIST.
IN AN ATTEMPT TO PULL MYSELF OUT OF IT, I TRIED ALL SORTS OF THINGS.
I WENT THROUGH PRIMAL SCREAMING.
I EVEN THOUGHT THAT MEDITATING WOULD SAVE ME.
AND TODAY, I'M HERE. I WOULD SO LIKE TO RELAX.
I'D SO LIKE A CLEAN SLATE.
I'M HAUNTED BY HORRIBLE MEMORIES FROM MY CHILDHOOD AND FROM TERRIBLE ACTS THAT I'VE DONE.
I HAD SO MUCH VIOLENCE IN ME.
PERHAPS THE TIME HAS COME TO OFFLOAD ALL THAT CRAP.

second session
THE BEATLES NO LONGER EXIST

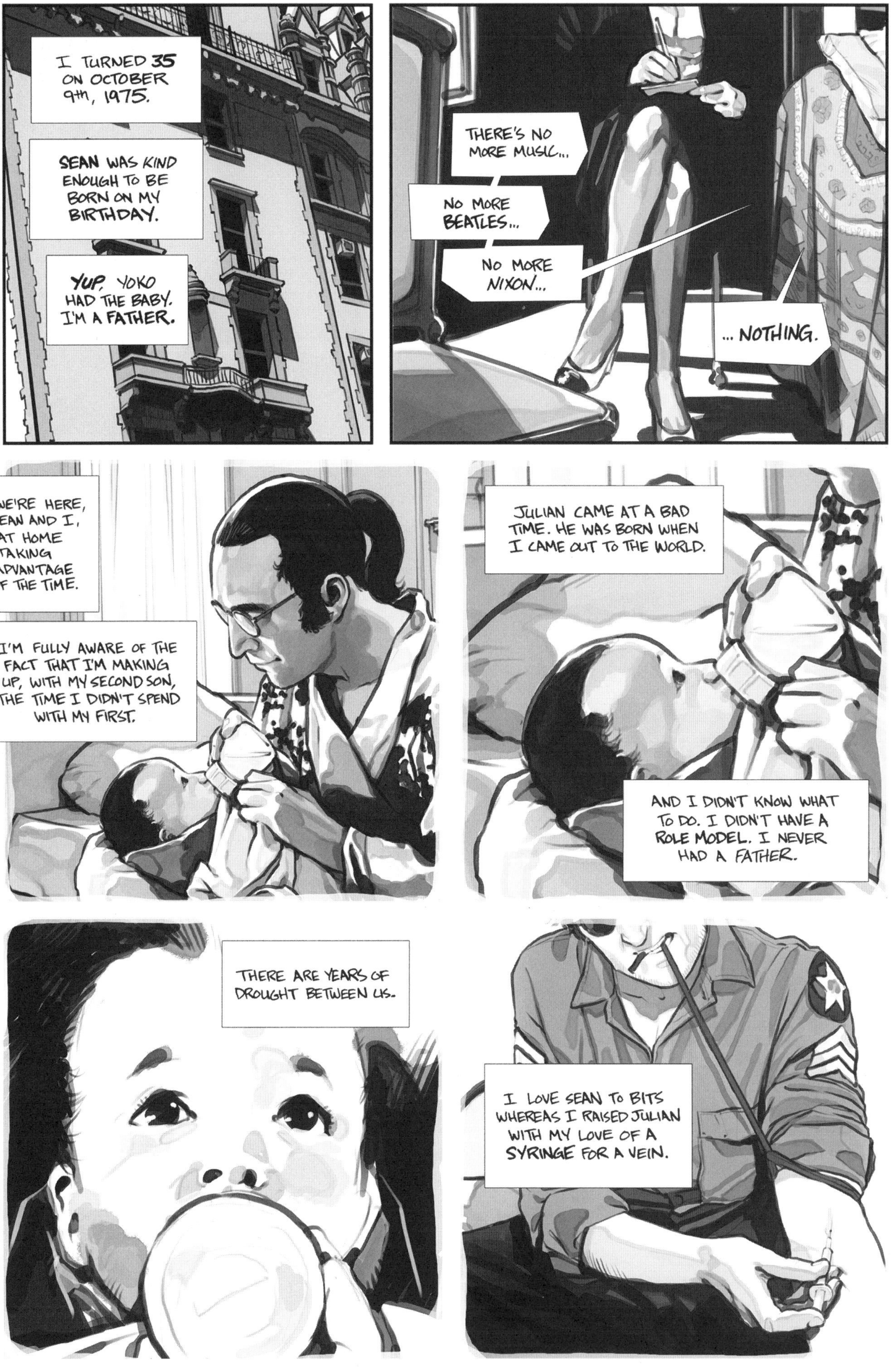
I TURNED 35 ON OCTOBER 9th, 1975.
SEAN WAS KIND ENOUGH TO BE BORN ON MY BIRTHDAY.
YUP, YOKO HAD THE BABY. I'M A FATHER.
THERE'S NO MORE MUSIC...
NO MORE BEATLES...
NO MORE NIXON...
... NOTHING.
WE'RE HERE, SEAN AND I, AT HOME TAKING ADVANTAGE OF THE TIME.
I'M FULLY AWARE OF THE FACT THAT I'M MAKING UP, WITH MY SECOND SON, THE TIME I DIDN'T SPEND WITH MY FIRST.
JULIAN CAME AT A BAD TIME. HE WAS BORN WHEN I CAME OUT TO THE WORLD.
AND I DIDN'T KNOW WHAT TO DO. I DIDN'T HAVE A ROLE MODEL. I NEVER HAD A FATHER.
THERE ARE YEARS OF DROUGHT BETWEEN US.
I LOVE SEAN TO BITS WHEREAS I RAISED JULIAN WITH MY LOVE OF A SYRINGE FOR A VEIN.

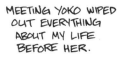

MEETING YOKO WIPED OUT EVERYTHING ABOUT MY LIFE BEFORE HER.

WHEN I KISSED HER I GOT AMNESIA AND JULIAN, LIKE EVERYTHING ELSE, FELL AWAY.

I TRY TO FIND REASONS BUT IT'S *RIDICULOUS* TO CONTEMPLATE OUR LOVE.

TOGETHER, WITH YOKO, WE OFFER SEAN A STABLE ENVIRONMENT, *WARM LOVE*, BUT WITH JULIAN, I RECREATED WHAT I HAD LIVED THROUGH.

I PASSED ON THE ROOTS OF MY ILLS.

I GAVE HIM ALL MY SUFFERING.

I WAS *INCAPABLE* OF SHOWING ANY TENDERNESS.

I WAS EVEN *CRUEL* AT TIMES.

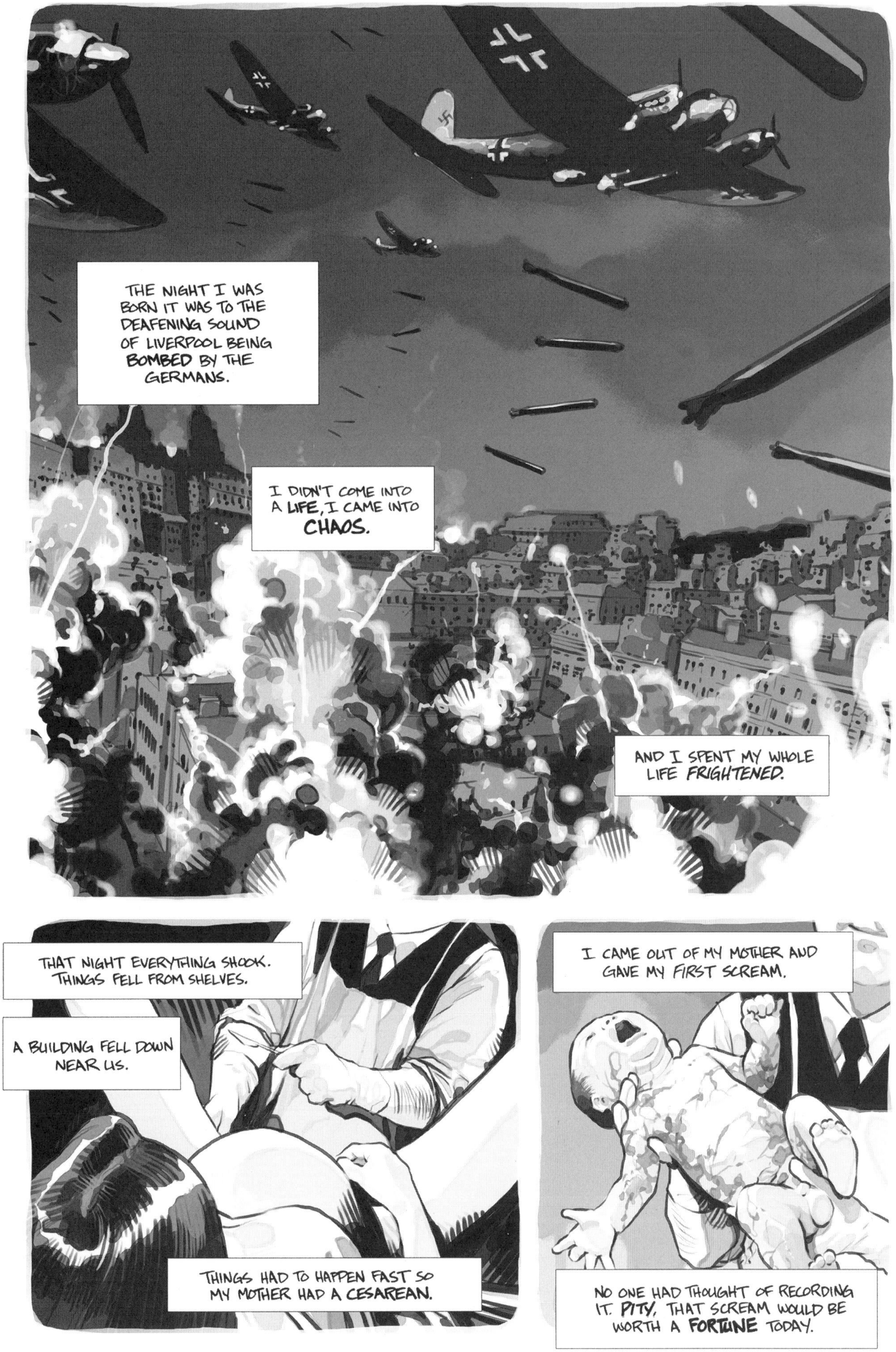
THE NIGHT I WAS BORN IT WAS TO THE DEAFENING SOUND OF LIVERPOOL BEING BOMBED BY THE GERMANS.
I DIDN'T COME INTO A LIFE, I CAME INTO CHAOS.
AND I SPENT MY WHOLE LIFE FRIGHTENED.
THAT NIGHT EVERYTHING SHOOK. THINGS FELL FROM SHELVES.
A BUILDING FELL DOWN NEAR US.
THINGS HAD TO HAPPEN FAST SO MY MOTHER HAD A CESAREAN.
I CAME OUT OF MY MOTHER AND GAVE MY FIRST SCREAM.
NO ONE HAD THOUGHT OF RECORDING IT. PITY, THAT SCREAM WOULD BE WORTH A FORTUNE TODAY.

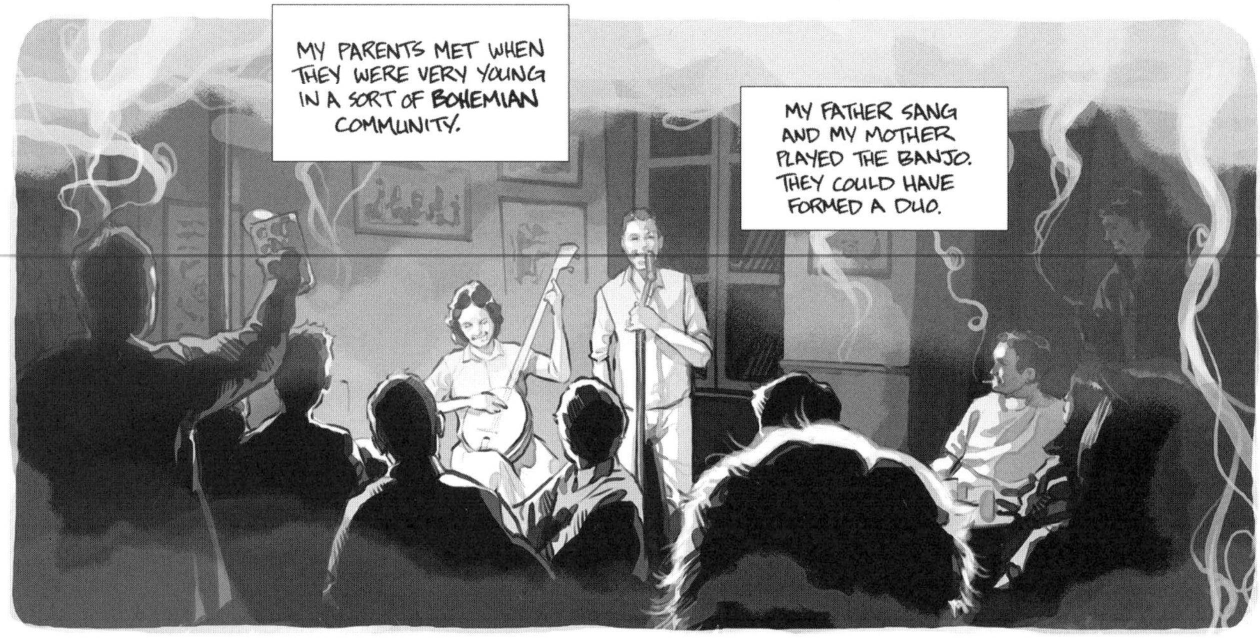
MY PARENTS MET WHEN THEY WERE VERY YOUNG IN A SORT OF BOHEMIAN COMMUNITY.
MY FATHER SANG AND MY MOTHER PLAYED THE BANJO. THEY COULD HAVE FORMED A DUO.

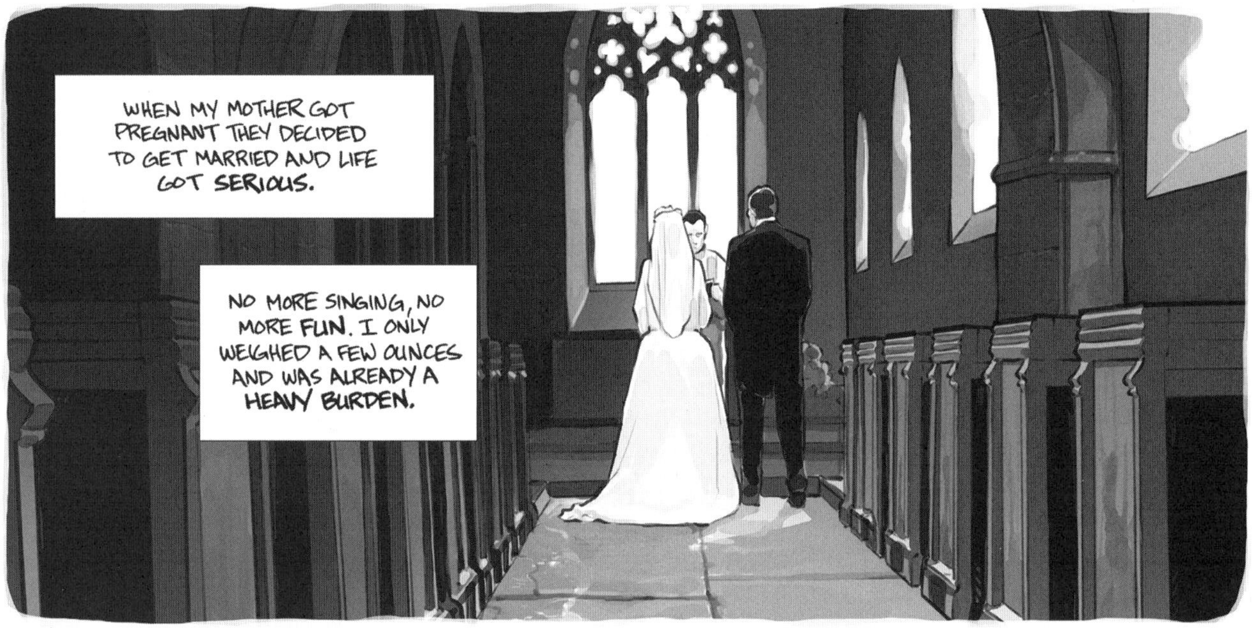
WHEN MY MOTHER GOT PREGNANT THEY DECIDED TO GET MARRIED AND LIFE GOT SERIOUS.
NO MORE SINGING, NO MORE FUN. I ONLY WEIGHED A FEW OUNCES AND WAS ALREADY A HEAVY BURDEN.

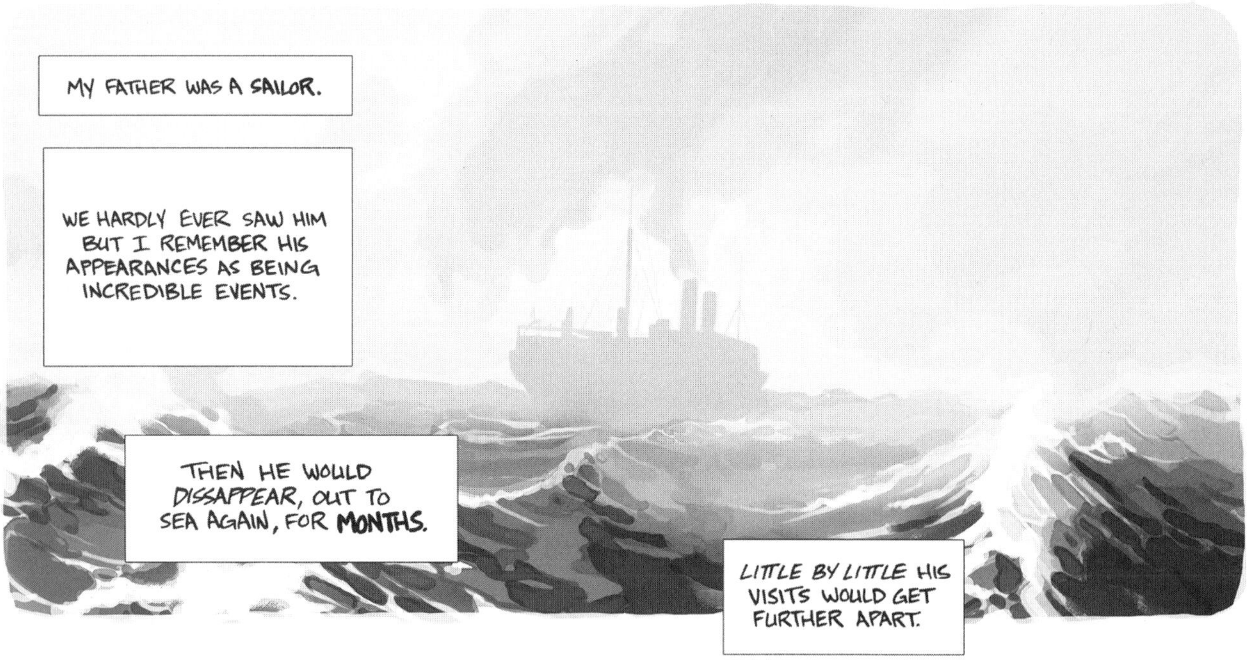
MY FATHER WAS A SAILOR.
WE HARDLY EVER SAW HIM BUT I REMEMBER HIS APPEARANCES AS BEING INCREDIBLE EVENTS.
THEN HE WOULD DISSAPPEAR, OUT TO SEA AGAIN, FOR MONTHS.
LITTLE BY LITTLE HIS VISITS WOULD GET FURTHER APART.

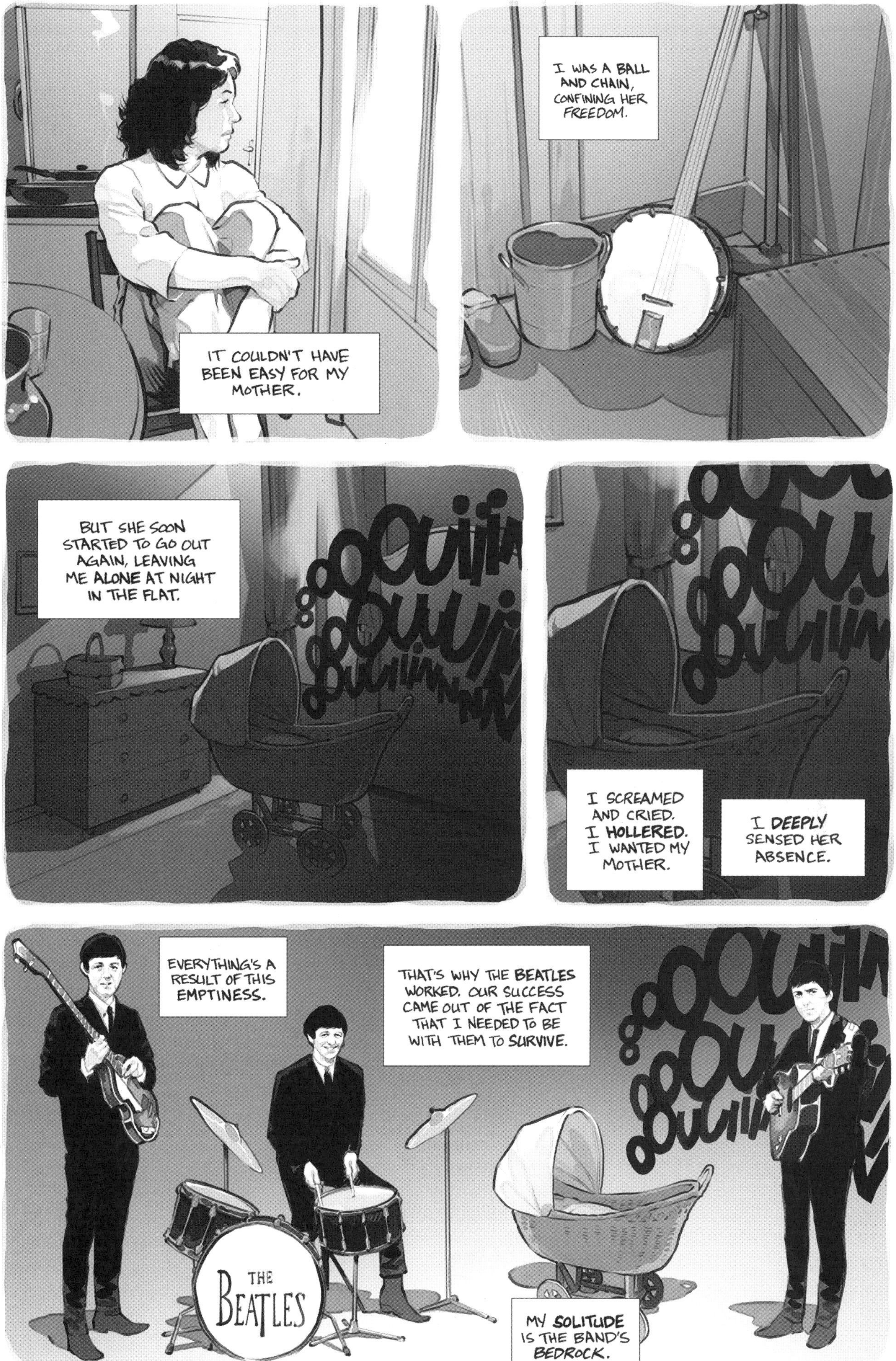
IT COULDN'T HAVE BEEN EASY FOR MY MOTHER.
I WAS A BALL AND CHAIN, CONFINING HER FREEDOM.
BUT SHE SOON STARTED TO GO OUT AGAIN, LEAVING ME **ALONE** AT NIGHT IN THE FLAT.
I SCREAMED AND CRIED. I **HOLLERED.** I WANTED MY MOTHER.
I **DEEPLY** SENSED HER ABSENCE.
EVERYTHING'S A RESULT OF THIS **EMPTINESS.**
THAT'S WHY THE **BEATLES** WORKED. OUR SUCCESS CAME OUT OF THE FACT THAT I NEEDED TO BE WITH THEM TO **SURVIVE.**
THE BEATLES
MY **SOLITUDE** IS THE BAND'S **BEDROCK.**

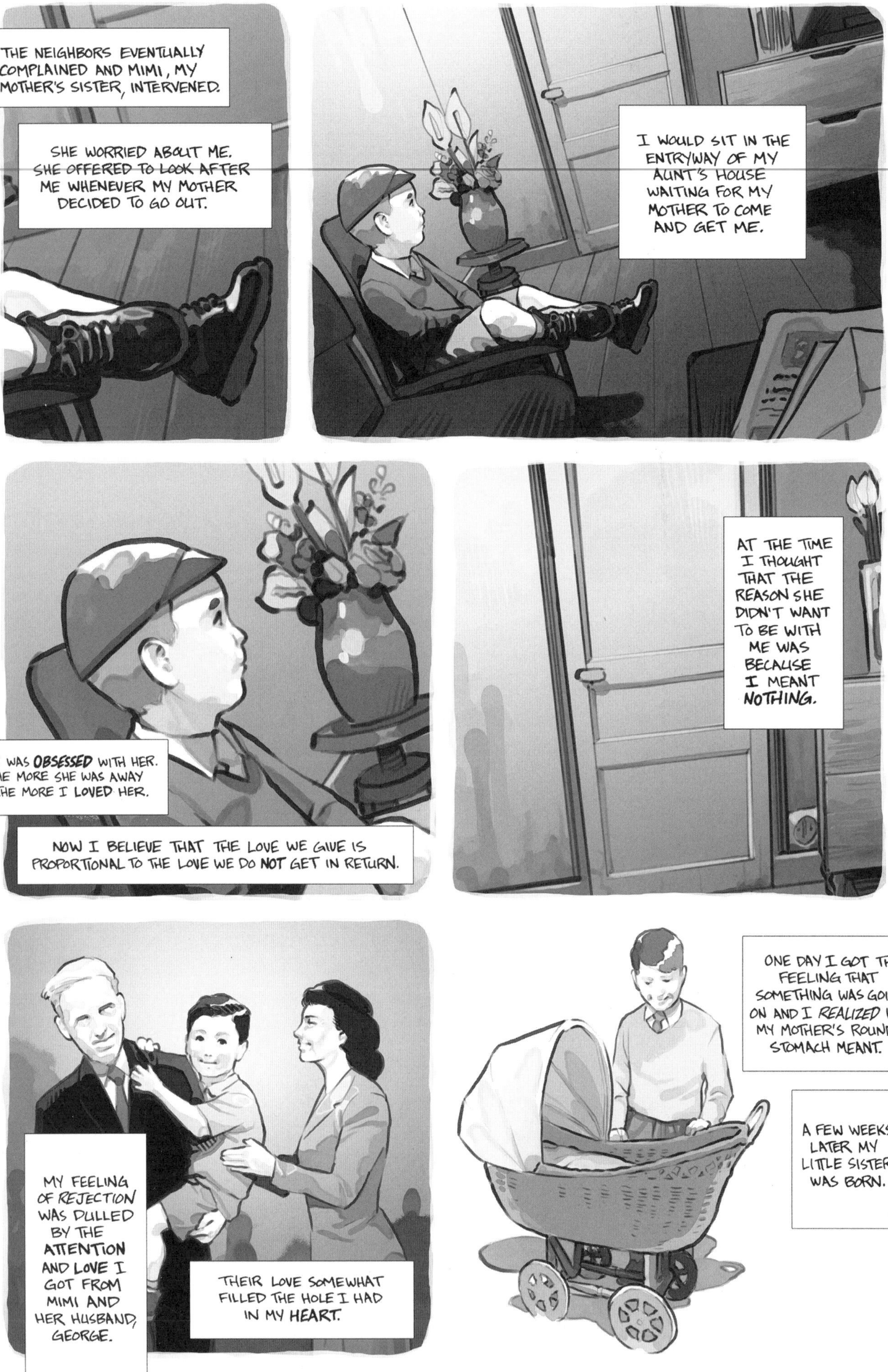
THE NEIGHBORS EVENTUALLY COMPLAINED AND MIMI, MY MOTHER'S SISTER, INTERVENED.
SHE WORRIED ABOUT ME. SHE OFFERED TO LOOK AFTER ME WHENEVER MY MOTHER DECIDED TO GO OUT.
I WOULD SIT IN THE ENTRYWAY OF MY AUNT'S HOUSE WAITING FOR MY MOTHER TO COME AND GET ME.
I WAS **OBSESSED** WITH HER. THE MORE SHE WAS AWAY THE MORE I **LOVED** HER.
NOW I BELIEVE THAT THE LOVE WE GIVE IS PROPORTIONAL TO THE LOVE WE DO **NOT** GET IN RETURN.
AT THE TIME I THOUGHT THAT THE REASON SHE DIDN'T WANT TO BE WITH ME WAS BECAUSE I MEANT **NOTHING.**
MY FEELING OF REJECTION WAS DULLED BY THE **ATTENTION** AND **LOVE** I GOT FROM MIMI AND HER HUSBAND, GEORGE.
THEIR LOVE SOMEWHAT FILLED THE HOLE I HAD IN MY **HEART.**
ONE DAY I GOT THE FEELING THAT SOMETHING WAS GOING ON AND I *REALIZED* WHAT MY MOTHER'S ROUNDED STOMACH MEANT.
A FEW WEEKS LATER MY LITTLE SISTER WAS BORN.

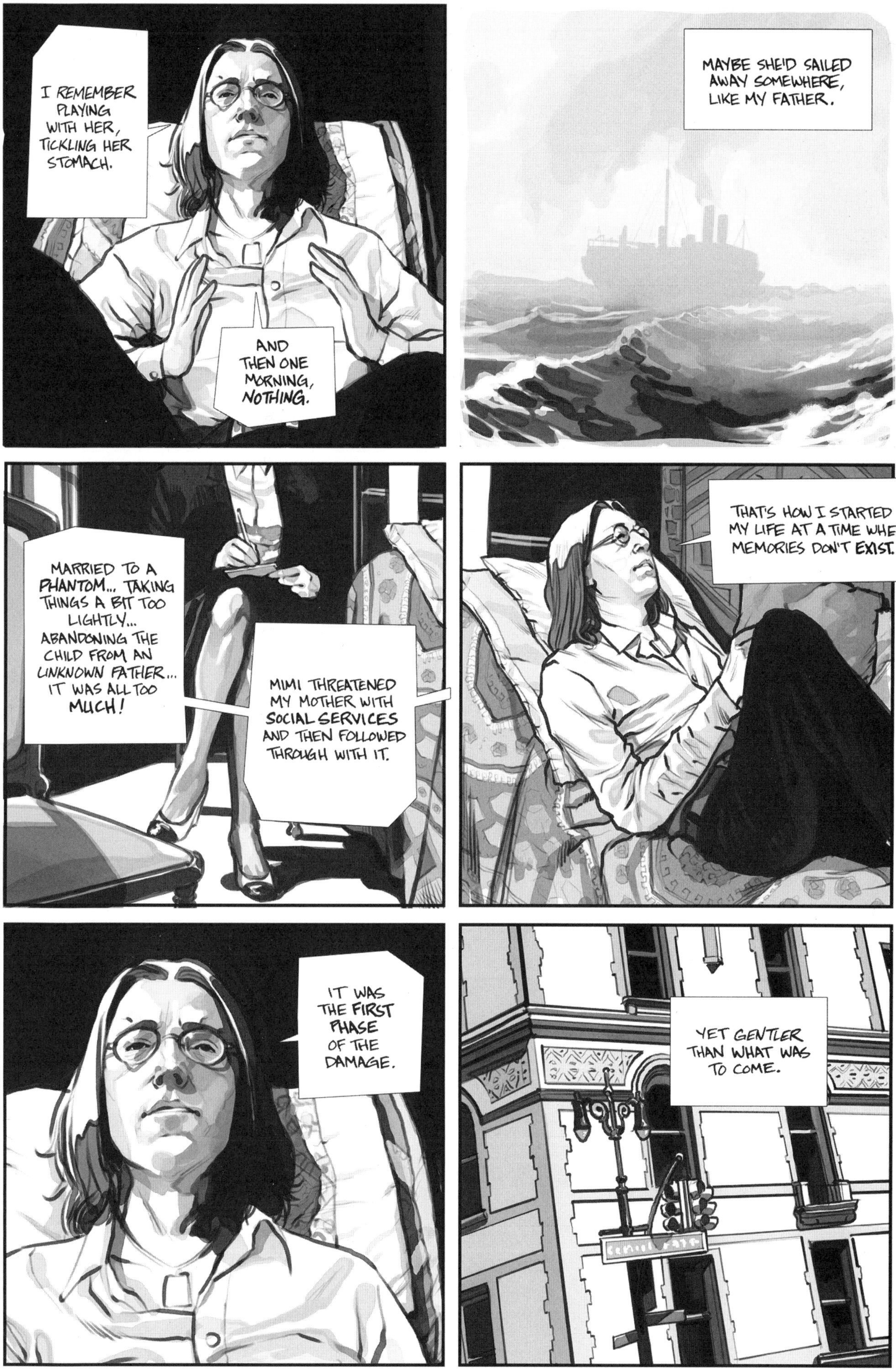
I REMEMBER PLAYING WITH HER, TICKLING HER STOMACH.
AND THEN ONE MORNING, NOTHING.
MAYBE SHE'D SAILED AWAY SOMEWHERE, LIKE MY FATHER.
MARRIED TO A PHANTOM... TAKING THINGS A BIT TOO LIGHTLY... ABANDONING THE CHILD FROM AN UNKNOWN FATHER... IT WAS ALL TOO MUCH!
MIMI THREATENED MY MOTHER WITH SOCIAL SERVICES AND THEN FOLLOWED THROUGH WITH IT.
THAT'S HOW I STARTED MY LIFE AT A TIME WHEN MEMORIES DON'T EXIST.
IT WAS THE FIRST PHASE OF THE DAMAGE.
YET GENTLER THAN WHAT WAS TO COME.

third session
IT'S ALL JUST TEMPORARY

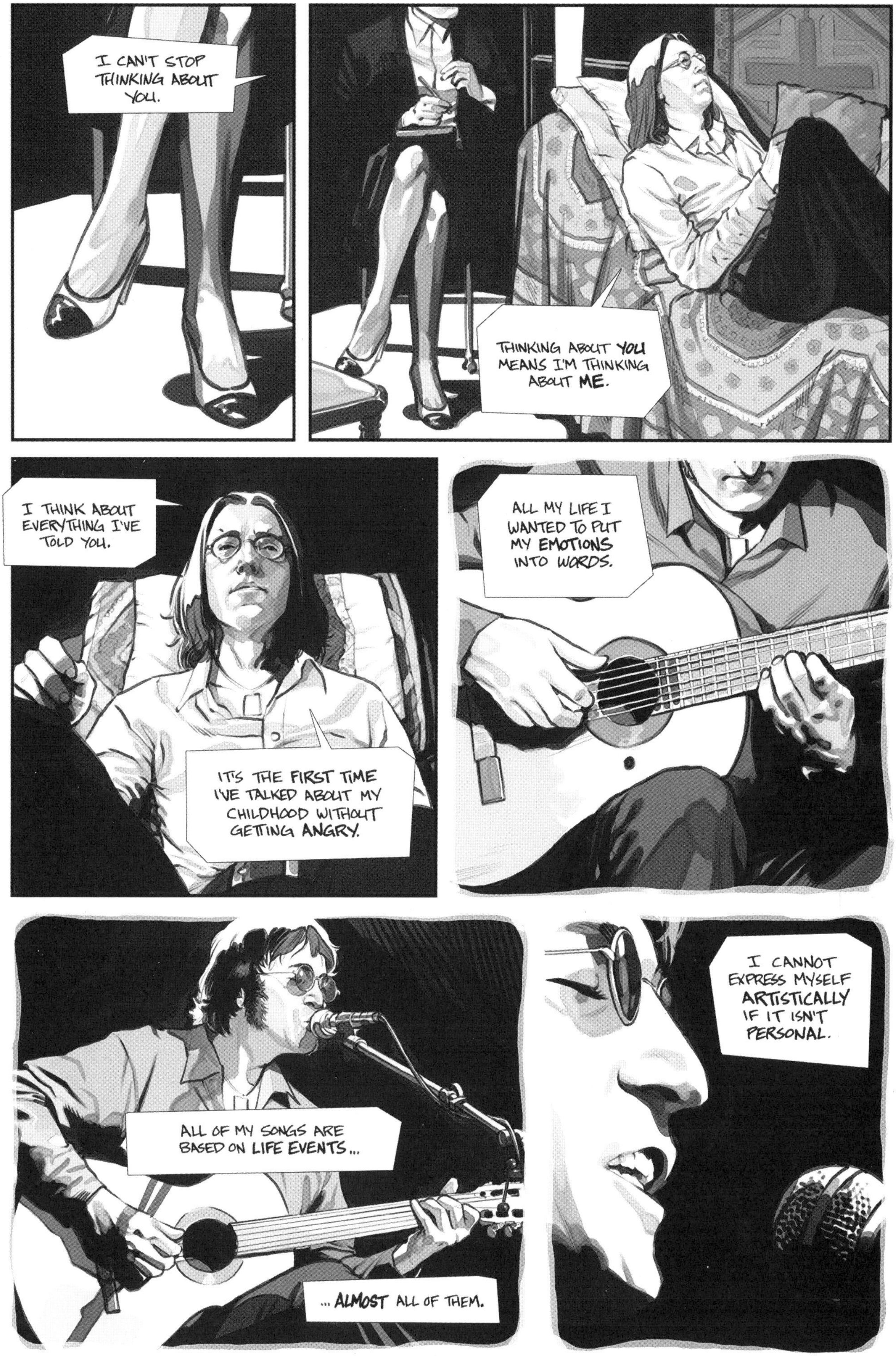

I CAN'T STOP THINKING ABOUT YOU.
THINKING ABOUT YOU MEANS I'M THINKING ABOUT ME.
I THINK ABOUT EVERYTHING I'VE TOLD YOU.
IT'S THE FIRST TIME I'VE TALKED ABOUT MY CHILDHOOD WITHOUT GETTING ANGRY.
ALL MY LIFE I WANTED TO PUT MY EMOTIONS INTO WORDS.
ALL OF MY SONGS ARE BASED ON LIFE EVENTS...
...ALMOST ALL OF THEM.
I CANNOT EXPRESS MYSELF ARTISTICALLY IF IT ISN'T PERSONAL.

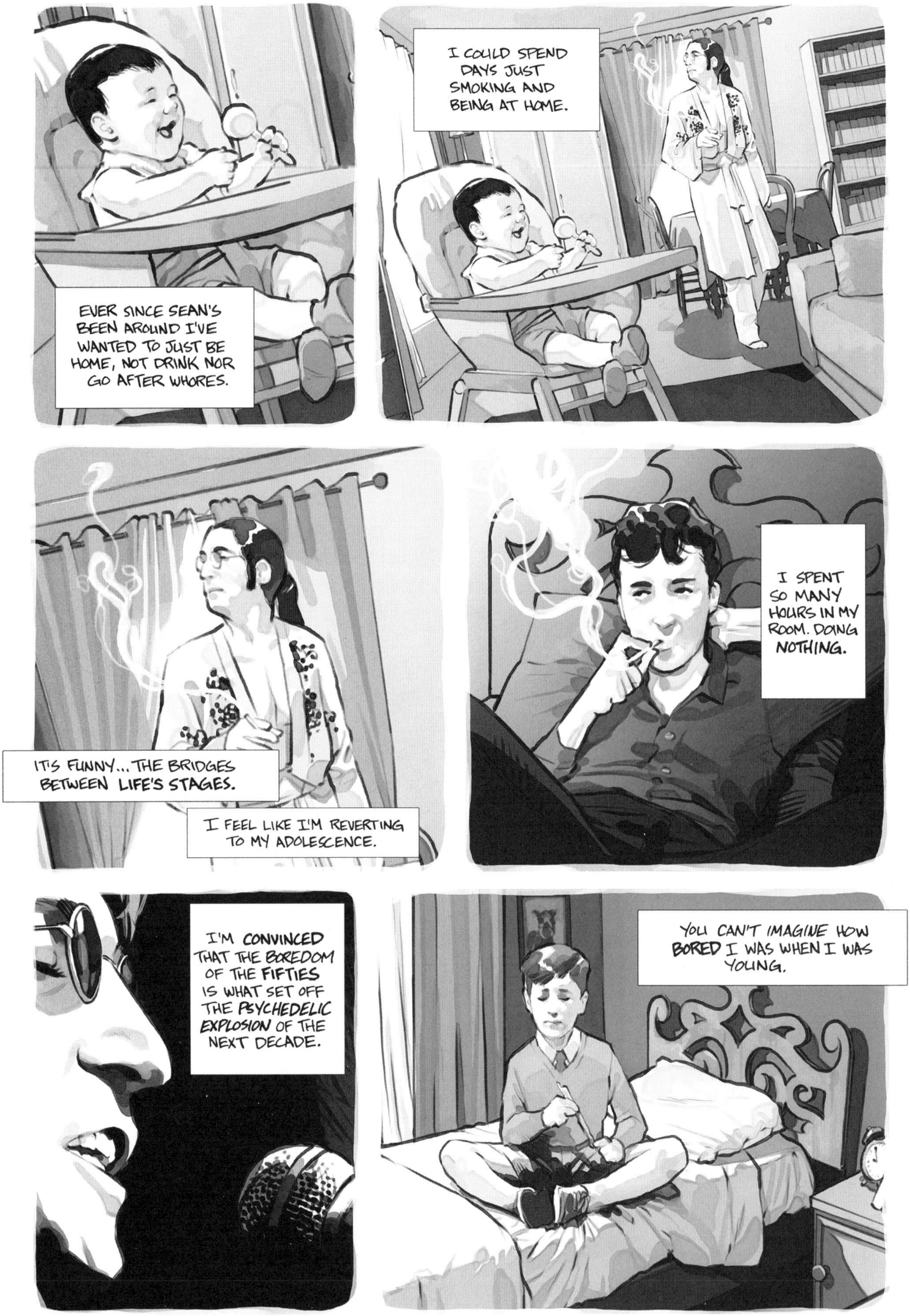
EVER SINCE SEAN'S BEEN AROUND I'VE WANTED TO JUST BE HOME, NOT DRINK NOR GO AFTER WHORES.
I COULD SPEND DAYS JUST SMOKING AND BEING AT HOME.
IT'S FUNNY... THE BRIDGES BETWEEN LIFE'S STAGES.
I FEEL LIKE I'M REVERTING TO MY ADOLESCENCE.
I SPENT SO MANY HOURS IN MY ROOM. DOING NOTHING.
I'M CONVINCED THAT THE BOREDOM OF THE FIFTIES IS WHAT SET OFF THE PSYCHEDELIC EXPLOSION OF THE NEXT DECADE.
YOU CAN'T IMAGINE HOW BORED I WAS WHEN I WAS YOUNG.

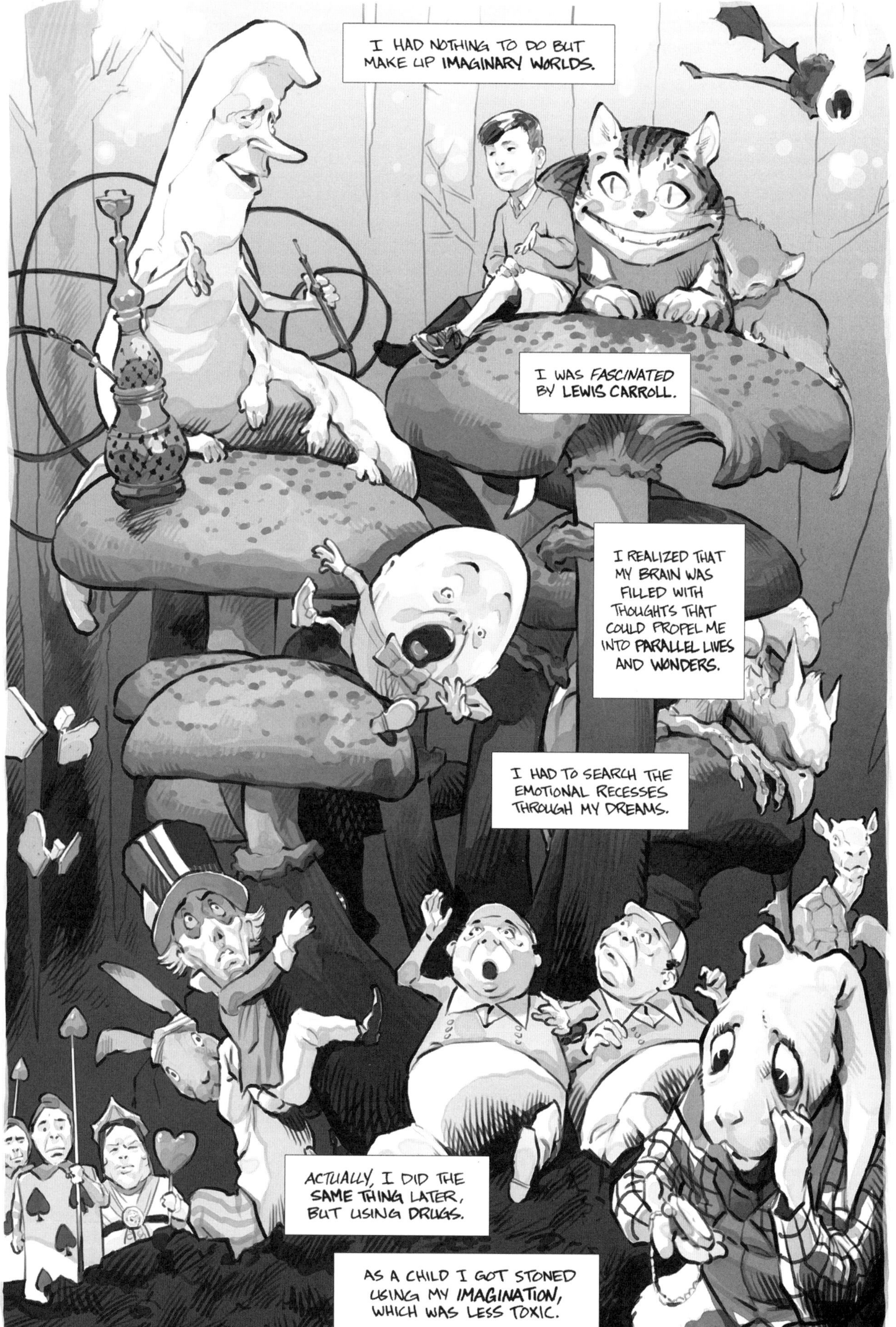
I HAD NOTHING TO DO BUT MAKE UP IMAGINARY WORLDS.
I WAS FASCINATED BY LEWIS CARROLL.
I REALIZED THAT MY BRAIN WAS FILLED WITH THOUGHTS THAT COULD PROPEL ME INTO PARALLEL LIVES AND WONDERS.
I HAD TO SEARCH THE EMOTIONAL RECESSES THROUGH MY DREAMS.
ACTUALLY, I DID THE SAME THING LATER, BUT USING DRUGS.
AS A CHILD I GOT STONED USING MY IMAGINATION, WHICH WAS LESS TOXIC.

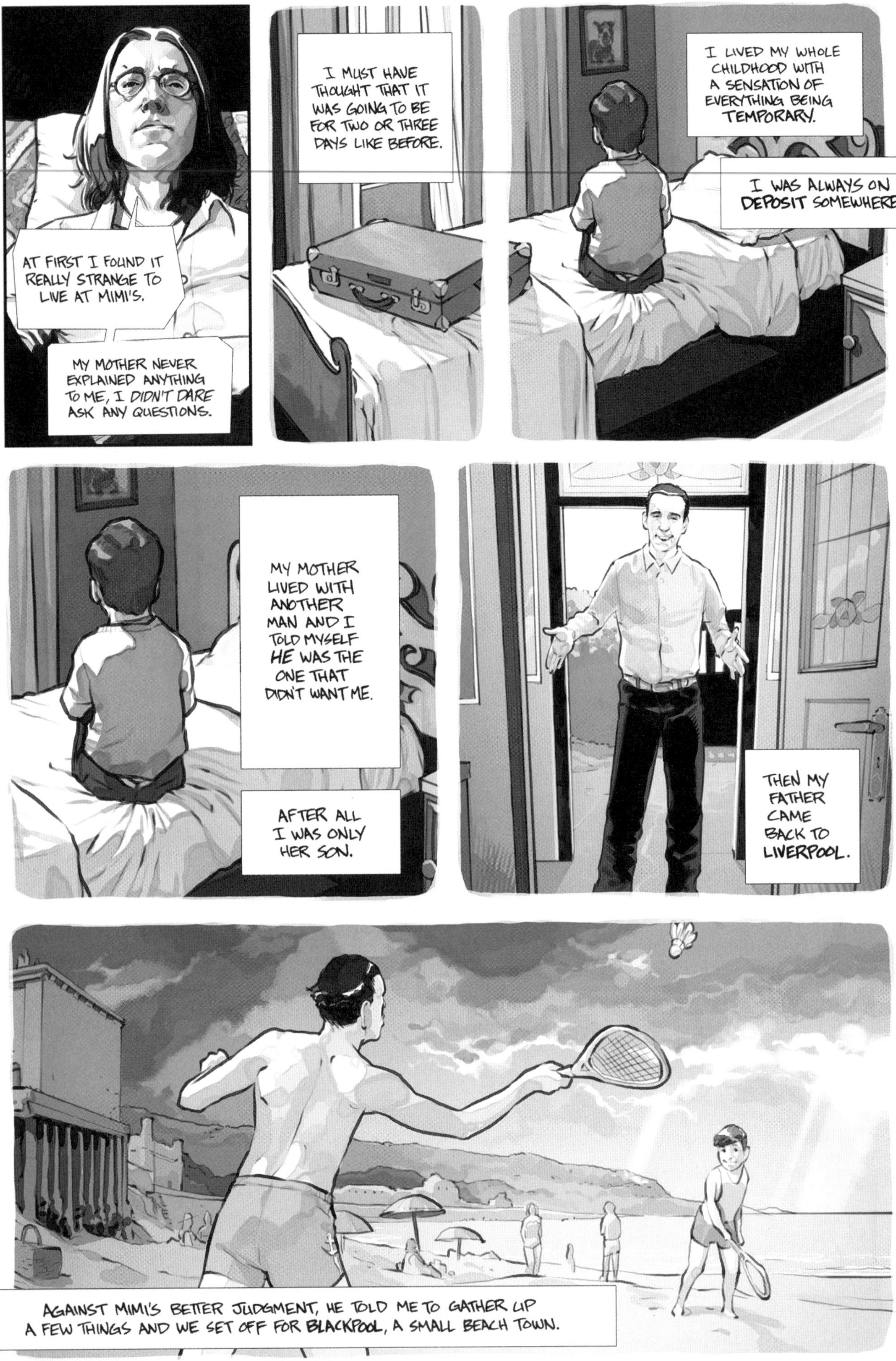
AT FIRST I FOUND IT REALLY STRANGE TO LIVE AT MIMI'S.
MY MOTHER NEVER EXPLAINED ANYTHING TO ME, I DIDN'T DARE ASK ANY QUESTIONS.
I MUST HAVE THOUGHT THAT IT WAS GOING TO BE FOR TWO OR THREE DAYS LIKE BEFORE.
I LIVED MY WHOLE CHILDHOOD WITH A SENSATION OF EVERYTHING BEING TEMPORARY.
I WAS ALWAYS ON DEPOSIT SOMEWHERE.
MY MOTHER LIVED WITH ANOTHER MAN AND I TOLD MYSELF HE WAS THE ONE THAT DIDN'T WANT ME.
AFTER ALL I WAS ONLY HER SON.
THEN MY FATHER CAME BACK TO LIVERPOOL.
AGAINST MIMI'S BETTER JUDGMENT, HE TOLD ME TO GATHER UP A FEW THINGS AND WE SET OFF FOR BLACKPOOL, A SMALL BEACH TOWN.

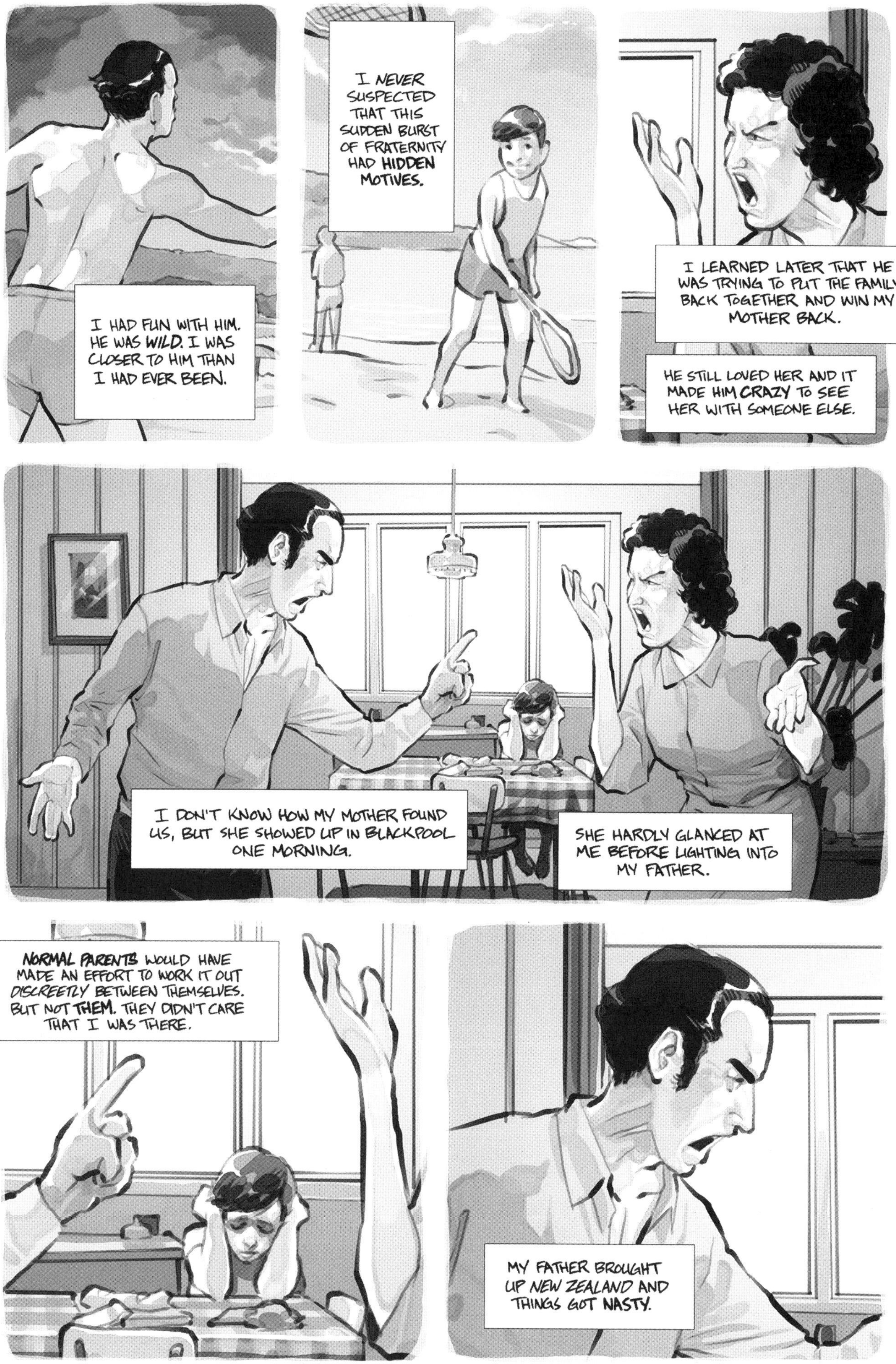
I HAD FUN WITH HIM. HE WAS **WILD**. I WAS CLOSER TO HIM THAN I HAD EVER BEEN.
I ***NEVER*** SUSPECTED THAT THIS SUDDEN BURST OF FRATERNITY HAD **HIDDEN** MOTIVES.
I LEARNED LATER THAT HE WAS TRYING TO PUT THE FAMILY BACK TOGETHER AND WIN MY MOTHER BACK.
HE STILL LOVED HER AND IT MADE HIM **CRAZY** TO SEE HER WITH SOMEONE ELSE.
I DON'T KNOW HOW MY MOTHER FOUND US, BUT SHE SHOWED UP IN BLACKPOOL ONE MORNING.
SHE HARDLY GLANCED AT ME BEFORE LIGHTING INTO MY FATHER.
NORMAL PARENTS WOULD HAVE MADE AN EFFORT TO WORK IT OUT *DISCREETLY* BETWEEN THEMSELVES. BUT NOT **THEM**. THEY DIDN'T CARE THAT I WAS THERE.
MY FATHER BROUGHT UP *NEW ZEALAND* AND THINGS GOT **NASTY**.

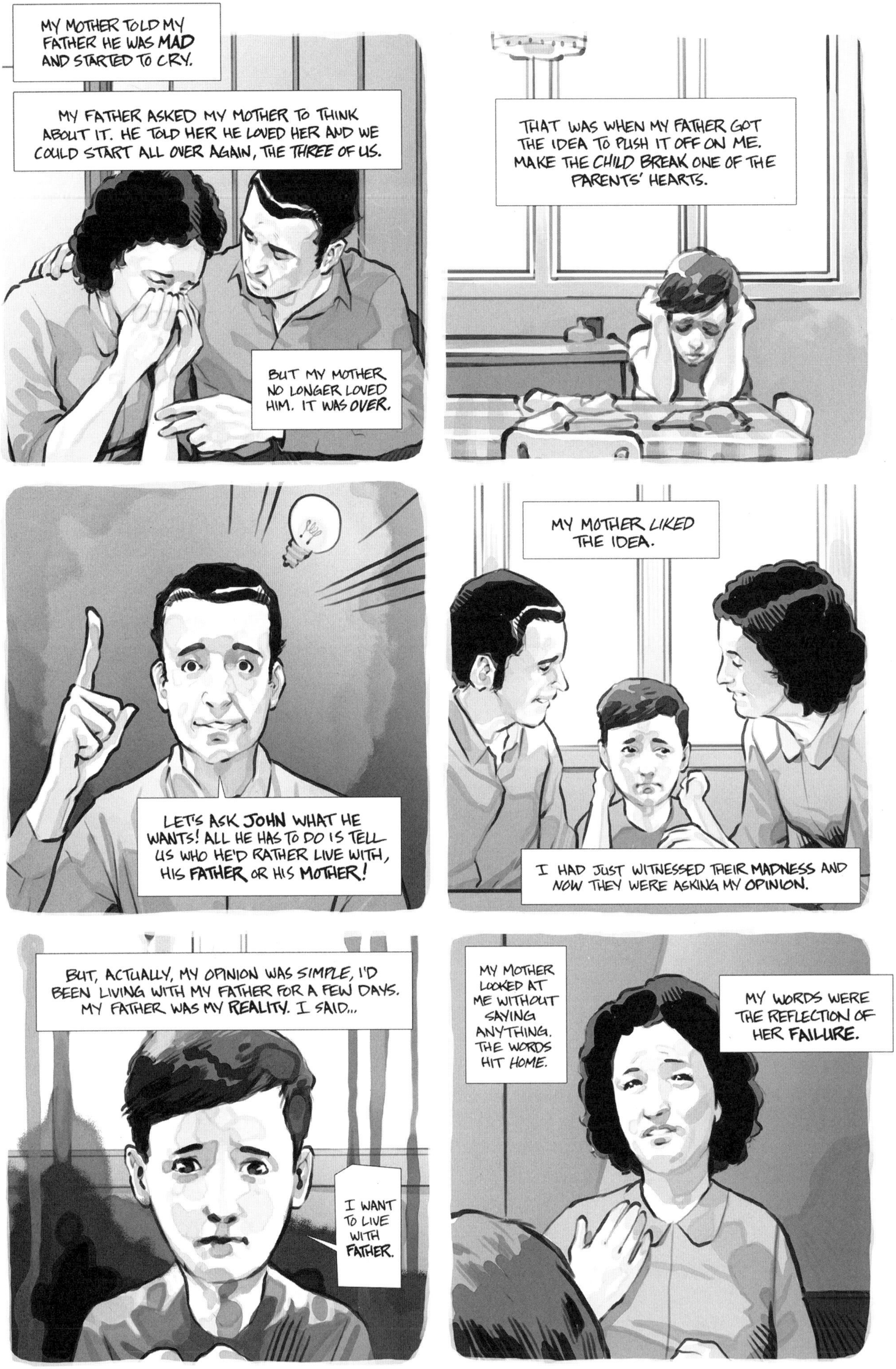
MY MOTHER TOLD MY FATHER HE WAS MAD AND STARTED TO CRY.
MY FATHER ASKED MY MOTHER TO THINK ABOUT IT. HE TOLD HER HE LOVED HER AND WE COULD START ALL OVER AGAIN, THE THREE OF US.
BUT MY MOTHER NO LONGER LOVED HIM. IT WAS OVER.
THAT WAS WHEN MY FATHER GOT THE IDEA TO PUSH IT OFF ON ME. MAKE THE CHILD BREAK ONE OF THE PARENTS' HEARTS.
LET'S ASK JOHN WHAT HE WANTS! ALL HE HAS TO DO IS TELL US WHO HE'D RATHER LIVE WITH, HIS FATHER OR HIS MOTHER!
MY MOTHER LIKED THE IDEA.
I HAD JUST WITNESSED THEIR MADNESS AND NOW THEY WERE ASKING MY OPINION.
BUT, ACTUALLY, MY OPINION WAS SIMPLE, I'D BEEN LIVING WITH MY FATHER FOR A FEW DAYS. MY FATHER WAS MY REALITY. I SAID...
I WANT TO LIVE WITH FATHER.
MY MOTHER LOOKED AT ME WITHOUT SAYING ANYTHING. THE WORDS HIT HOME.
MY WORDS WERE THE REFLECTION OF HER FAILURE.

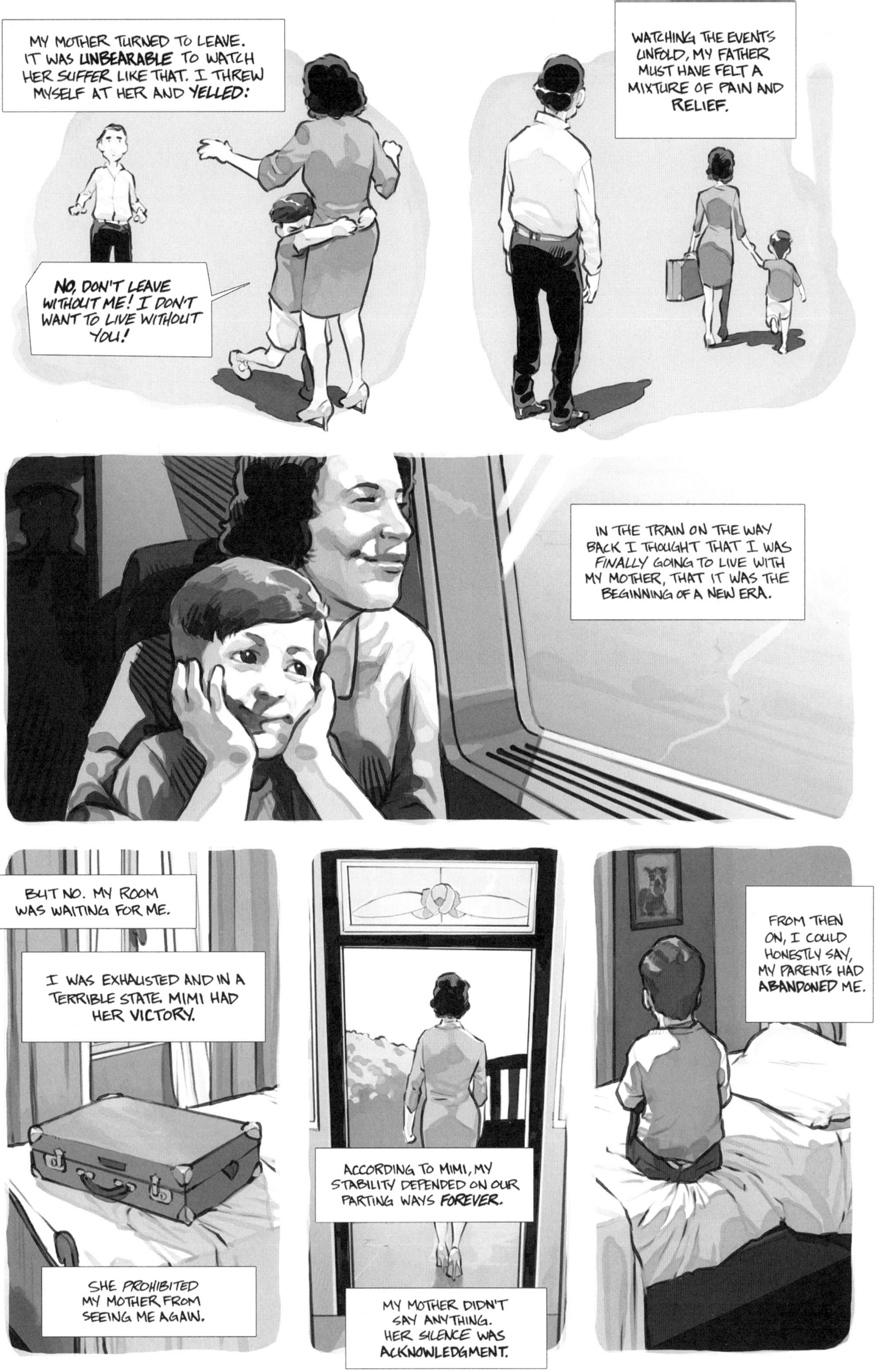
MY MOTHER TURNED TO LEAVE. IT WAS **UNBEARABLE** TO WATCH HER SUFFER LIKE THAT. I THREW MYSELF AT HER AND **YELLED:**
NO, DON'T LEAVE WITHOUT ME! I DON'T WANT TO LIVE WITHOUT YOU!
WATCHING THE EVENTS UNFOLD, MY FATHER MUST HAVE FELT A MIXTURE OF PAIN AND **RELIEF.**
IN THE TRAIN ON THE WAY BACK I THOUGHT THAT I WAS *FINALLY* GOING TO LIVE WITH MY MOTHER, THAT IT WAS THE BEGINNING OF A NEW ERA.
BUT NO. MY ROOM WAS WAITING FOR ME.
I WAS EXHAUSTED AND IN A TERRIBLE STATE. MIMI HAD HER **VICTORY.**
SHE *PROHIBITED* MY MOTHER FROM SEEING ME AGAIN.
ACCORDING TO MIMI, MY STABILITY DEPENDED ON OUR PARTING WAYS **FOREVER.**
MY MOTHER DIDN'T SAY ANYTHING. HER SILENCE WAS **ACKNOWLEDGMENT.**
FROM THEN ON, I COULD HONESTLY SAY, MY PARENTS HAD **ABANDONED** ME.

fourth session

I JUST WANTED TO HURT HIM

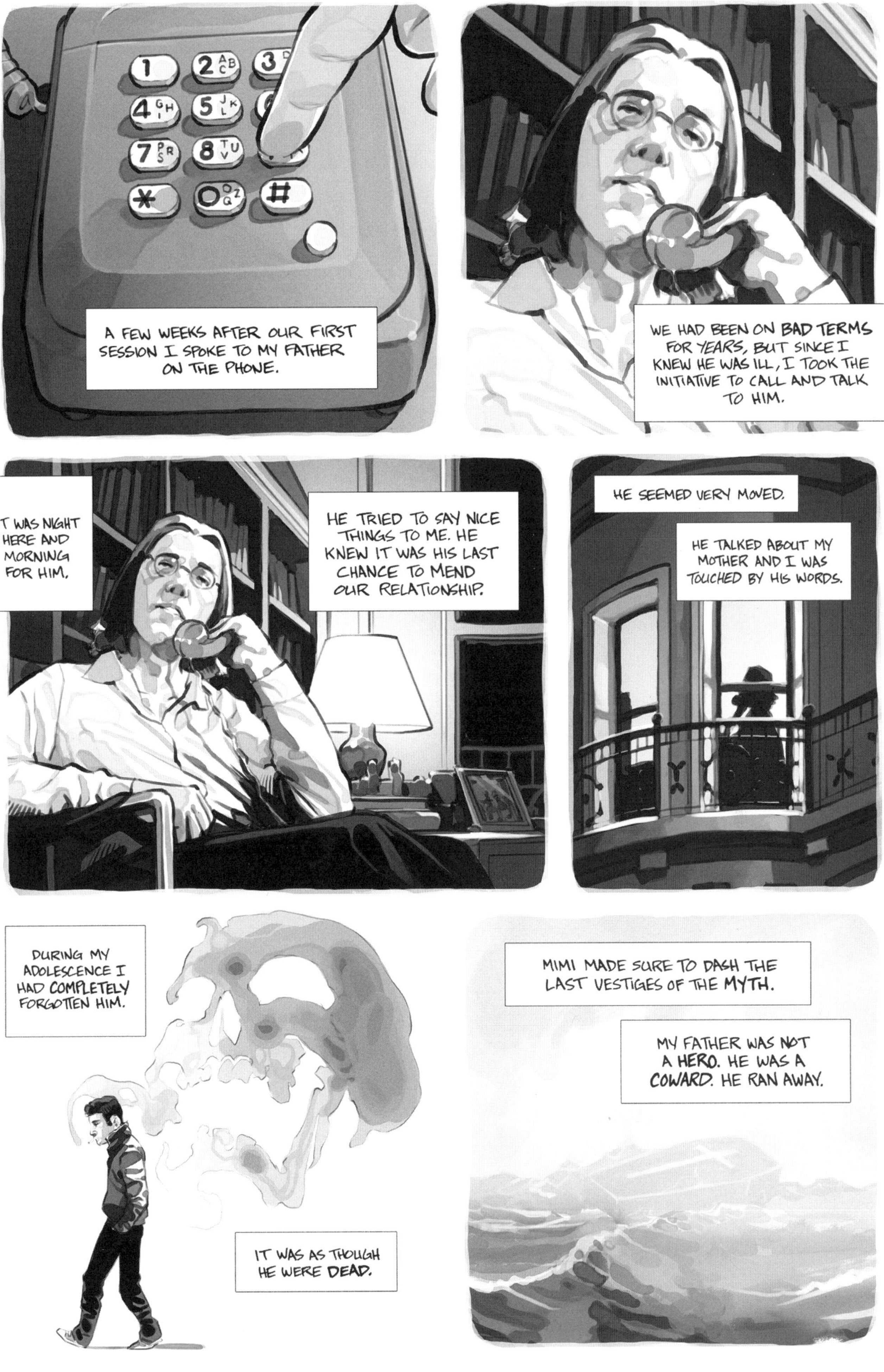
A FEW WEEKS AFTER OUR FIRST SESSION I SPOKE TO MY FATHER ON THE PHONE.
WE HAD BEEN ON BAD TERMS FOR YEARS, BUT SINCE I KNEW HE WAS ILL, I TOOK THE INITIATIVE TO CALL AND TALK TO HIM.
IT WAS NIGHT HERE AND MORNING FOR HIM.
HE TRIED TO SAY NICE THINGS TO ME. HE KNEW IT WAS HIS LAST CHANCE TO MEND OUR RELATIONSHIP.
HE SEEMED VERY MOVED.
HE TALKED ABOUT MY MOTHER AND I WAS TOUCHED BY HIS WORDS.
DURING MY ADOLESCENCE I HAD COMPLETELY FORGOTTEN HIM.
IT WAS AS THOUGH HE WERE DEAD.
MIMI MADE SURE TO DASH THE LAST VESTIGES OF THE MYTH.
MY FATHER WAS NOT A HERO. HE WAS A COWARD. HE RAN AWAY.

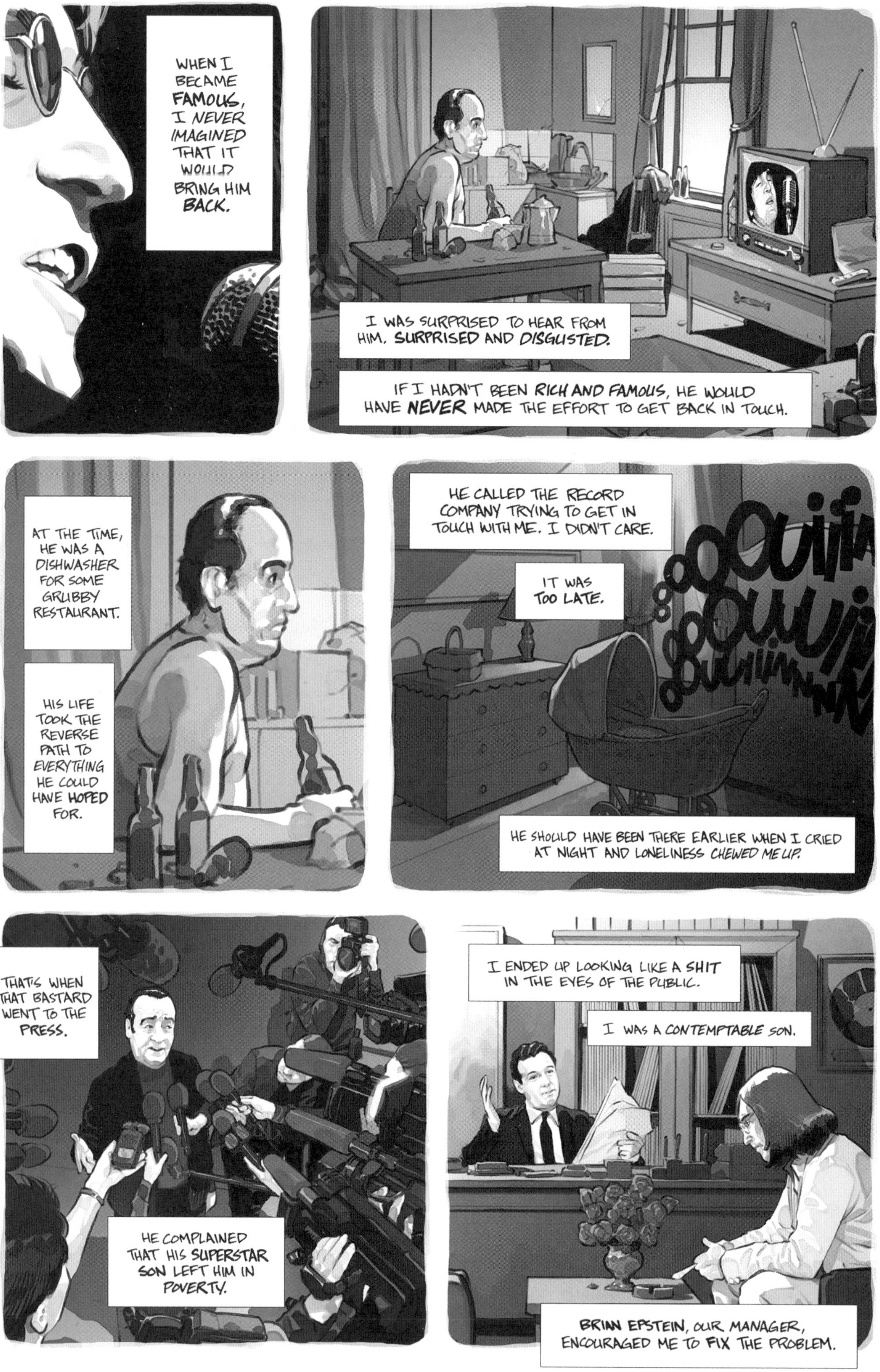
WHEN I BECAME FAMOUS, I NEVER IMAGINED THAT IT WOULD BRING HIM BACK.
I WAS SURPRISED TO HEAR FROM HIM, SURPRISED AND DISGUSTED.
IF I HADN'T BEEN RICH AND FAMOUS, HE WOULD HAVE NEVER MADE THE EFFORT TO GET BACK IN TOUCH.
AT THE TIME, HE WAS A DISHWASHER FOR SOME GRUBBY RESTAURANT.
HIS LIFE TOOK THE REVERSE PATH TO EVERYTHING HE COULD HAVE HOPED FOR.
HE CALLED THE RECORD COMPANY TRYING TO GET IN TOUCH WITH ME. I DIDN'T CARE.
IT WAS TOO LATE.
HE SHOULD HAVE BEEN THERE EARLIER WHEN I CRIED AT NIGHT AND LONELINESS CHEWED ME UP.
THAT'S WHEN THAT BASTARD WENT TO THE PRESS.
HE COMPLAINED THAT HIS SUPERSTAR SON LEFT HIM IN POVERTY.
I ENDED UP LOOKING LIKE A SHIT IN THE EYES OF THE PUBLIC.
I WAS A CONTEMPTABLE SON.
BRIAN EPSTEIN, OUR MANAGER, ENCOURAGED ME TO FIX THE PROBLEM.

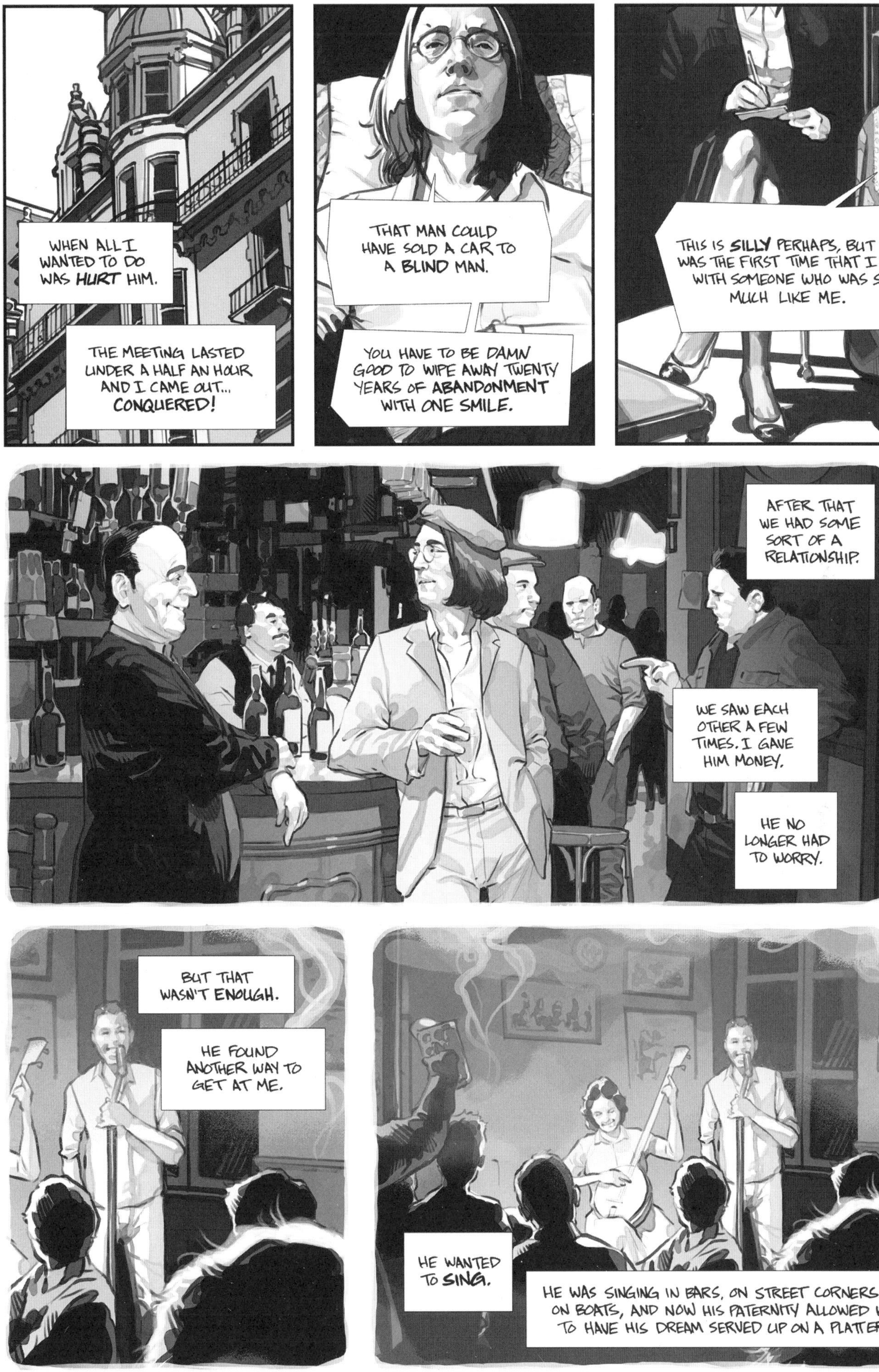
WHEN ALL I WANTED TO DO WAS HURT HIM.
THE MEETING LASTED UNDER A HALF AN HOUR AND I CAME OUT... CONQUERED!
THAT MAN COULD HAVE SOLD A CAR TO A BLIND MAN.
YOU HAVE TO BE DAMN GOOD TO WIPE AWAY TWENTY YEARS OF ABANDONMENT WITH ONE SMILE.
THIS IS SILLY PERHAPS, BUT IT WAS THE FIRST TIME THAT I WAS WITH SOMEONE WHO WAS SO MUCH LIKE ME.
AFTER THAT WE HAD SOME SORT OF A RELATIONSHIP.
WE SAW EACH OTHER A FEW TIMES. I GAVE HIM MONEY.
HE NO LONGER HAD TO WORRY.
BUT THAT WASN'T ENOUGH.
HE FOUND ANOTHER WAY TO GET AT ME.
HE WANTED TO SING.
HE WAS SINGING IN BARS, ON STREET CORNERS AND ON BOATS, AND NOW HIS PATERNITY ALLOWED HIM TO HAVE HIS DREAM SERVED UP ON A PLATTER.

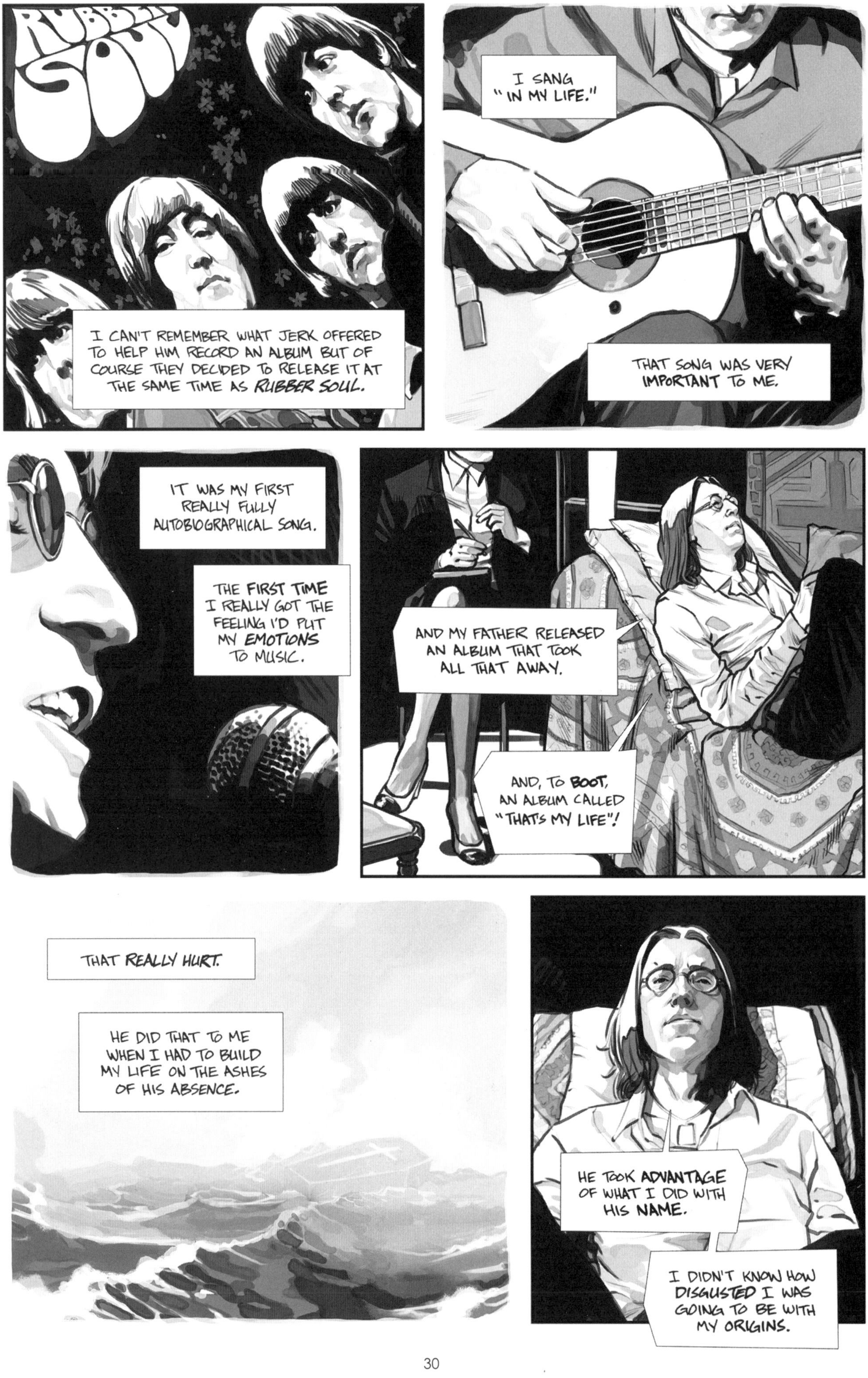
RUBBER SOUL
I CAN'T REMEMBER WHAT JERK OFFERED TO HELP HIM RECORD AN ALBUM BUT OF COURSE THEY DECIDED TO RELEASE IT AT THE SAME TIME AS RUBBER SOUL.
I SANG "IN MY LIFE."
THAT SONG WAS VERY IMPORTANT TO ME.
IT WAS MY FIRST REALLY FULLY AUTOBIOGRAPHICAL SONG.
THE FIRST TIME I REALLY GOT THE FEELING I'D PUT MY EMOTIONS TO MUSIC.
AND MY FATHER RELEASED AN ALBUM THAT TOOK ALL THAT AWAY.
AND, TO BOOT, AN ALBUM CALLED "THAT'S MY LIFE"!
THAT REALLY HURT.
HE DID THAT TO ME WHEN I HAD TO BUILD MY LIFE ON THE ASHES OF HIS ABSENCE.
HE TOOK ADVANTAGE OF WHAT I DID WITH HIS NAME.
I DIDN'T KNOW HOW DISGUSTED I WAS GOING TO BE WITH MY ORIGINS.

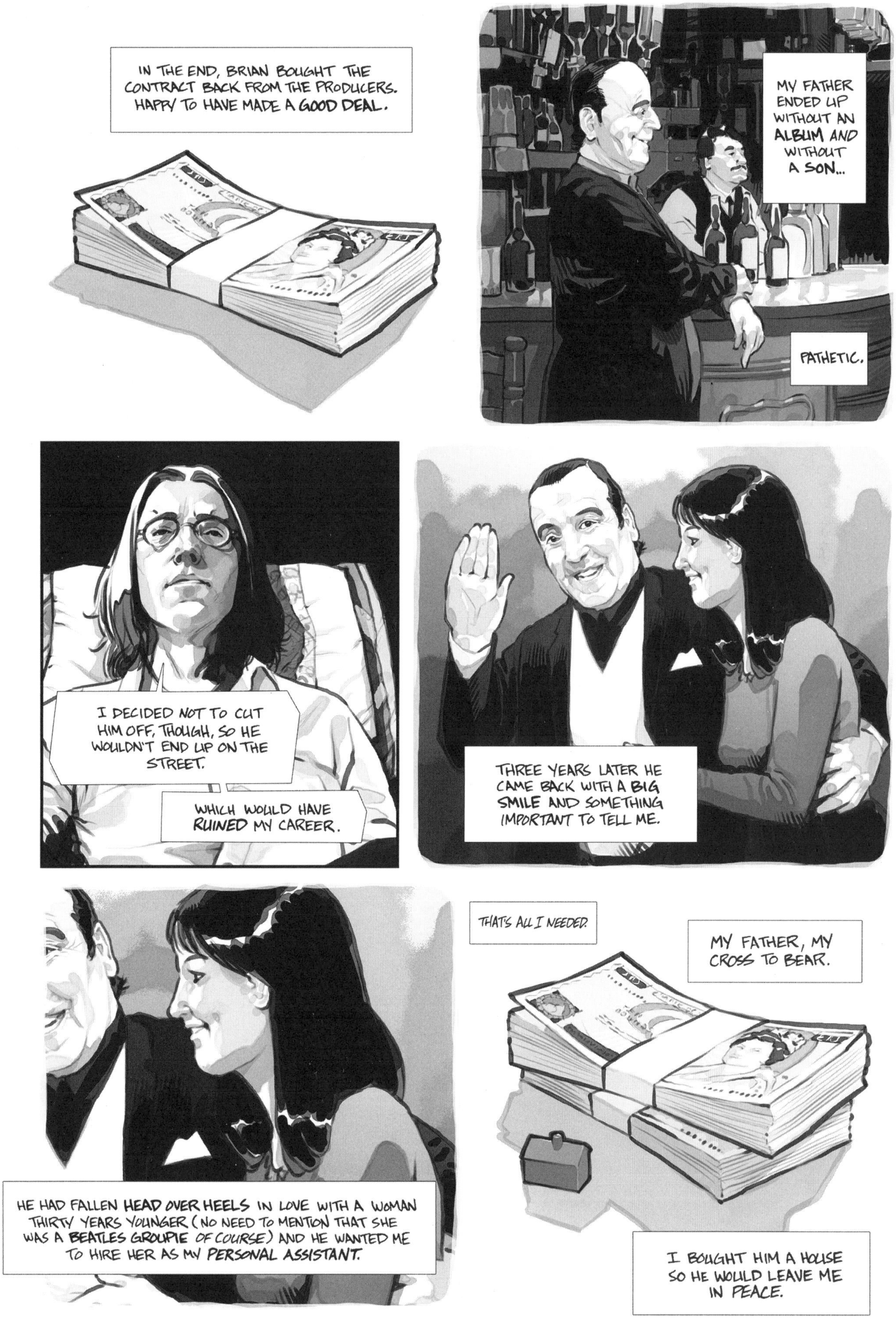

IN THE END, BRIAN BOUGHT THE CONTRACT BACK FROM THE PRODUCERS. HAPPY TO HAVE MADE A GOOD DEAL.
MY FATHER ENDED UP WITHOUT AN ALBUM AND WITHOUT A SON...
PATHETIC.
I DECIDED NOT TO CUT HIM OFF, THOUGH, SO HE WOULDN'T END UP ON THE STREET.
WHICH WOULD HAVE RUINED MY CAREER.
THREE YEARS LATER HE CAME BACK WITH A BIG SMILE AND SOMETHING IMPORTANT TO TELL ME.
HE HAD FALLEN HEAD OVER HEELS IN LOVE WITH A WOMAN THIRTY YEARS YOUNGER (NO NEED TO MENTION THAT SHE WAS A BEATLES GROUPIE OF COURSE) AND HE WANTED ME TO HIRE HER AS MY PERSONAL ASSISTANT.
THAT'S ALL I NEEDED.
MY FATHER, MY CROSS TO BEAR.
I BOUGHT HIM A HOUSE SO HE WOULD LEAVE ME IN PEACE.

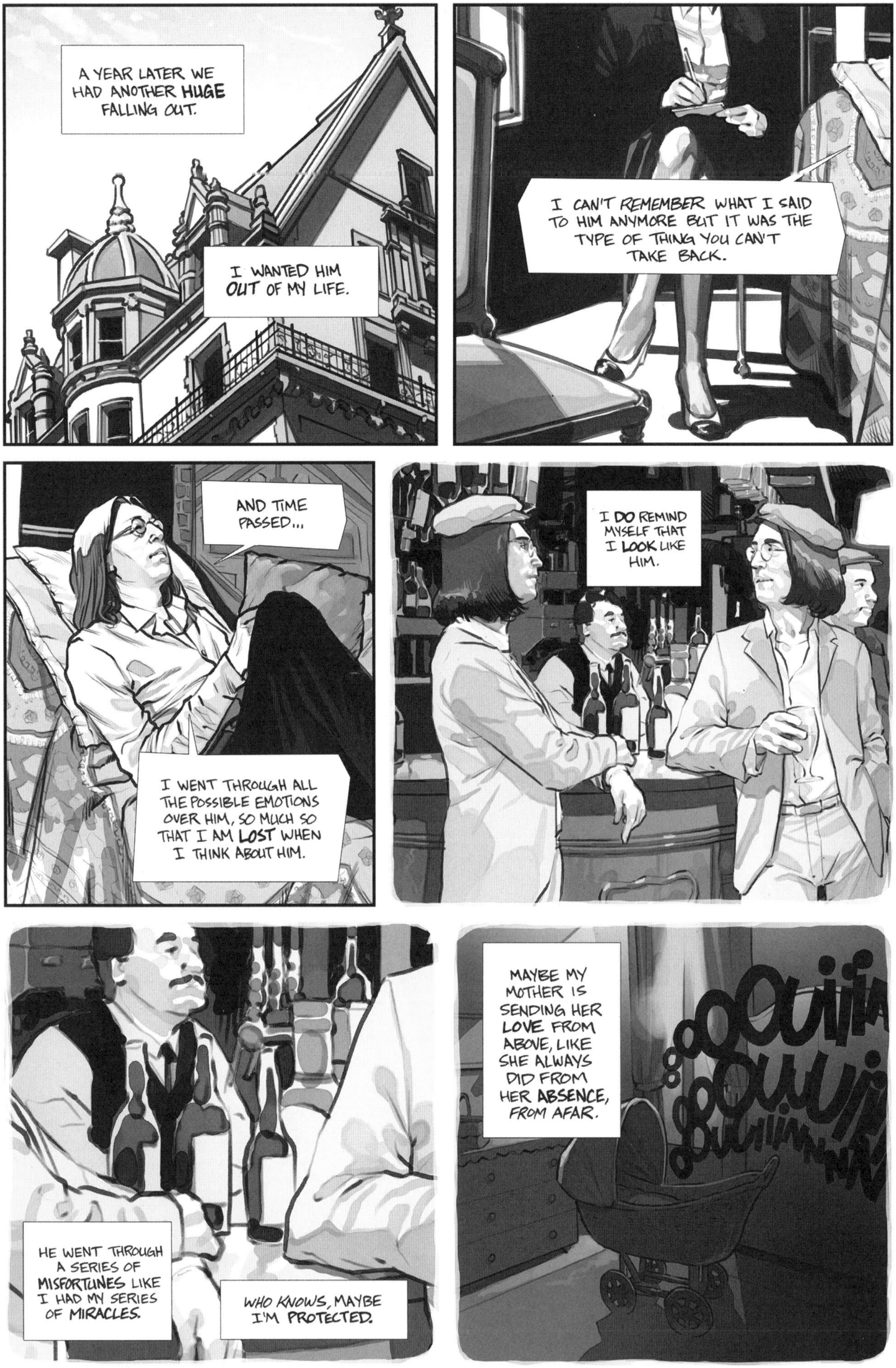
A YEAR LATER WE HAD ANOTHER HUGE FALLING OUT.
I WANTED HIM OUT OF MY LIFE.
I CAN'T REMEMBER WHAT I SAID TO HIM ANYMORE BUT IT WAS THE TYPE OF THING YOU CAN'T TAKE BACK.
AND TIME PASSED...
I WENT THROUGH ALL THE POSSIBLE EMOTIONS OVER HIM, SO MUCH SO THAT I AM LOST WHEN I THINK ABOUT HIM.
I DO REMIND MYSELF THAT I LOOK LIKE HIM.
HE WENT THROUGH A SERIES OF MISFORTUNES LIKE I HAD MY SERIES OF MIRACLES.
WHO KNOWS, MAYBE I'M PROTECTED.
MAYBE MY MOTHER IS SENDING HER LOVE FROM ABOVE, LIKE SHE ALWAYS DID FROM HER ABSENCE, FROM AFAR.

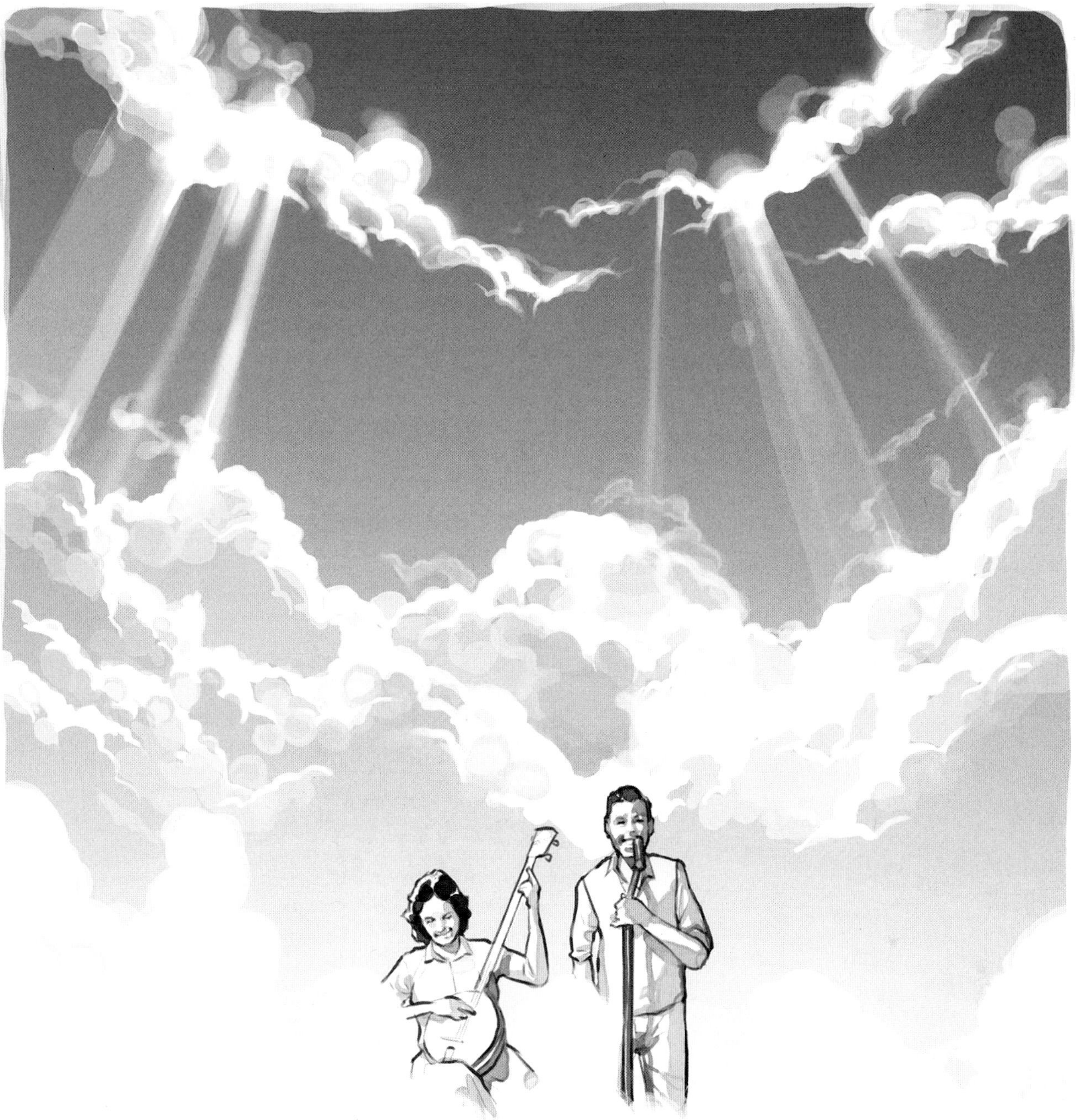

MY PARENTS ARE PROBABLY BACK TOGETHER NOW SOMEWHERE IN THE **GREAT BEYOND.**

fifth session

I'M NOT AN ADULT

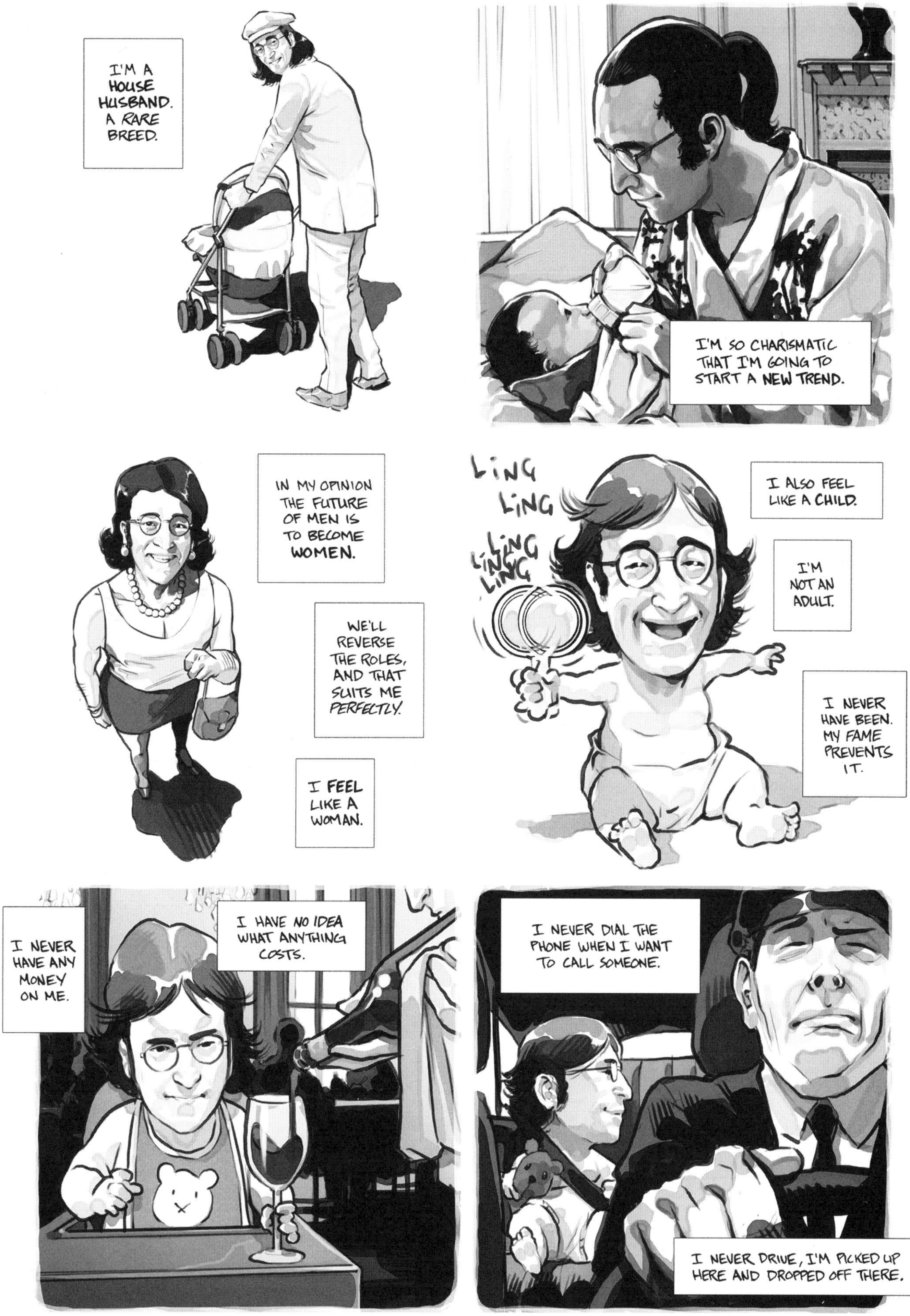

I'M A HOUSE HUSBAND. A RARE BREED.
I'M SO CHARISMATIC THAT I'M GOING TO START A NEW TREND.
IN MY OPINION THE FUTURE OF MEN IS TO BECOME WOMEN.
WE'LL REVERSE THE ROLES, AND THAT SUITS ME PERFECTLY.
I FEEL LIKE A WOMAN.
LING LING LING LING LING
I ALSO FEEL LIKE A CHILD.
I'M NOT AN ADULT.
I NEVER HAVE BEEN. MY FAME PREVENTS IT.
I NEVER HAVE ANY MONEY ON ME.
I HAVE NO IDEA WHAT ANYTHING COSTS.
I NEVER DIAL THE PHONE WHEN I WANT TO CALL SOMEONE.
I NEVER DRIVE, I'M PICKED UP HERE AND DROPPED OFF THERE.

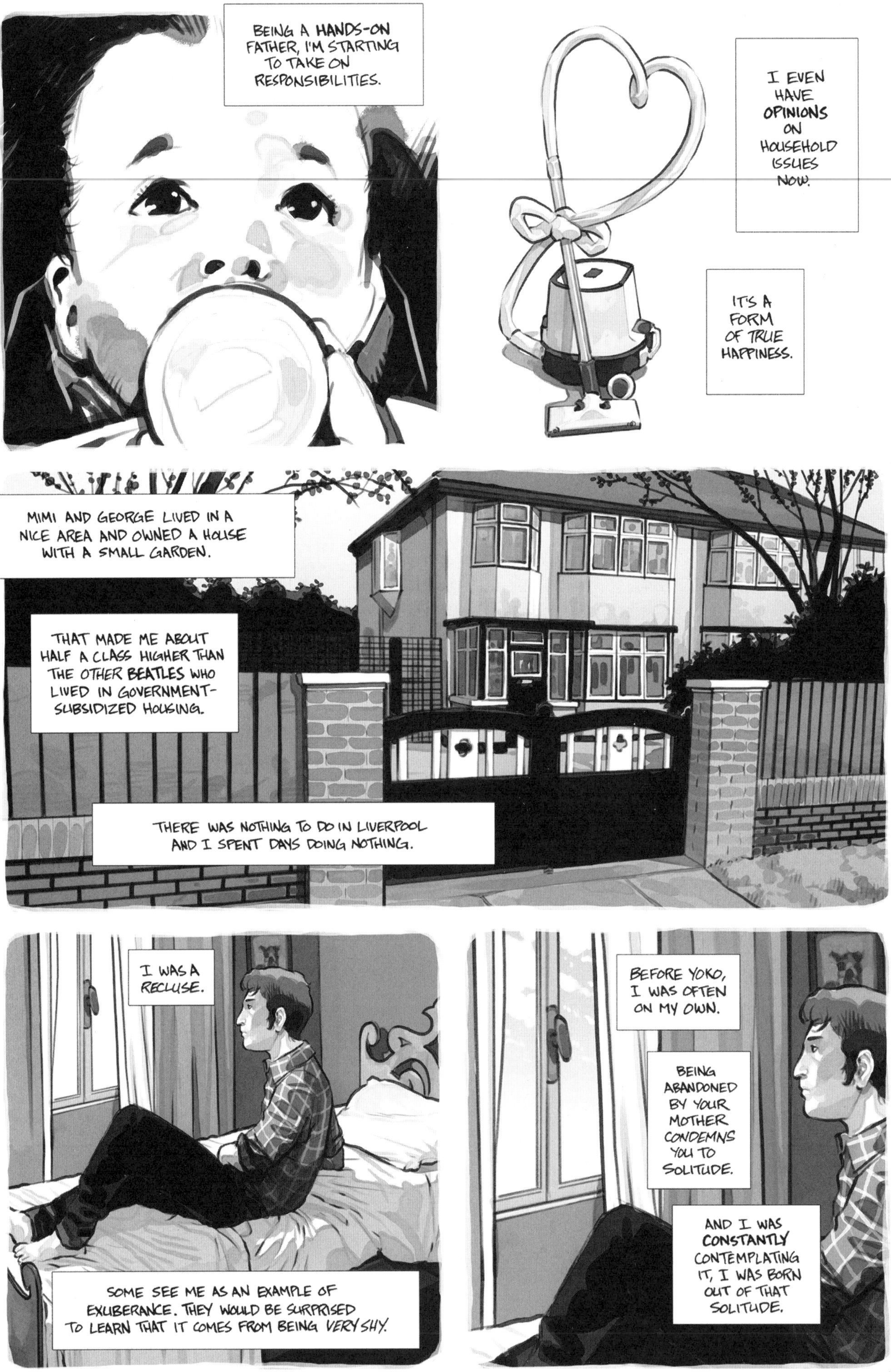
BEING A HANDS-ON FATHER, I'M STARTING TO TAKE ON RESPONSIBILITIES.
I EVEN HAVE OPINIONS ON HOUSEHOLD ISSUES NOW.
IT'S A FORM OF TRUE HAPPINESS.
MIMI AND GEORGE LIVED IN A NICE AREA AND OWNED A HOUSE WITH A SMALL GARDEN.
THAT MADE ME ABOUT HALF A CLASS HIGHER THAN THE OTHER BEATLES WHO LIVED IN GOVERNMENT-SUBSIDIZED HOUSING.
THERE WAS NOTHING TO DO IN LIVERPOOL AND I SPENT DAYS DOING NOTHING.
I WAS A RECLUSE.
SOME SEE ME AS AN EXAMPLE OF EXUBERANCE. THEY WOULD BE SURPRISED TO LEARN THAT IT COMES FROM BEING VERY SHY.
BEFORE YOKO, I WAS OFTEN ON MY OWN.
BEING ABANDONED BY YOUR MOTHER CONDEMNS YOU TO SOLITUDE.
AND I WAS CONSTANTLY CONTEMPLATING IT, I WAS BORN OUT OF THAT SOLITUDE.

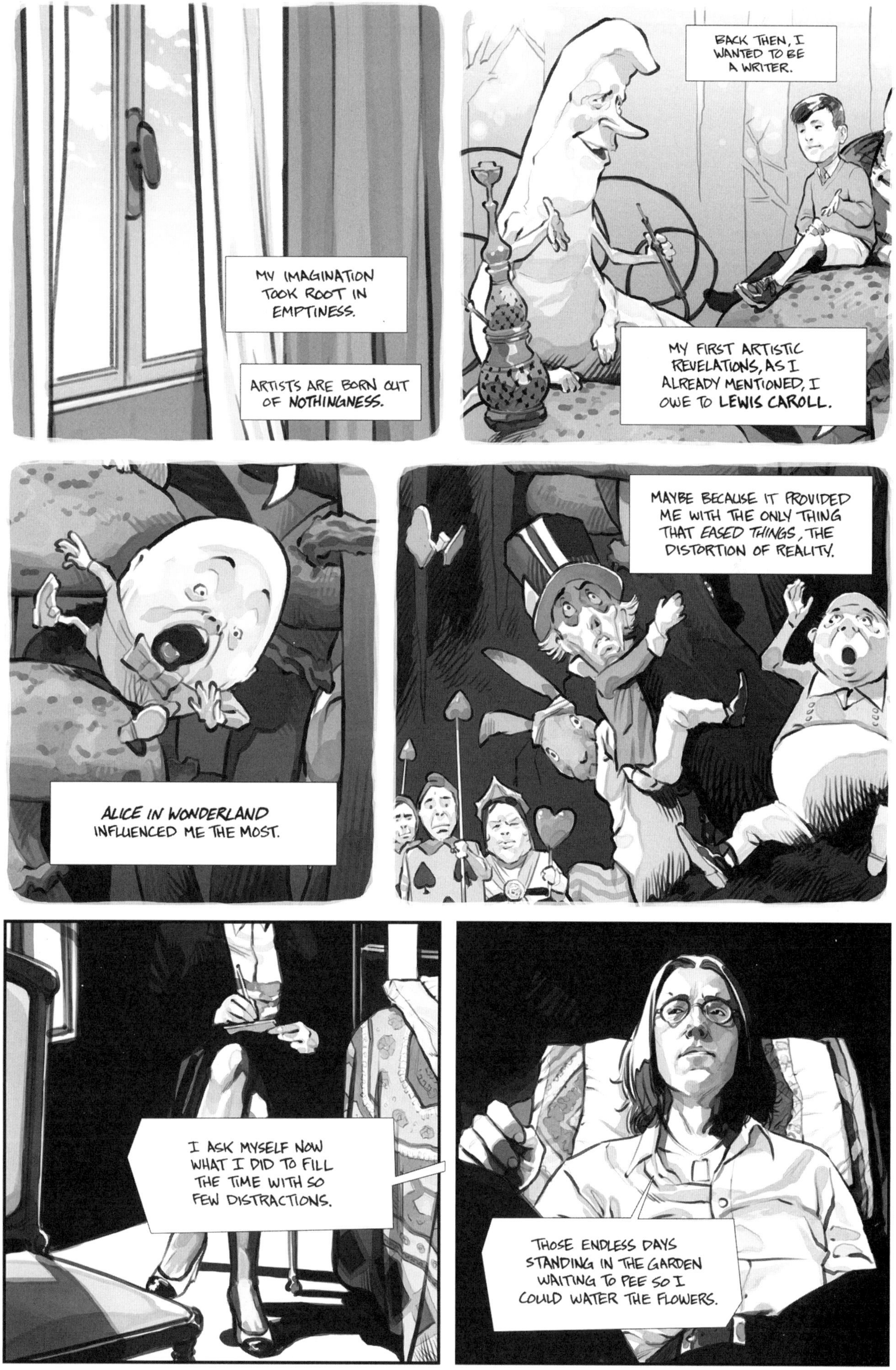
MY IMAGINATION TOOK ROOT IN EMPTINESS.
ARTISTS ARE BORN OUT OF NOTHINGNESS.
BACK THEN, I WANTED TO BE A WRITER.
MY FIRST ARTISTIC REVELATIONS, AS I ALREADY MENTIONED, I OWE TO LEWIS CAROLL.
ALICE IN WONDERLAND INFLUENCED ME THE MOST.
MAYBE BECAUSE IT PROVIDED ME WITH THE ONLY THING THAT EASED THINGS, THE DISTORTION OF REALITY.
I ASK MYSELF NOW WHAT I DID TO FILL THE TIME WITH SO FEW DISTRACTIONS.
THOSE ENDLESS DAYS STANDING IN THE GARDEN WAITING TO PEE SO I COULD WATER THE FLOWERS.

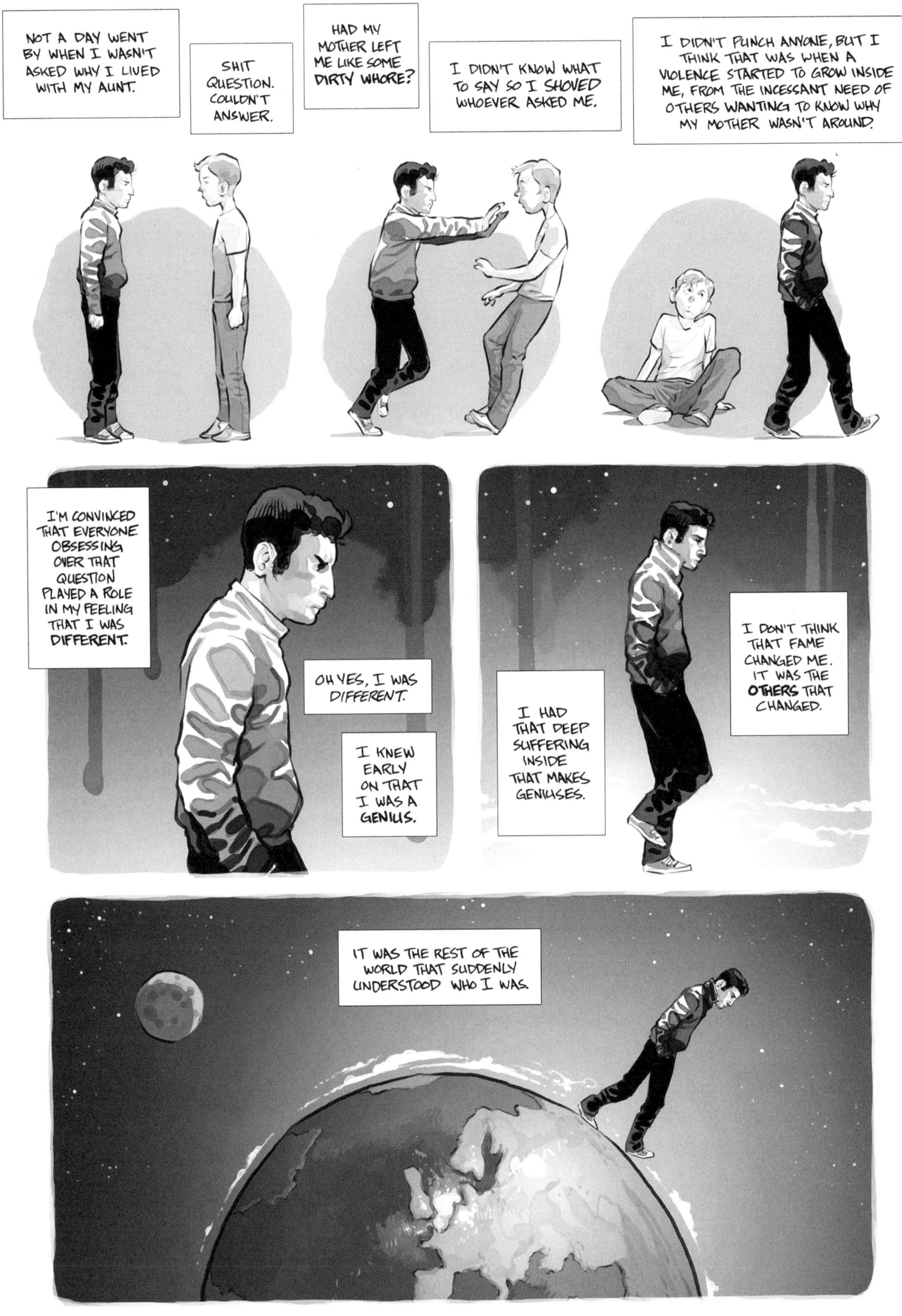
NOT A DAY WENT BY WHEN I WASN'T ASKED WHY I LIVED WITH MY AUNT.
SHIT QUESTION. COULDN'T ANSWER.
HAD MY MOTHER LEFT ME LIKE SOME DIRTY WHORE?
I DIDN'T KNOW WHAT TO SAY SO I SHOVED WHOEVER ASKED ME.
I DIDN'T PUNCH ANYONE, BUT I THINK THAT WAS WHEN A VIOLENCE STARTED TO GROW INSIDE ME, FROM THE INCESSANT NEED OF OTHERS WANTING TO KNOW WHY MY MOTHER WASN'T AROUND.
I'M CONVINCED THAT EVERYONE OBSESSING OVER THAT QUESTION PLAYED A ROLE IN MY FEELING THAT I WAS DIFFERENT.
OH YES, I WAS DIFFERENT.
I KNEW EARLY ON THAT I WAS A GENIUS.
I HAD THAT DEEP SUFFERING INSIDE THAT MAKES GENIUSES.
I DON'T THINK THAT FAME CHANGED ME. IT WAS THE OTHERS THAT CHANGED.
IT WAS THE REST OF THE WORLD THAT SUDDENLY UNDERSTOOD WHO I WAS.

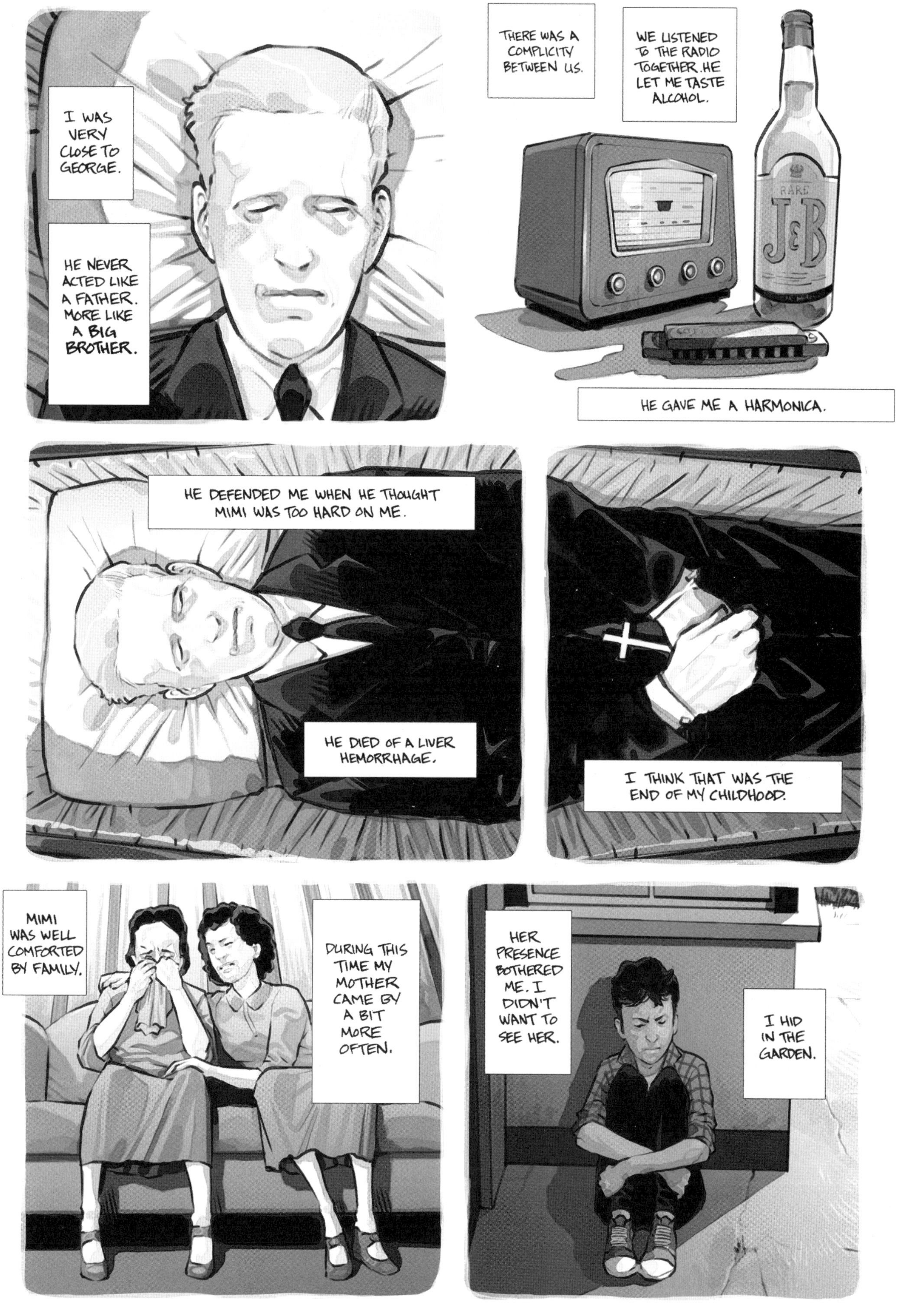
I WAS VERY CLOSE TO GEORGE.
HE NEVER ACTED LIKE A FATHER. MORE LIKE A **BIG BROTHER.**
THERE WAS A COMPLICITY BETWEEN US.
WE LISTENED TO THE RADIO TOGETHER. HE LET ME TASTE ALCOHOL.
RARE
J&B
HE GAVE ME A HARMONICA.
HE DEFENDED ME WHEN HE THOUGHT MIMI WAS TOO HARD ON ME.
HE DIED OF A LIVER HEMORRHAGE.
I THINK THAT WAS THE END OF MY CHILDHOOD.
MIMI WAS WELL COMFORTED BY FAMILY.
DURING THIS TIME MY MOTHER CAME BY A BIT MORE OFTEN.
HER PRESENCE BOTHERED ME. I DIDN'T WANT TO SEE HER.
I HID IN THE GARDEN.

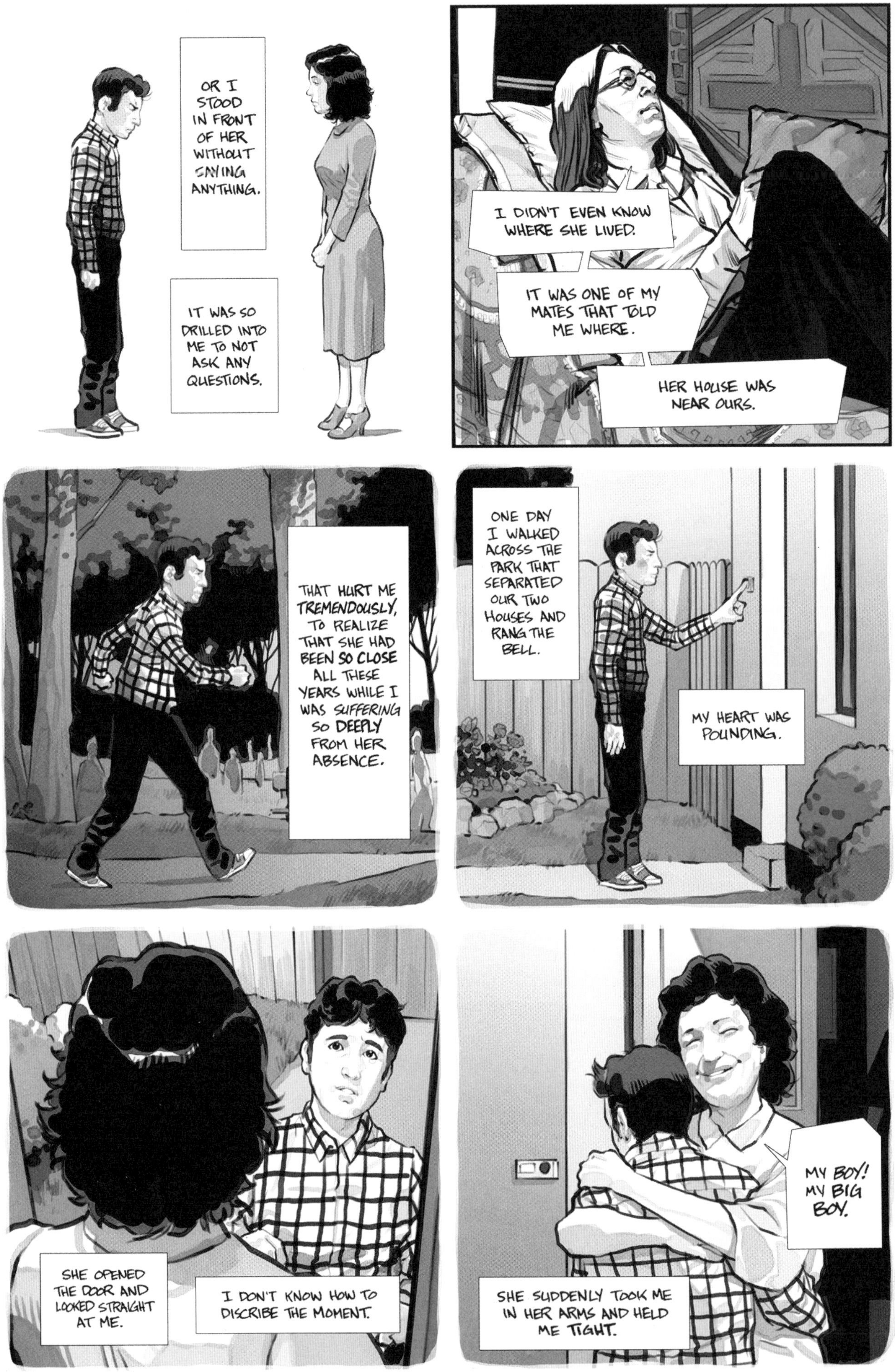
OR I STOOD IN FRONT OF HER WITHOUT SAYING ANYTHING.
IT WAS SO DRILLED INTO ME TO NOT ASK ANY QUESTIONS.
I DIDN'T EVEN KNOW WHERE SHE LIVED.
IT WAS ONE OF MY MATES THAT TOLD ME WHERE.
HER HOUSE WAS NEAR OURS.
THAT HURT ME TREMENDOUSLY, TO REALIZE THAT SHE HAD BEEN SO CLOSE ALL THESE YEARS WHILE I WAS SUFFERING SO DEEPLY FROM HER ABSENCE.
ONE DAY I WALKED ACROSS THE PARK THAT SEPARATED OUR TWO HOUSES AND RANG THE BELL.
MY HEART WAS POUNDING.
SHE OPENED THE DOOR AND LOOKED STRAIGHT AT ME.
I DON'T KNOW HOW TO DISCRIBE THE MOMENT.
MY BOY! MY BIG BOY.
SHE SUDDENLY TOOK ME IN HER ARMS AND HELD ME TIGHT.

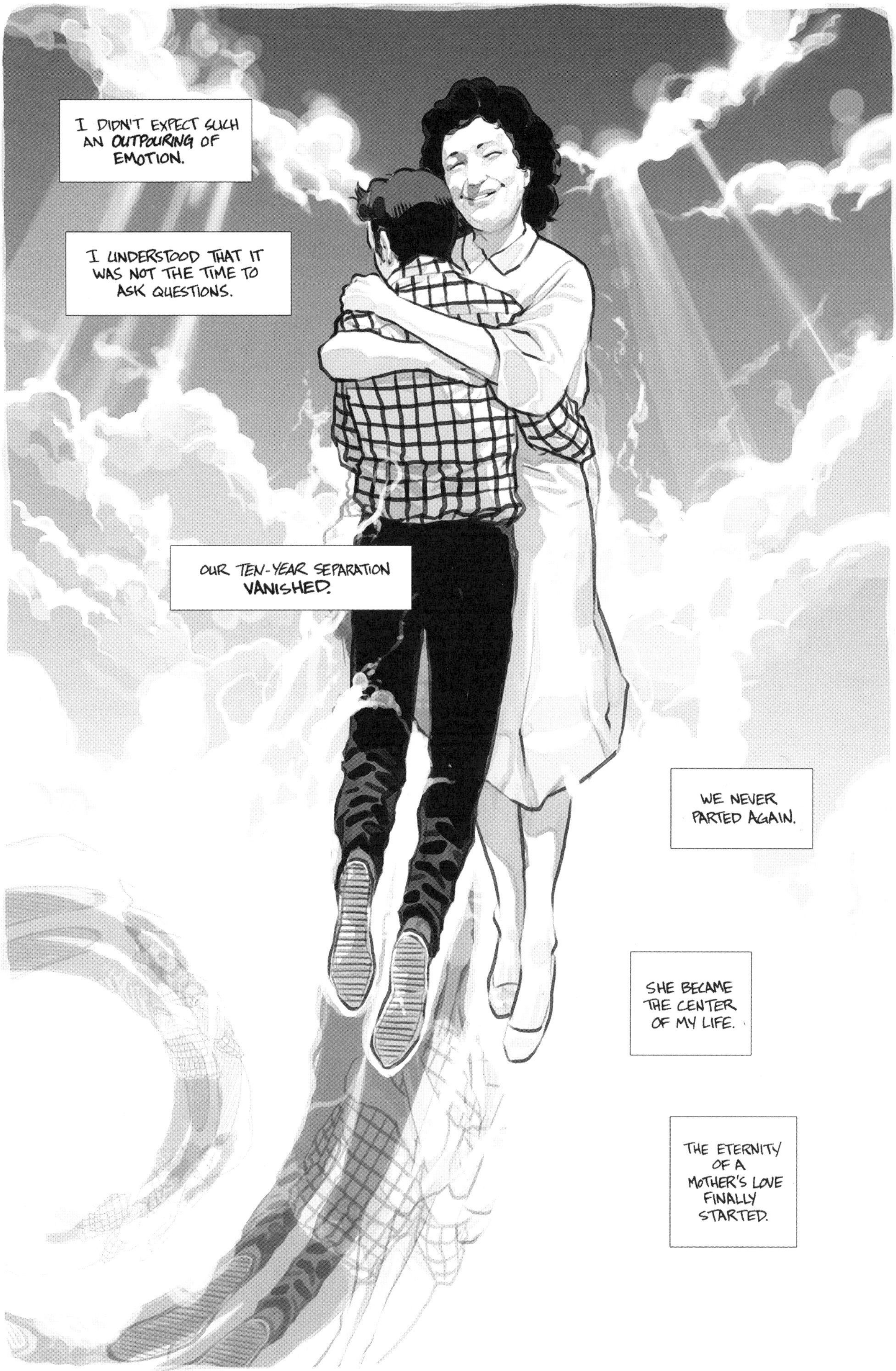

I DIDN'T EXPECT SUCH AN OUTPOURING OF EMOTION.
I UNDERSTOOD THAT IT WAS NOT THE TIME TO ASK QUESTIONS.
OUR TEN-YEAR SEPARATION VANISHED.
WE NEVER PARTED AGAIN.
SHE BECAME THE CENTER OF MY LIFE.
THE ETERNITY OF A MOTHER'S LOVE FINALLY STARTED.

sixth session

I FELT AS THOUGH
MY EARS HAD WINGS

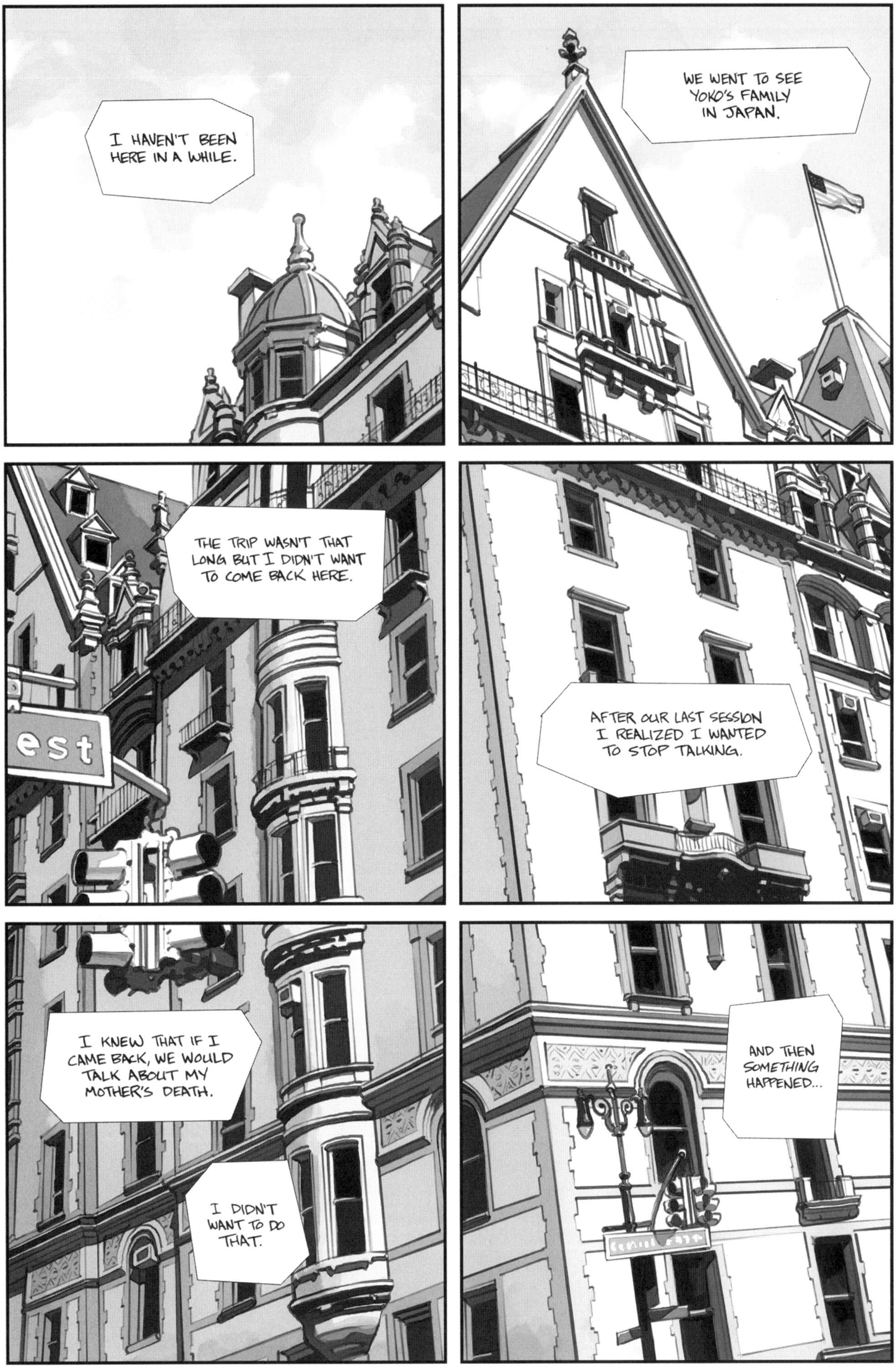
I HAVEN'T BEEN HERE IN A WHILE.
WE WENT TO SEE YOKO'S FAMILY IN JAPAN.
THE TRIP WASN'T THAT LONG BUT I DIDN'T WANT TO COME BACK HERE.
est
AFTER OUR LAST SESSION I REALIZED I WANTED TO STOP TALKING.
I KNEW THAT IF I CAME BACK, WE WOULD TALK ABOUT MY MOTHER'S DEATH.
I DIDN'T WANT TO DO THAT.
AND THEN SOMETHING HAPPENED...

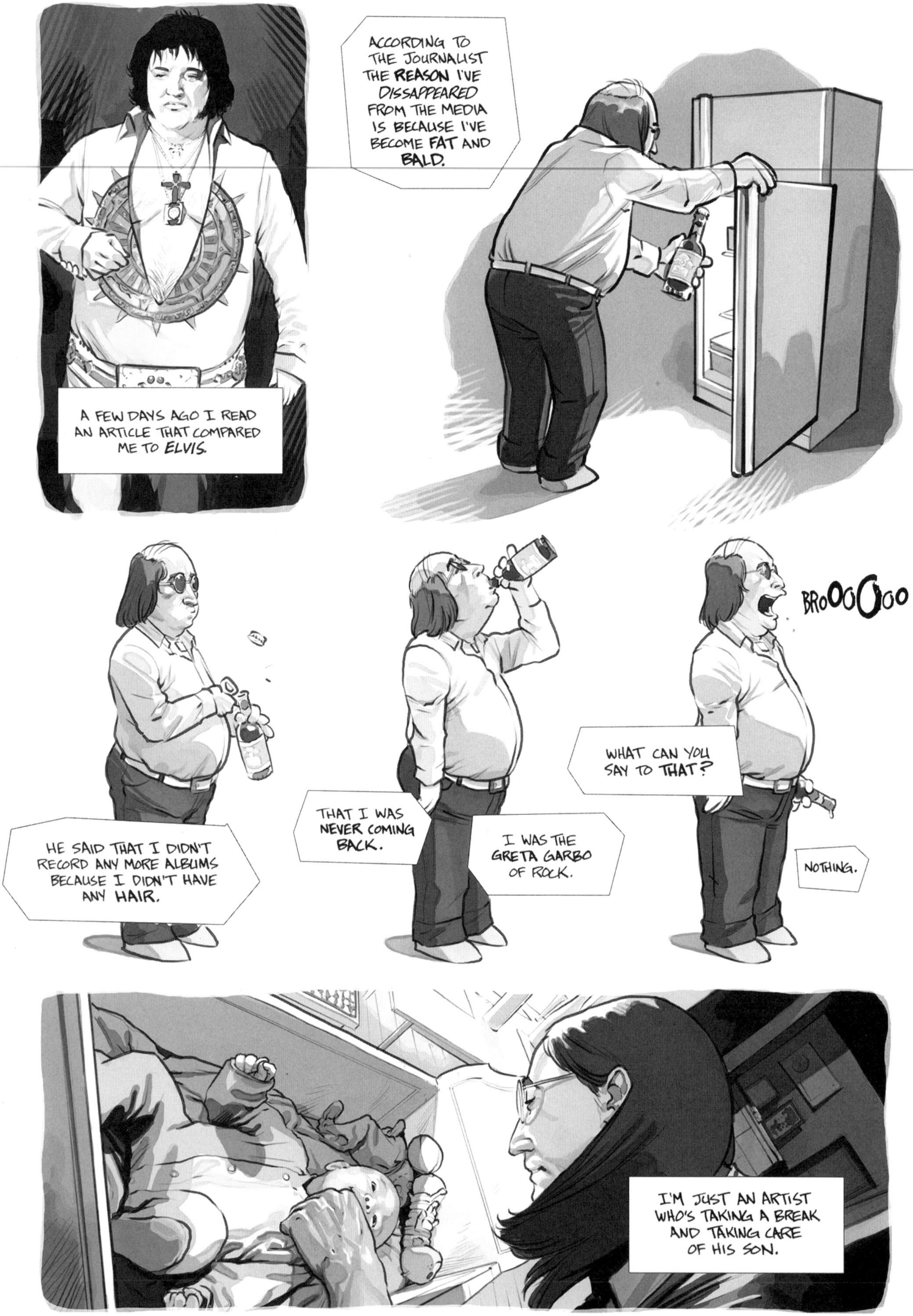
A FEW DAYS AGO I READ AN ARTICLE THAT COMPARED ME TO ELVIS.
ACCORDING TO THE JOURNALIST THE REASON I'VE DISSAPPEARED FROM THE MEDIA IS BECAUSE I'VE BECOME FAT AND BALD.
HE SAID THAT I DIDN'T RECORD ANY MORE ALBUMS BECAUSE I DIDN'T HAVE ANY HAIR.
THAT I WAS NEVER COMING BACK.
I WAS THE GRETA GARBO OF ROCK.
BROOOOoo
WHAT CAN YOU SAY TO THAT?
NOTHING.
I'M JUST AN ARTIST WHO'S TAKING A BREAK AND TAKING CARE OF HIS SON.

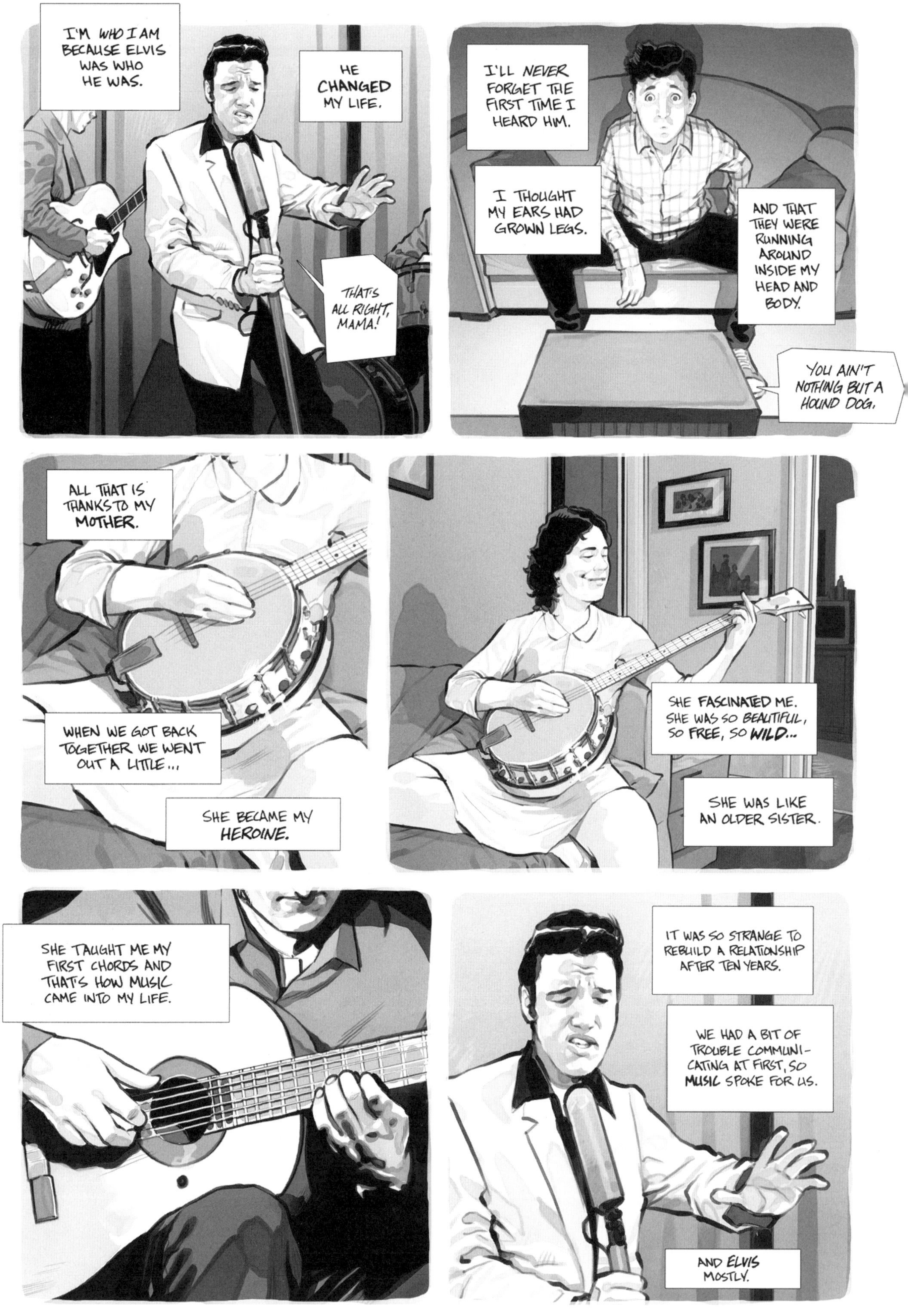
I'M WHO I AM BECAUSE ELVIS WAS WHO HE WAS.
HE CHANGED MY LIFE.
THAT'S ALL RIGHT, MAMA!
I'LL NEVER FORGET THE FIRST TIME I HEARD HIM.
I THOUGHT MY EARS HAD GROWN LEGS.
AND THAT THEY WERE RUNNING AROUND INSIDE MY HEAD AND BODY.
YOU AIN'T NOTHING BUT A HOUND DOG.
ALL THAT IS THANKS TO MY MOTHER.
WHEN WE GOT BACK TOGETHER WE WENT OUT A LITTLE...
SHE BECAME MY HEROINE.
SHE FASCINATED ME. SHE WAS SO BEAUTIFUL, SO FREE, SO WILD...
SHE WAS LIKE AN OLDER SISTER.
SHE TAUGHT ME MY FIRST CHORDS AND THAT'S HOW MUSIC CAME INTO MY LIFE.
IT WAS SO STRANGE TO REBUILD A RELATIONSHIP AFTER TEN YEARS.
WE HAD A BIT OF TROUBLE COMMUNI-CATING AT FIRST, SO MUSIC SPOKE FOR US.
AND ELVIS MOSTLY.

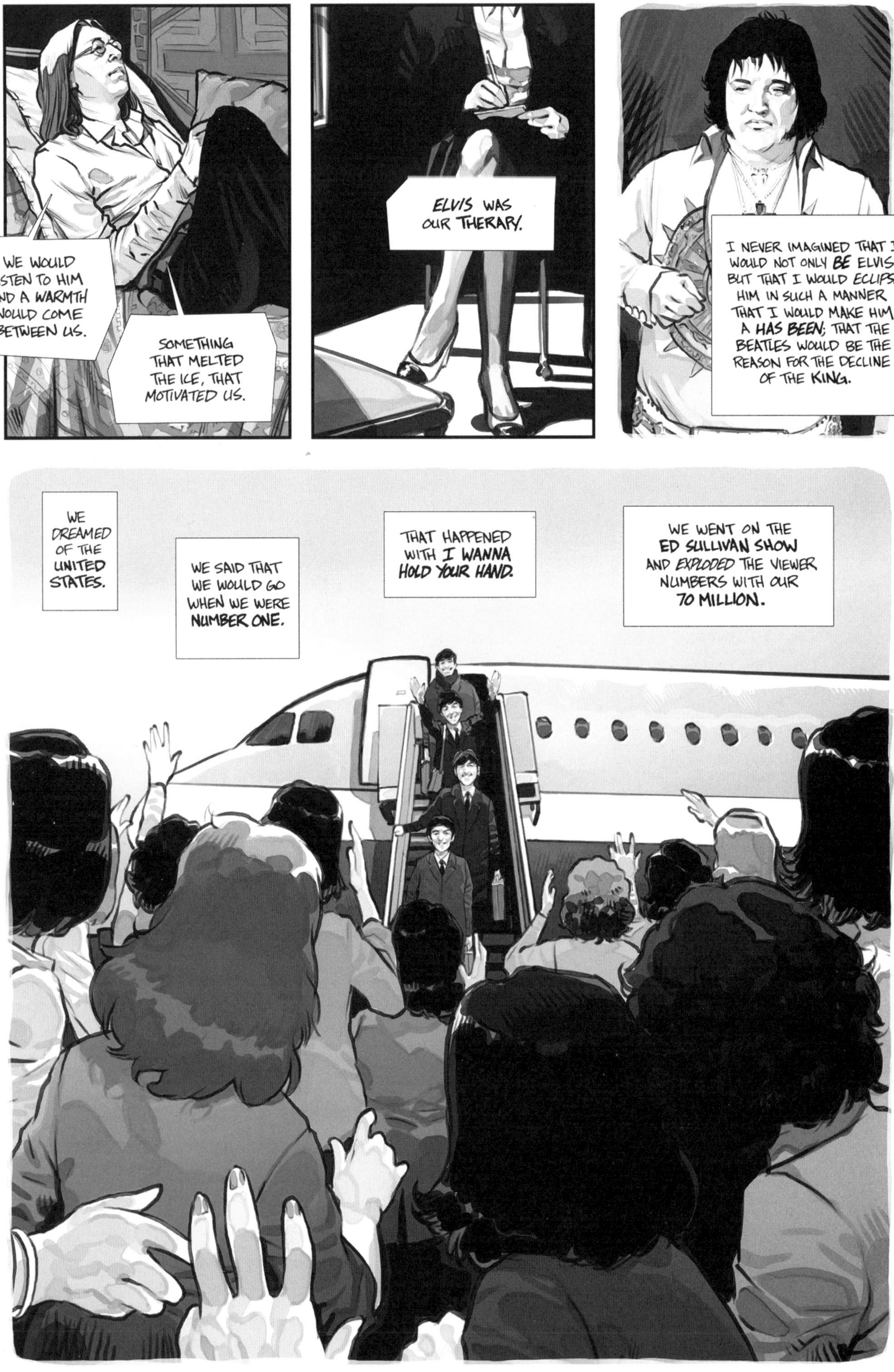
WE WOULD LISTEN TO HIM AND A WARMTH WOULD COME BETWEEN US.
SOMETHING THAT MELTED THE ICE, THAT MOTIVATED US.
ELVIS WAS OUR THERAPY.
I NEVER IMAGINED THAT I WOULD NOT ONLY BE ELVIS BUT THAT I WOULD ECLIPSE HIM IN SUCH A MANNER THAT I WOULD MAKE HIM A HAS BEEN; THAT THE BEATLES WOULD BE THE REASON FOR THE DECLINE OF THE KING.
WE DREAMED OF THE UNITED STATES.
WE SAID THAT WE WOULD GO WHEN WE WERE NUMBER ONE.
THAT HAPPENED WITH I WANNA HOLD YOUR HAND.
WE WENT ON THE ED SULLIVAN SHOW AND EXPLODED THE VIEWER NUMBERS WITH OUR 70 MILLION.

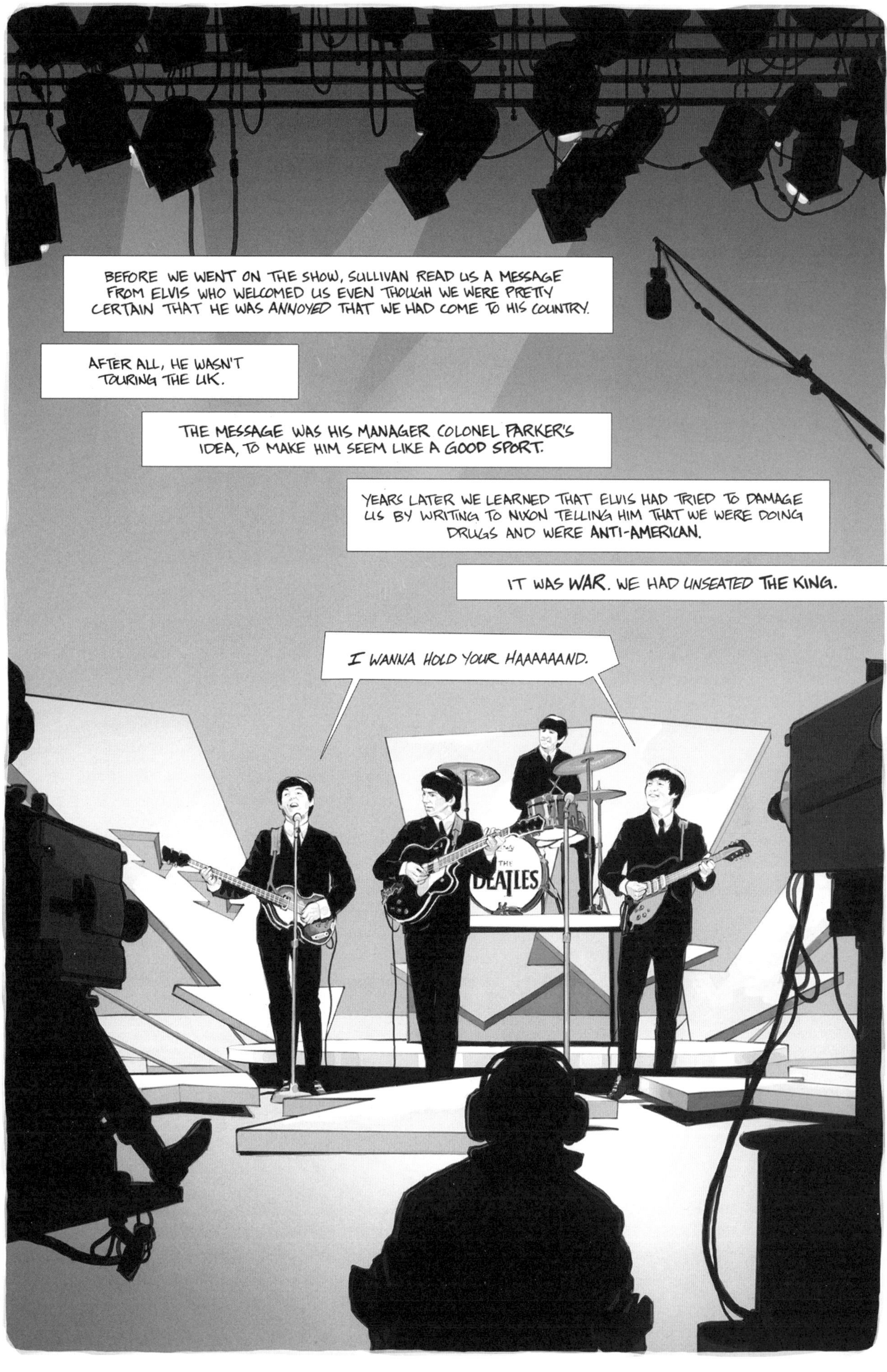
BEFORE WE WENT ON THE SHOW, SULLIVAN READ US A MESSAGE FROM ELVIS WHO WELCOMED US EVEN THOUGH WE WERE PRETTY CERTAIN THAT HE WAS ANNOYED THAT WE HAD COME TO HIS COUNTRY.
AFTER ALL, HE WASN'T TOURING THE UK.
THE MESSAGE WAS HIS MANAGER COLONEL PARKER'S IDEA, TO MAKE HIM SEEM LIKE A GOOD SPORT.
YEARS LATER WE LEARNED THAT ELVIS HAD TRIED TO DAMAGE US BY WRITING TO NIXON TELLING HIM THAT WE WERE DOING DRUGS AND WERE ANTI-AMERICAN.
IT WAS WAR. WE HAD UNSEATED THE KING.
I WANNA HOLD YOUR HAAAAAAND.
THE BEATLES

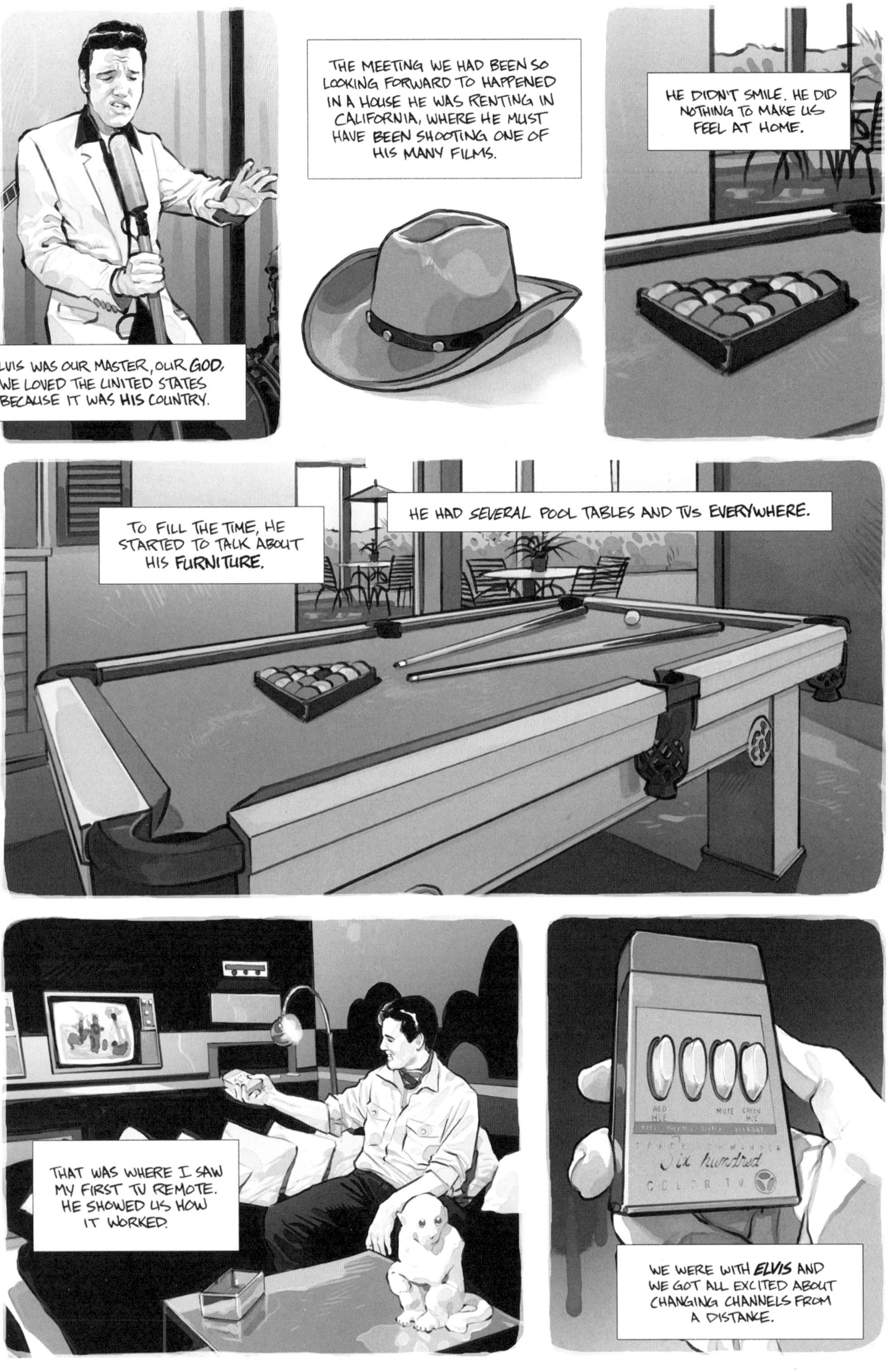

ELVIS WAS OUR MASTER, OUR **GOD**, WE LOVED THE UNITED STATES BECAUSE IT WAS **HIS** COUNTRY.
THE MEETING WE HAD BEEN SO LOOKING FORWARD TO HAPPENED IN A HOUSE HE WAS RENTING IN CALIFORNIA, WHERE HE MUST HAVE BEEN SHOOTING ONE OF HIS MANY FILMS.
HE DIDN'T SMILE. HE DID NOTHING TO MAKE US FEEL AT HOME.
TO FILL THE TIME, HE STARTED TO TALK ABOUT HIS **FURNITURE**.
HE HAD *SEVERAL* POOL TABLES AND TVs **EVERYWHERE**.
THAT WAS WHERE I SAW MY FIRST TV REMOTE. HE SHOWED US HOW IT WORKED.
RED HUE
MUTE
GREEN HUE
Six hundred
COLOR TV
WE WERE WITH ***ELVIS*** AND WE GOT ALL EXCITED ABOUT CHANGING CHANNELS FROM A DISTANCE.

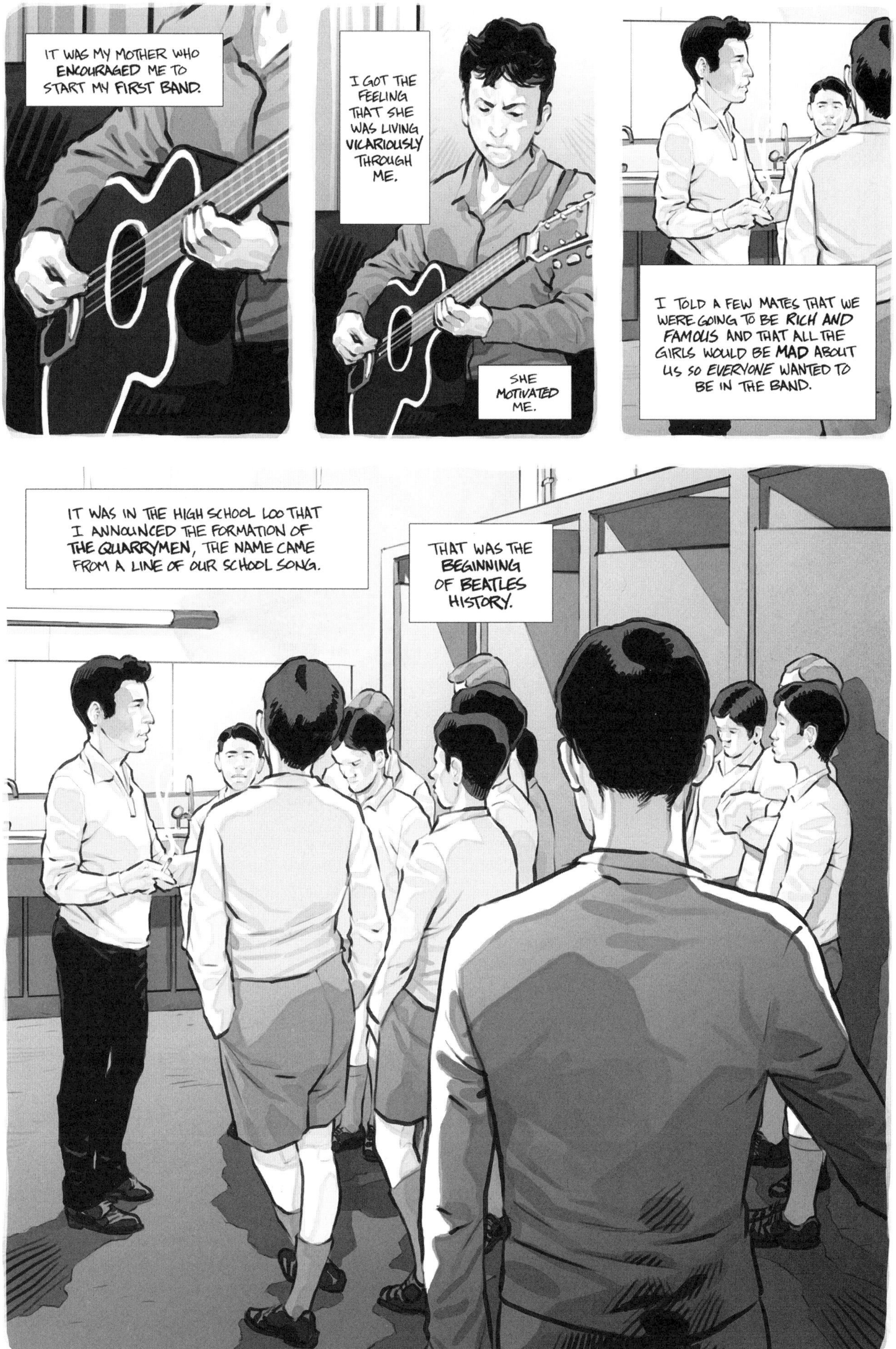
IT WAS MY MOTHER WHO ENCOURAGED ME TO START MY FIRST BAND.
I GOT THE FEELING THAT SHE WAS LIVING VICARIOUSLY THROUGH ME.
SHE MOTIVATED ME.
I TOLD A FEW MATES THAT WE WERE GOING TO BE RICH AND FAMOUS AND THAT ALL THE GIRLS WOULD BE MAD ABOUT US SO EVERYONE WANTED TO BE IN THE BAND.
IT WAS IN THE HIGH SCHOOL LOO THAT I ANNOUNCED THE FORMATION OF THE QUARRYMEN, THE NAME CAME FROM A LINE OF OUR SCHOOL SONG.
THAT WAS THE BEGINNING OF BEATLES HISTORY.

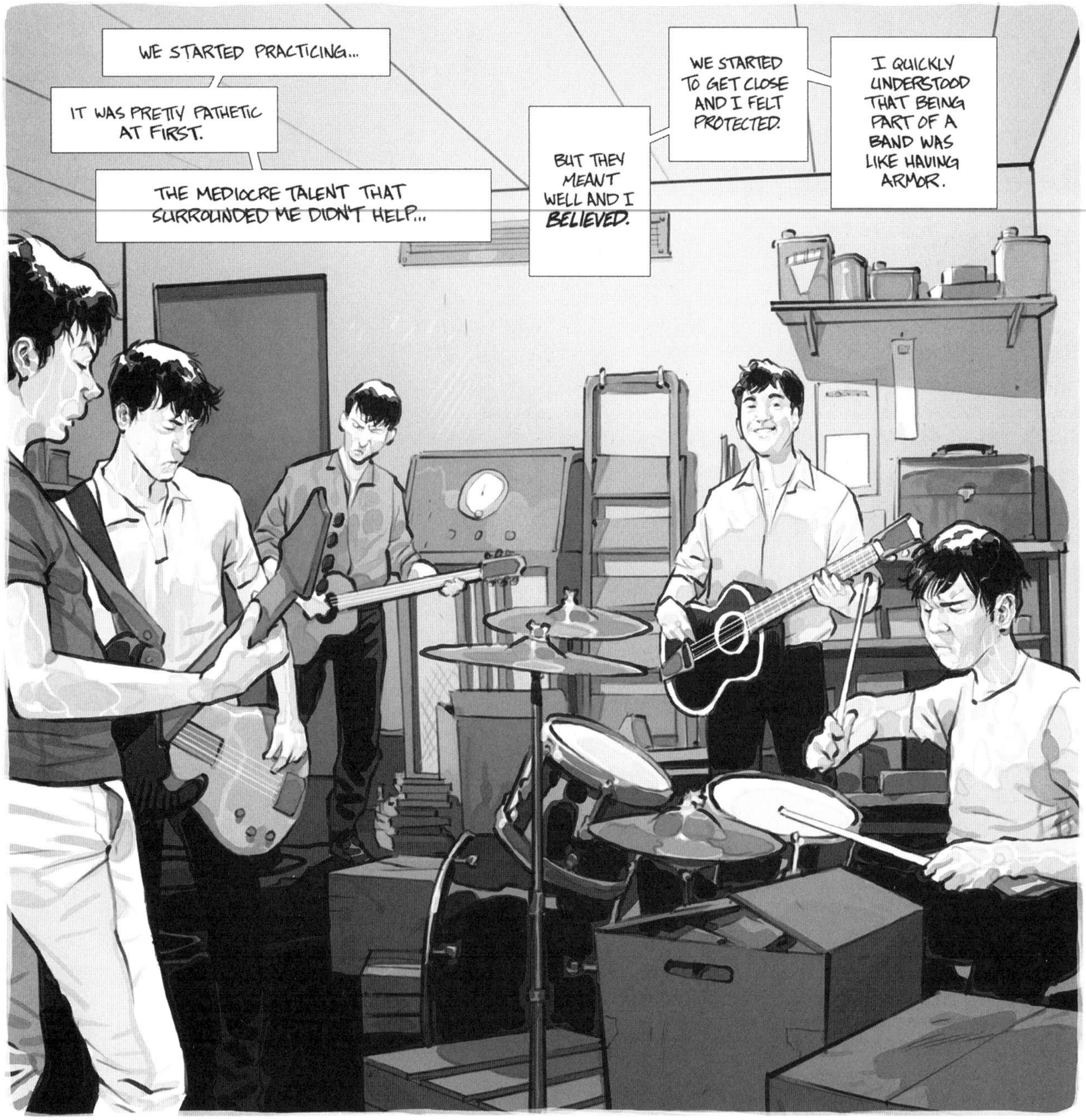
WE STARTED PRACTICING...
IT WAS PRETTY PATHETIC AT FIRST.
THE MEDIOCRE TALENT THAT SURROUNDED ME DIDN'T HELP...
BUT THEY MEANT WELL AND I BELIEVED.
WE STARTED TO GET CLOSE AND I FELT PROTECTED.
I QUICKLY UNDERSTOOD THAT BEING PART OF A BAND WAS LIKE HAVING ARMOR.

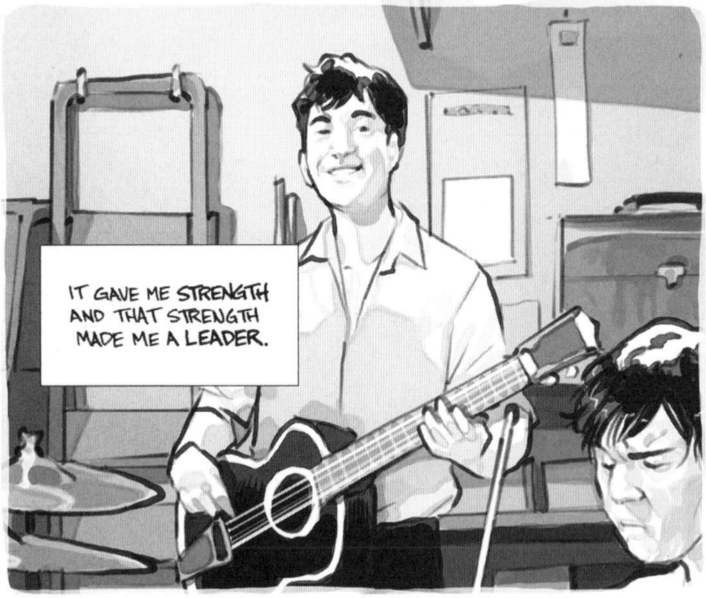
IT GAVE ME STRENGTH AND THAT STRENGTH MADE ME A LEADER.

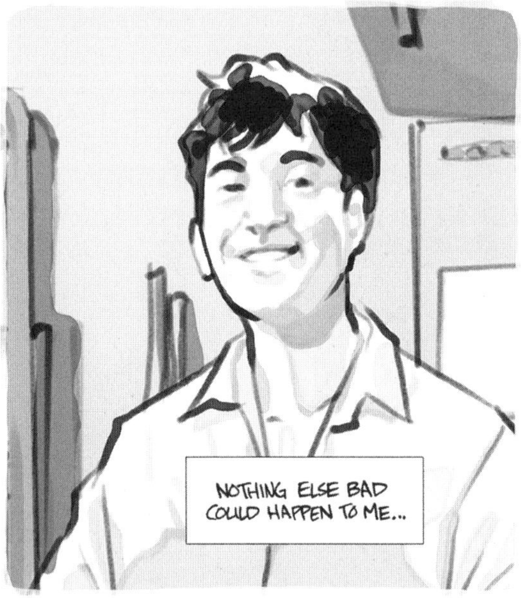
NOTHING ELSE BAD COULD HAPPEN TO ME...

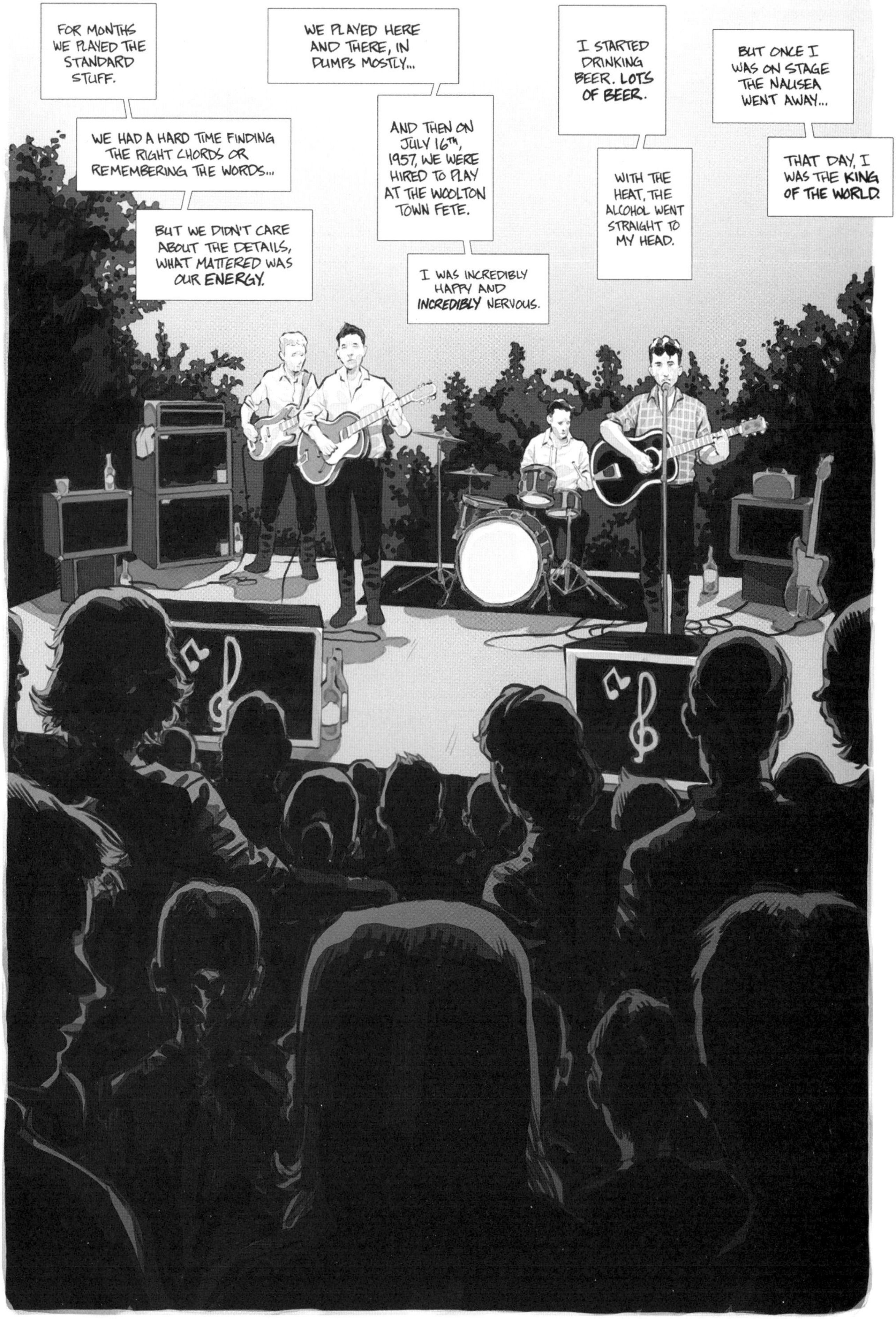
FOR MONTHS WE PLAYED THE STANDARD STUFF.
WE HAD A HARD TIME FINDING THE RIGHT CHORDS OR REMEMBERING THE WORDS...
BUT WE DIDN'T CARE ABOUT THE DETAILS, WHAT MATTERED WAS OUR **ENERGY**.
WE PLAYED HERE AND THERE, IN DUMPS MOSTLY...
AND THEN ON JULY 16TH, 1957, WE WERE HIRED TO PLAY AT THE WOOLTON TOWN FETE.
I WAS INCREDIBLY HAPPY AND ***INCREDIBLY*** NERVOUS.
I STARTED DRINKING BEER. **LOTS OF BEER**.
WITH THE HEAT, THE ALCOHOL WENT STRAIGHT TO MY HEAD.
BUT ONCE I WAS ON STAGE THE NAUSEA WENT AWAY...
THAT DAY, I WAS THE **KING OF THE WORLD**.

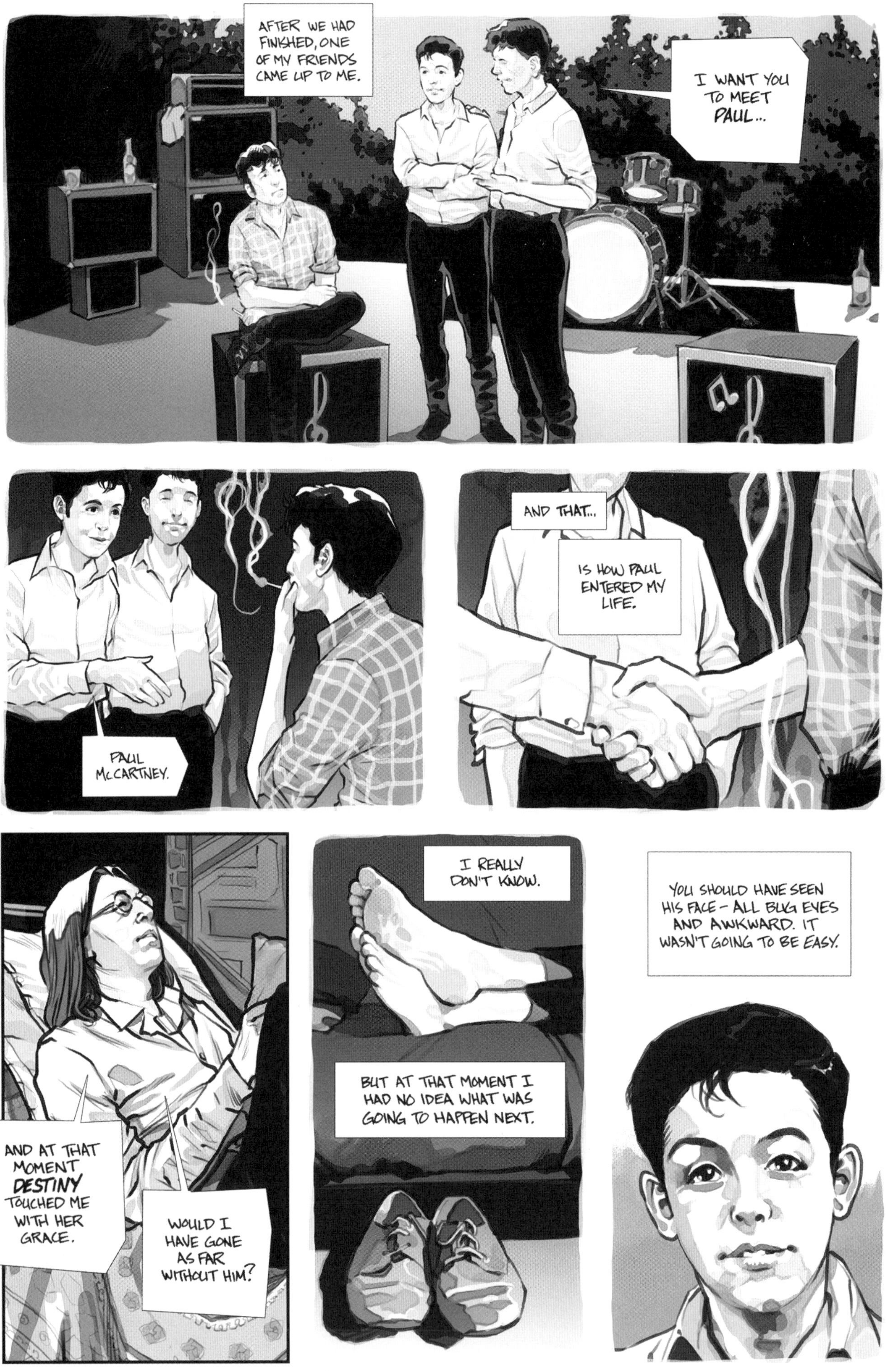
AFTER WE HAD FINISHED, ONE OF MY FRIENDS CAME UP TO ME.
I WANT YOU TO MEET PAUL...
PAUL McCARTNEY.
AND THAT...
IS HOW PAUL ENTERED MY LIFE.
AND AT THAT MOMENT DESTINY TOUCHED ME WITH HER GRACE.
WOULD I HAVE GONE AS FAR WITHOUT HIM?
I REALLY DON'T KNOW.
BUT AT THAT MOMENT I HAD NO IDEA WHAT WAS GOING TO HAPPEN NEXT.
YOU SHOULD HAVE SEEN HIS FACE - ALL BUG EYES AND AWKWARD. IT WASN'T GOING TO BE EASY.

THAT YOUNG BUGGER WAS GOOD

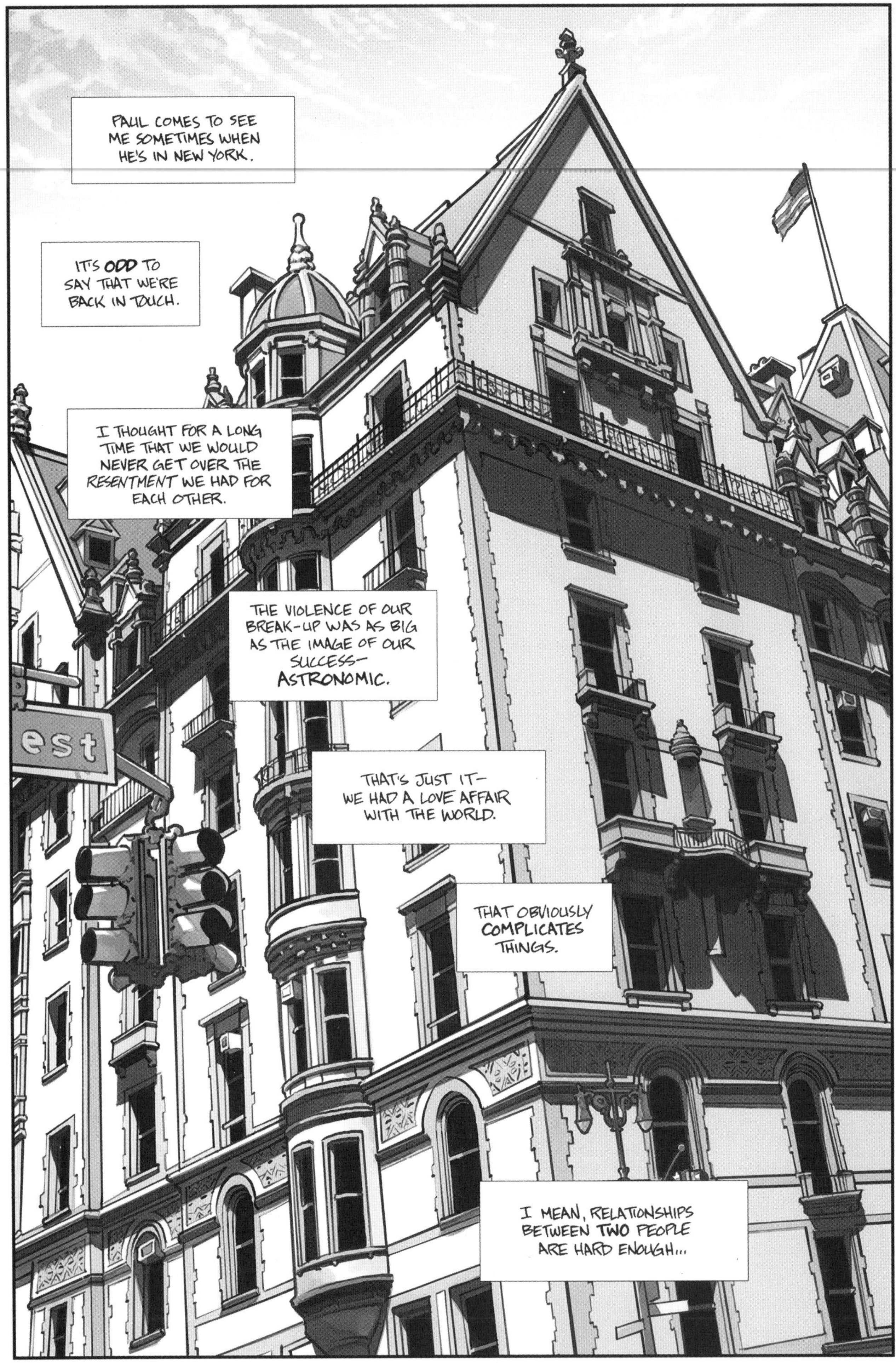
PAUL COMES TO SEE ME SOMETIMES WHEN HE'S IN NEW YORK.
IT'S ODD TO SAY THAT WE'RE BACK IN TOUCH.
I THOUGHT FOR A LONG TIME THAT WE WOULD NEVER GET OVER THE RESENTMENT WE HAD FOR EACH OTHER.
THE VIOLENCE OF OUR BREAK-UP WAS AS BIG AS THE IMAGE OF OUR SUCCESS— ASTRONOMIC.
THAT'S JUST IT— WE HAD A LOVE AFFAIR WITH THE WORLD.
THAT OBVIOUSLY COMPLICATES THINGS.
I MEAN, RELATIONSHIPS BETWEEN TWO PEOPLE ARE HARD ENOUGH...
est

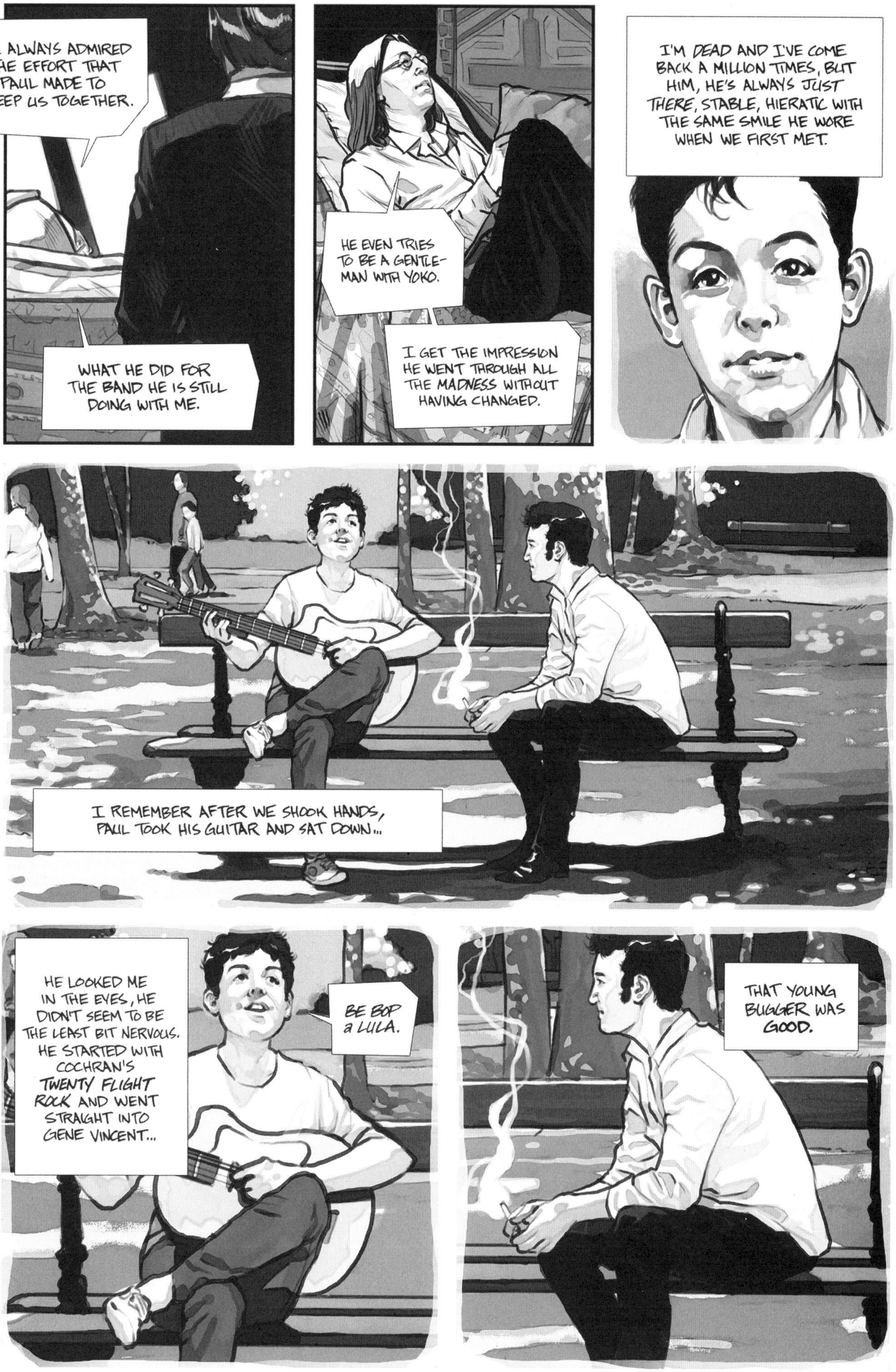
I ALWAYS ADMIRED THE EFFORT THAT PAUL MADE TO KEEP US TOGETHER.
WHAT HE DID FOR THE BAND HE IS STILL DOING WITH ME.
HE EVEN TRIES TO BE A GENTLE-MAN WITH YOKO.
I GET THE IMPRESSION HE WENT THROUGH ALL THE MADNESS WITHOUT HAVING CHANGED.
I'M DEAD AND I'VE COME BACK A MILLION TIMES, BUT HIM, HE'S ALWAYS JUST THERE, STABLE, HIERATIC WITH THE SAME SMILE HE WORE WHEN WE FIRST MET.
I REMEMBER AFTER WE SHOOK HANDS, PAUL TOOK HIS GUITAR AND SAT DOWN...
HE LOOKED ME IN THE EYES, HE DIDN'T SEEM TO BE THE LEAST BIT NERVOUS. HE STARTED WITH COCHRAN'S TWENTY FLIGHT ROCK AND WENT STRAIGHT INTO GENE VINCENT...
BE BOP a LULA.
THAT YOUNG BUGGER WAS GOOD.

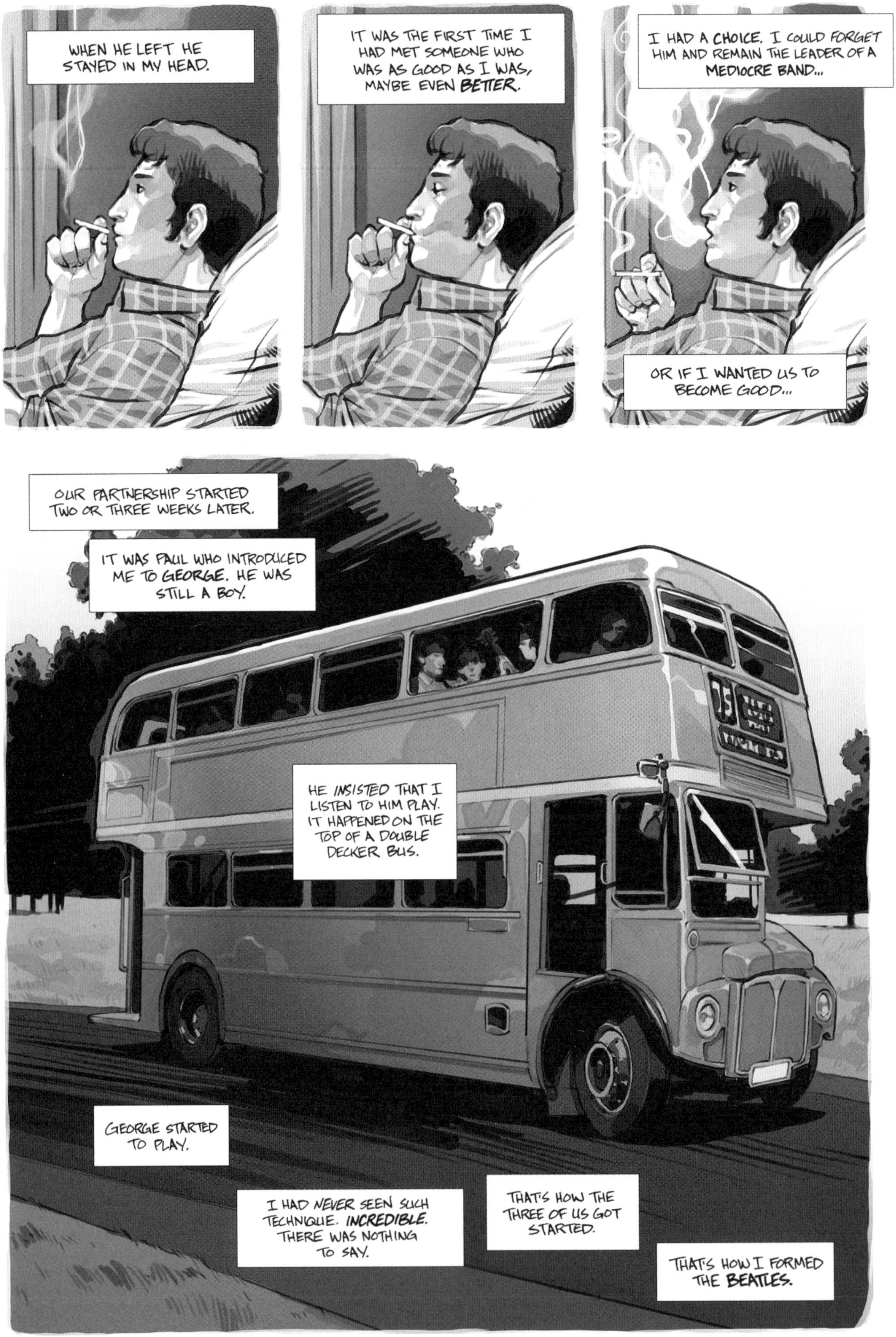
WHEN HE LEFT HE STAYED IN MY HEAD.
IT WAS THE FIRST TIME I HAD MET SOMEONE WHO WAS AS GOOD AS I WAS, MAYBE EVEN BETTER.
I HAD A CHOICE. I COULD FORGET HIM AND REMAIN THE LEADER OF A MEDIOCRE BAND...
OR IF I WANTED US TO BECOME GOOD...
OUR PARTNERSHIP STARTED TWO OR THREE WEEKS LATER.
IT WAS PAUL WHO INTRODUCED ME TO GEORGE. HE WAS STILL A BOY.
HE INSISTED THAT I LISTEN TO HIM PLAY. IT HAPPENED ON THE TOP OF A DOUBLE DECKER BUS.
GEORGE STARTED TO PLAY.
I HAD NEVER SEEN SUCH TECHNIQUE. INCREDIBLE. THERE WAS NOTHING TO SAY.
THAT'S HOW THE THREE OF US GOT STARTED.
THAT'S HOW I FORMED THE BEATLES.

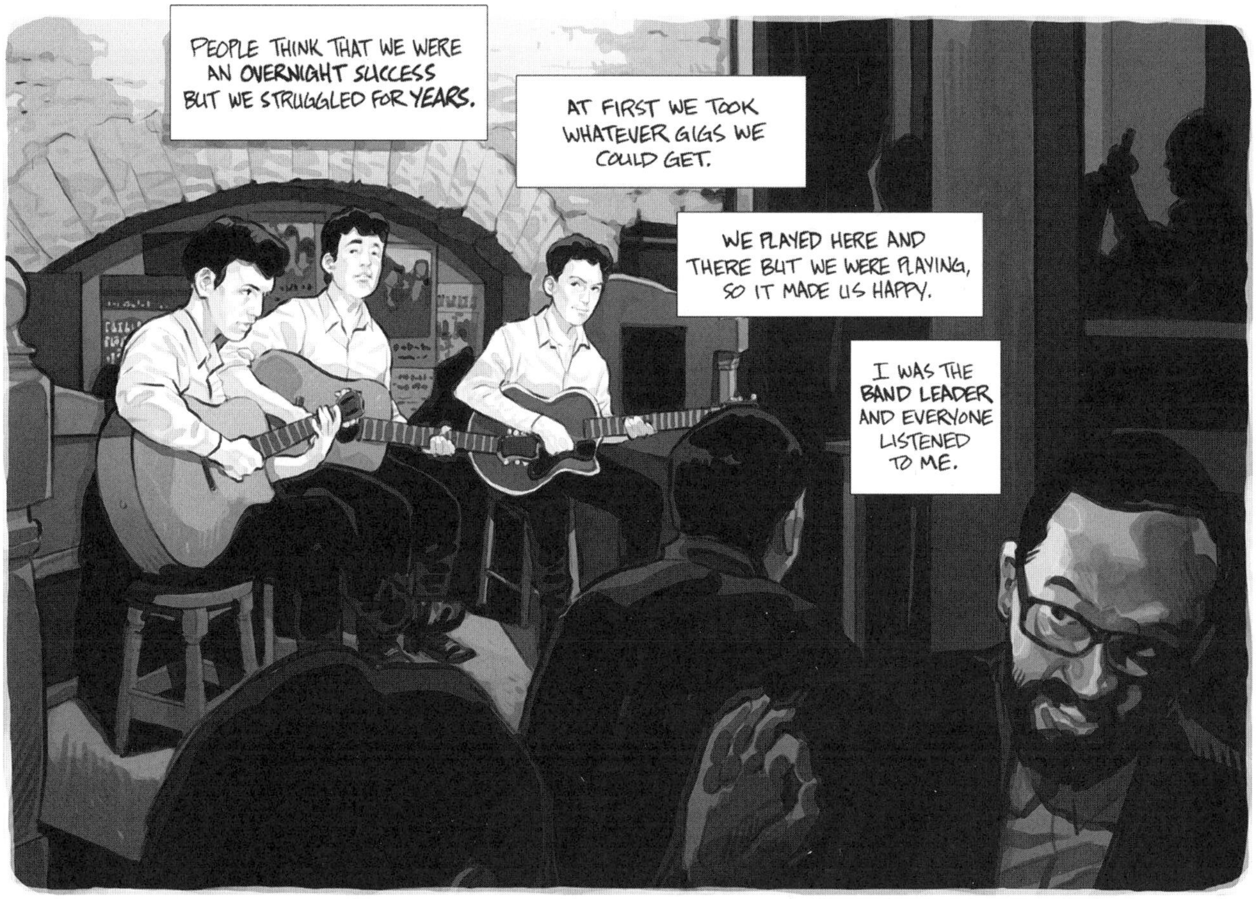
PEOPLE THINK THAT WE WERE AN OVERNIGHT SUCCESS BUT WE STRUGGLED FOR YEARS.
AT FIRST WE TOOK WHATEVER GIGS WE COULD GET.
WE PLAYED HERE AND THERE BUT WE WERE PLAYING, SO IT MADE US HAPPY.
I WAS THE BAND LEADER AND EVERYONE LISTENED TO ME.

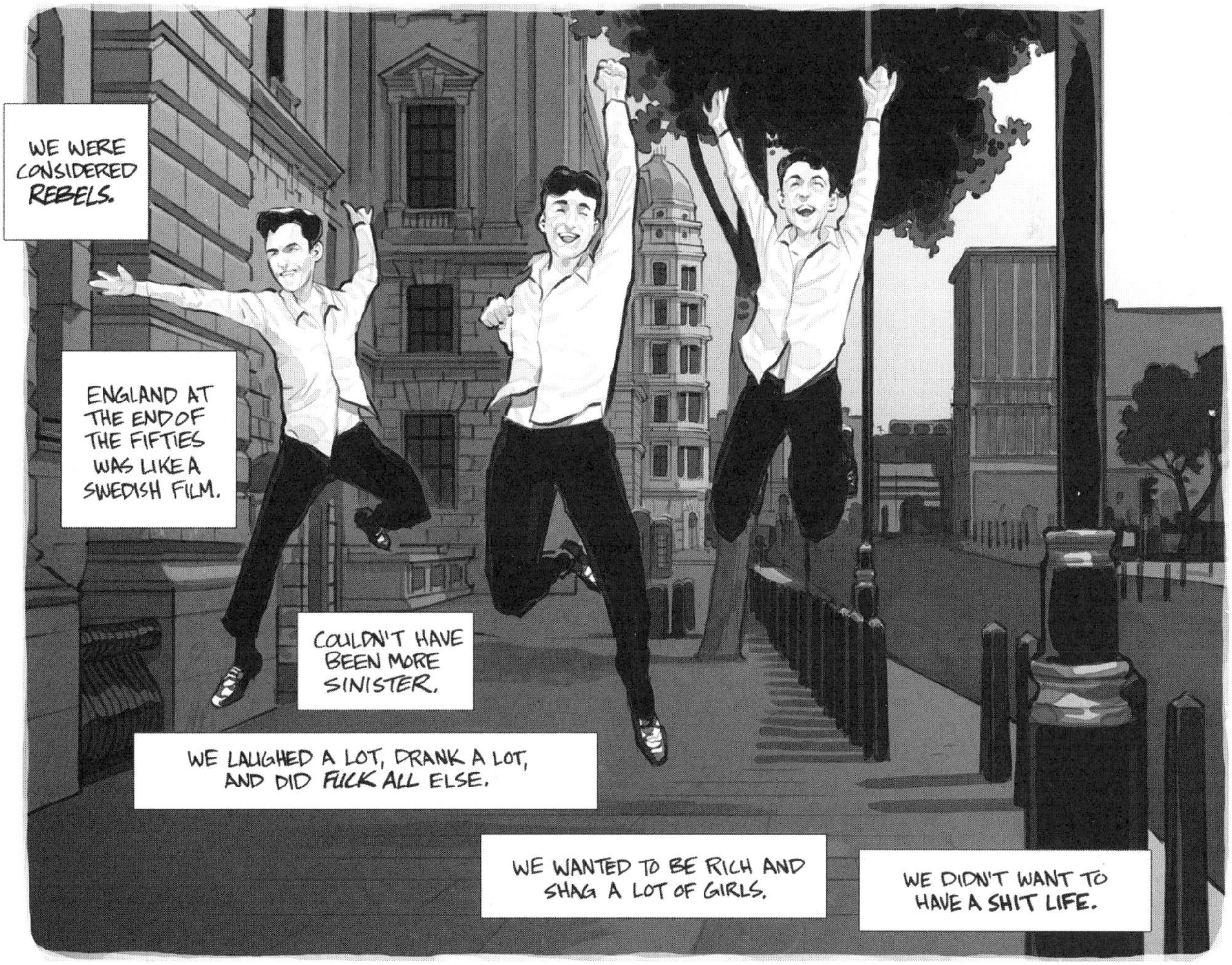
WE WERE CONSIDERED REBELS.
ENGLAND AT THE END OF THE FIFTIES WAS LIKE A SWEDISH FILM.
COULDN'T HAVE BEEN MORE SINISTER.
WE LAUGHED A LOT, DRANK A LOT, AND DID FUCK ALL ELSE.
WE WANTED TO BE RICH AND SHAG A LOT OF GIRLS.
WE DIDN'T WANT TO HAVE A SHIT LIFE.

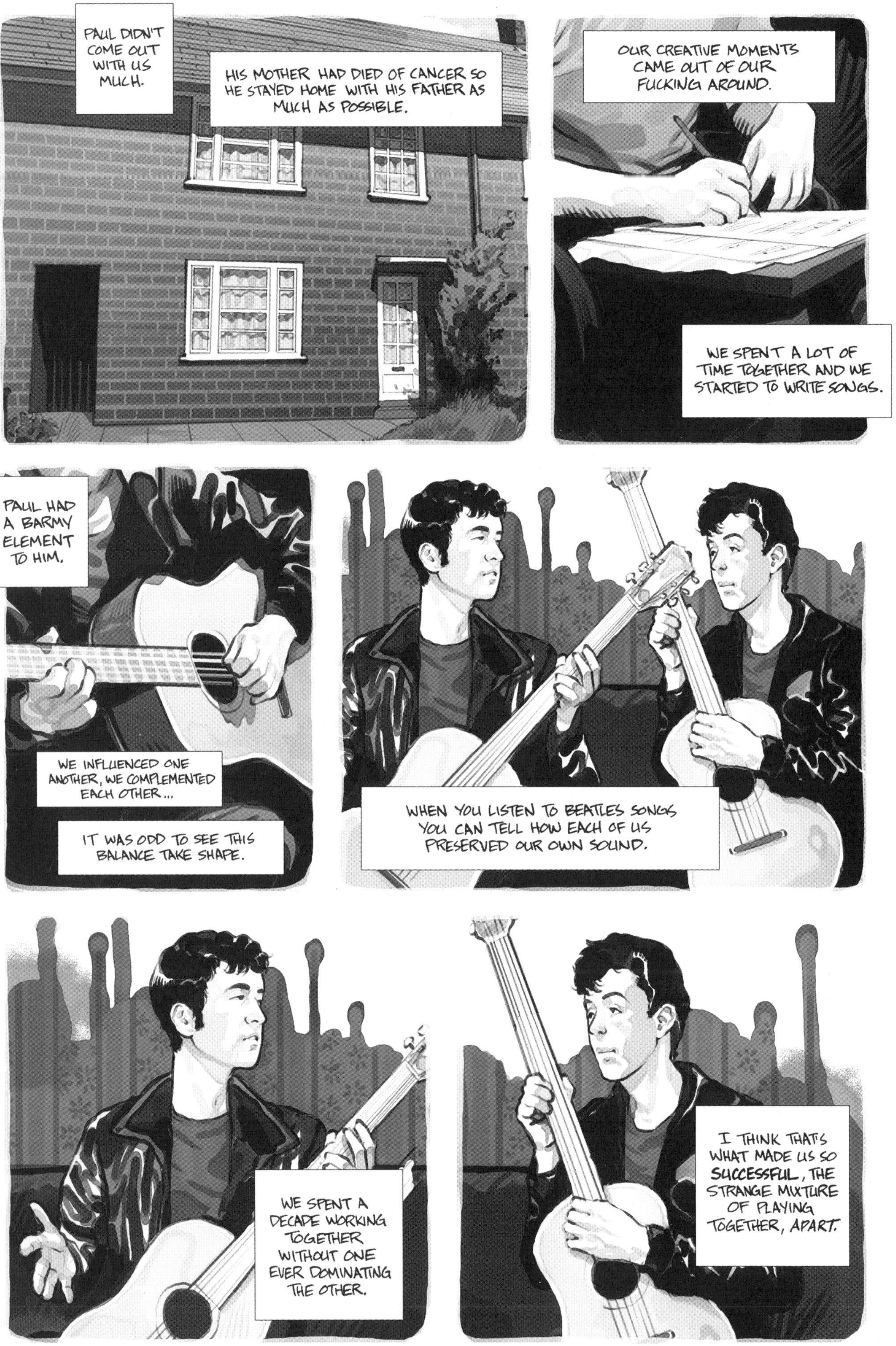
PAUL DIDN'T COME OUT WITH US MUCH.
HIS MOTHER HAD DIED OF CANCER SO HE STAYED HOME WITH HIS FATHER AS MUCH AS POSSIBLE.
OUR CREATIVE MOMENTS CAME OUT OF OUR FUCKING AROUND.
WE SPENT A LOT OF TIME TOGETHER AND WE STARTED TO WRITE SONGS.
PAUL HAD A BARMY ELEMENT TO HIM.
WE INFLUENCED ONE ANOTHER, WE COMPLEMENTED EACH OTHER...
IT WAS ODD TO SEE THIS BALANCE TAKE SHAPE.
WHEN YOU LISTEN TO BEATLES SONGS YOU CAN TELL HOW EACH OF US PRESERVED OUR OWN SOUND.
WE SPENT A DECADE WORKING TOGETHER WITHOUT ONE EVER DOMINATING THE OTHER.
I THINK THAT'S WHAT MADE US SO SUCCESSFUL, THE STRANGE MIXTURE OF PLAYING TOGETHER, APART.

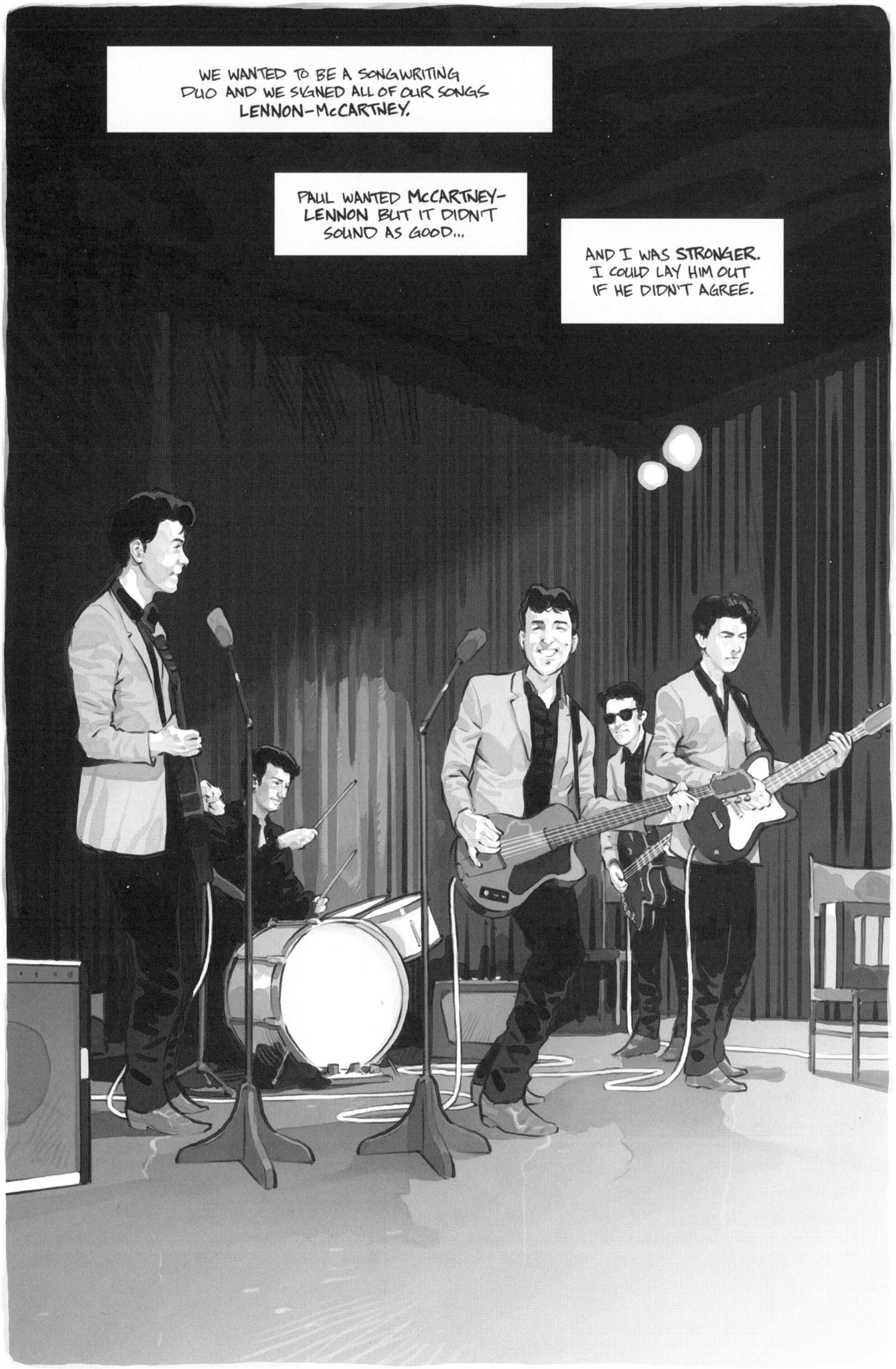
WE WANTED TO BE A SONGWRITING DUO AND WE SIGNED ALL OF OUR SONGS LENNON-McCARTNEY.
PAUL WANTED McCARTNEY-LENNON BUT IT DIDN'T SOUND AS GOOD...
AND I WAS STRONGER. I COULD LAY HIM OUT IF HE DIDN'T AGREE.

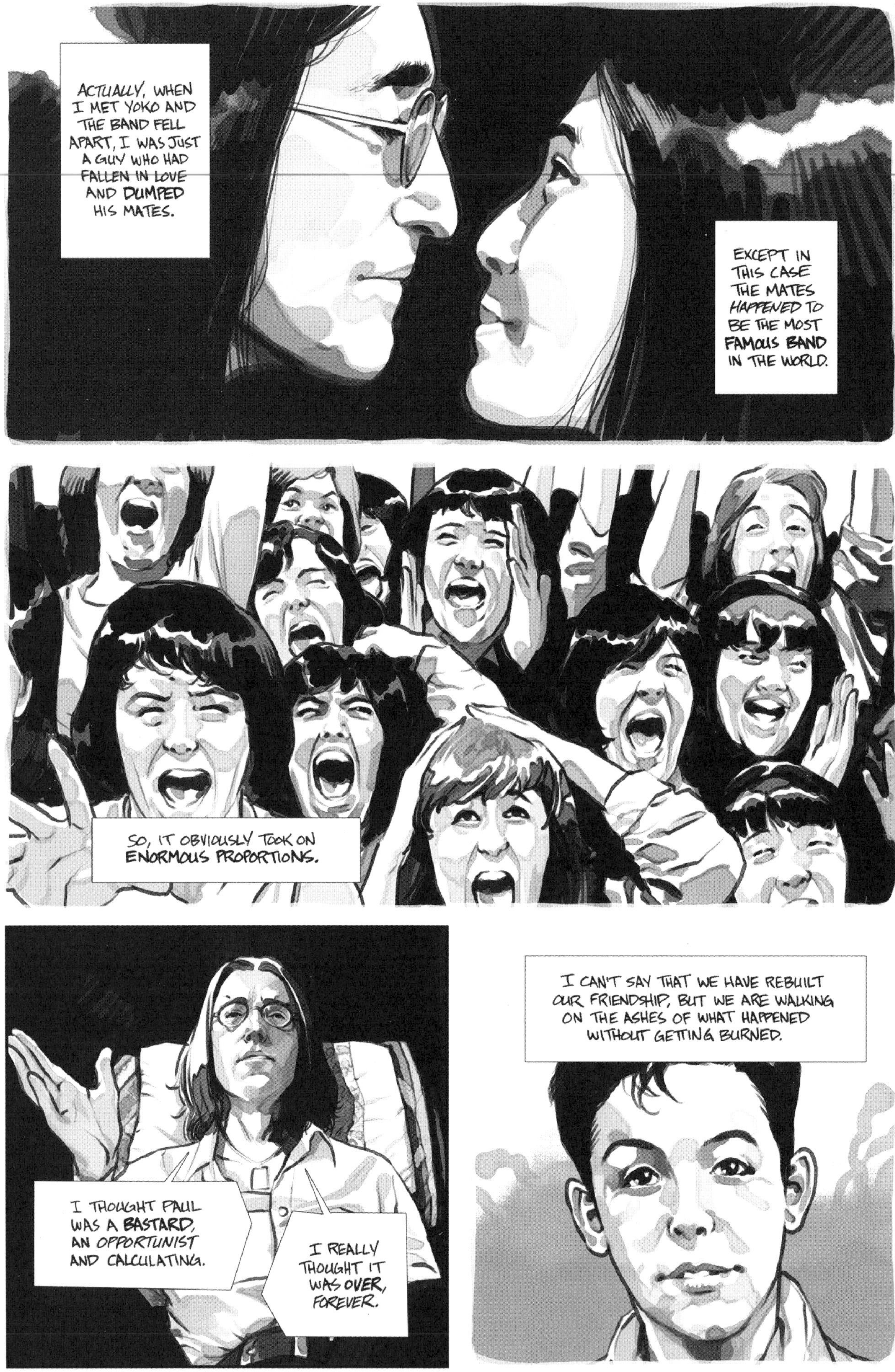

ACTUALLY, WHEN I MET YOKO AND THE BAND FELL APART, I WAS JUST A GUY WHO HAD FALLEN IN LOVE AND DUMPED HIS MATES.
EXCEPT IN THIS CASE THE MATES HAPPENED TO BE THE MOST FAMOUS BAND IN THE WORLD.
SO, IT OBVIOUSLY TOOK ON ENORMOUS PROPORTIONS.
I THOUGHT PAUL WAS A BASTARD, AN OPPORTUNIST AND CALCULATING.
I REALLY THOUGHT IT WAS OVER, FOREVER.
I CAN'T SAY THAT WE HAVE REBUILT OUR FRIENDSHIP, BUT WE ARE WALKING ON THE ASHES OF WHAT HAPPENED WITHOUT GETTING BURNED.

eighth session
BODIES BURIED IN THE MUSIC

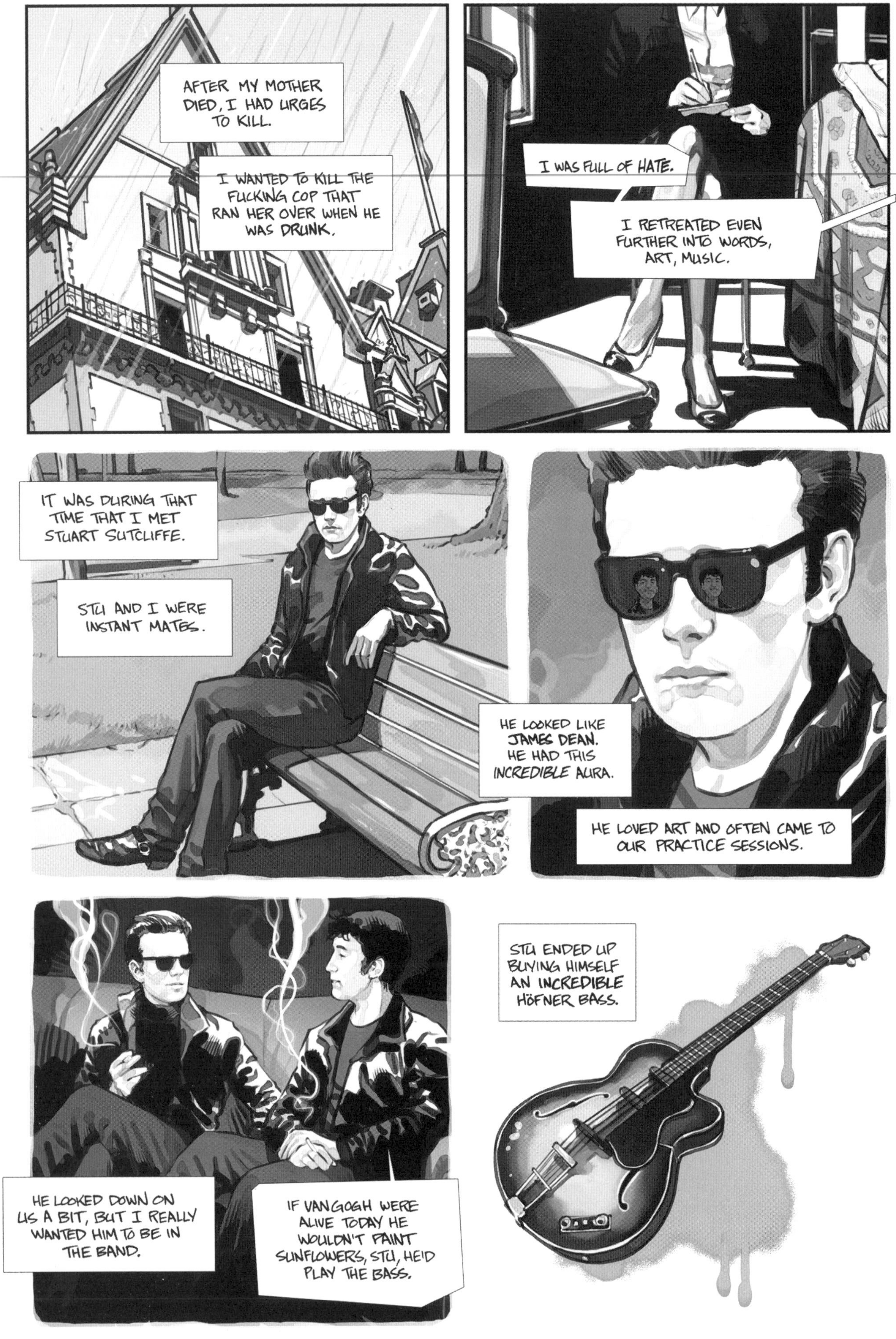
AFTER MY MOTHER DIED, I HAD URGES TO KILL.
I WANTED TO KILL THE FUCKING COP THAT RAN HER OVER WHEN HE WAS DRUNK.
I WAS FULL OF HATE.
I RETREATED EVEN FURTHER INTO WORDS, ART, MUSIC.
IT WAS DURING THAT TIME THAT I MET STUART SUTCLIFFE.
STU AND I WERE INSTANT MATES.
HE LOOKED LIKE JAMES DEAN. HE HAD THIS INCREDIBLE AURA.
HE LOVED ART AND OFTEN CAME TO OUR PRACTICE SESSIONS.
HE LOOKED DOWN ON US A BIT, BUT I REALLY WANTED HIM TO BE IN THE BAND.
IF VAN GOGH WERE ALIVE TODAY HE WOULDN'T PAINT SUNFLOWERS, STU, HE'D PLAY THE BASS.
STU ENDED UP BUYING HIMSELF AN INCREDIBLE HÖFNER BASS.

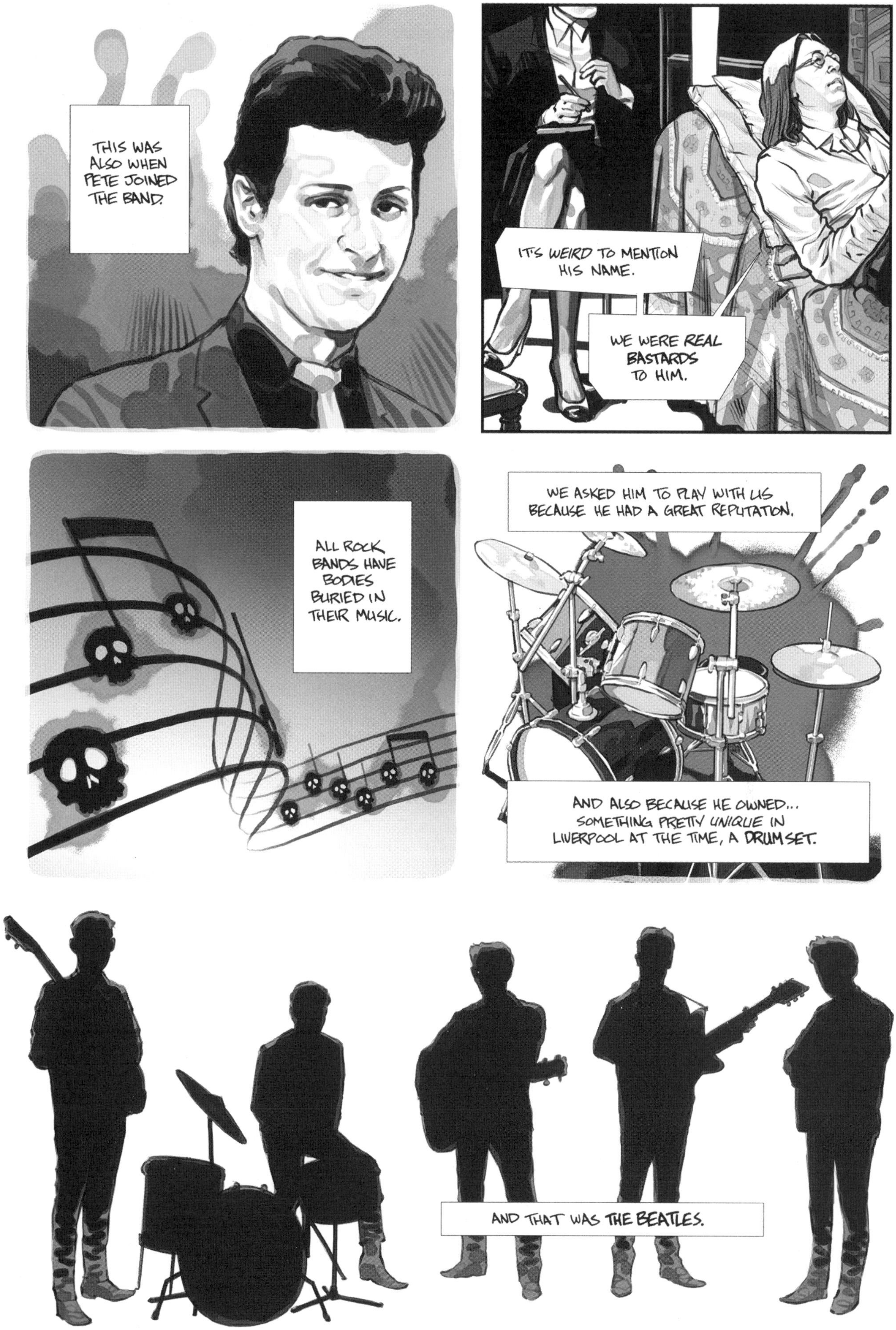
THIS WAS ALSO WHEN PETE JOINED THE BAND.
IT'S WEIRD TO MENTION HIS NAME.
WE WERE REAL BASTARDS TO HIM.
ALL ROCK BANDS HAVE BODIES BURIED IN THEIR MUSIC.
WE ASKED HIM TO PLAY WITH US BECAUSE HE HAD A GREAT REPUTATION.
AND ALSO BECAUSE HE OWNED... SOMETHING PRETTY UNIQUE IN LIVERPOOL AT THE TIME, A DRUM SET.
AND THAT WAS THE BEATLES.

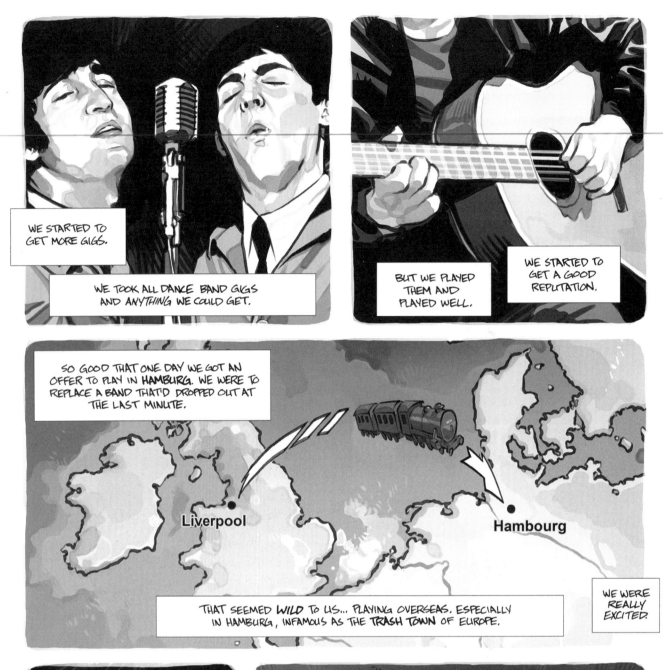

WE STARTED TO GET MORE GIGS.

WE TOOK ALL DANCE BAND GIGS AND ANYTHING WE COULD GET.

BUT WE PLAYED THEM AND PLAYED WELL.

WE STARTED TO GET A GOOD REPUTATION.

SO GOOD THAT ONE DAY WE GOT AN OFFER TO PLAY IN **HAMBURG**. WE WERE TO REPLACE A BAND THAT'D DROPPED OUT AT THE LAST MINUTE.

Liverpool

Hambourg

THAT SEEMED **WILD** TO US... PLAYING OVERSEAS. ESPECIALLY IN HAMBURG, INFAMOUS AS THE **TRASH TOWN** OF EUROPE.

WE WERE REALLY EXCITED.

I STILL REMEMBER THE CLUB OWNER'S FACE WHEN WE SHOWED UP.

?!?

YOU'RE THE ENGLISH GUYS THAT ARE SO **HOT**?

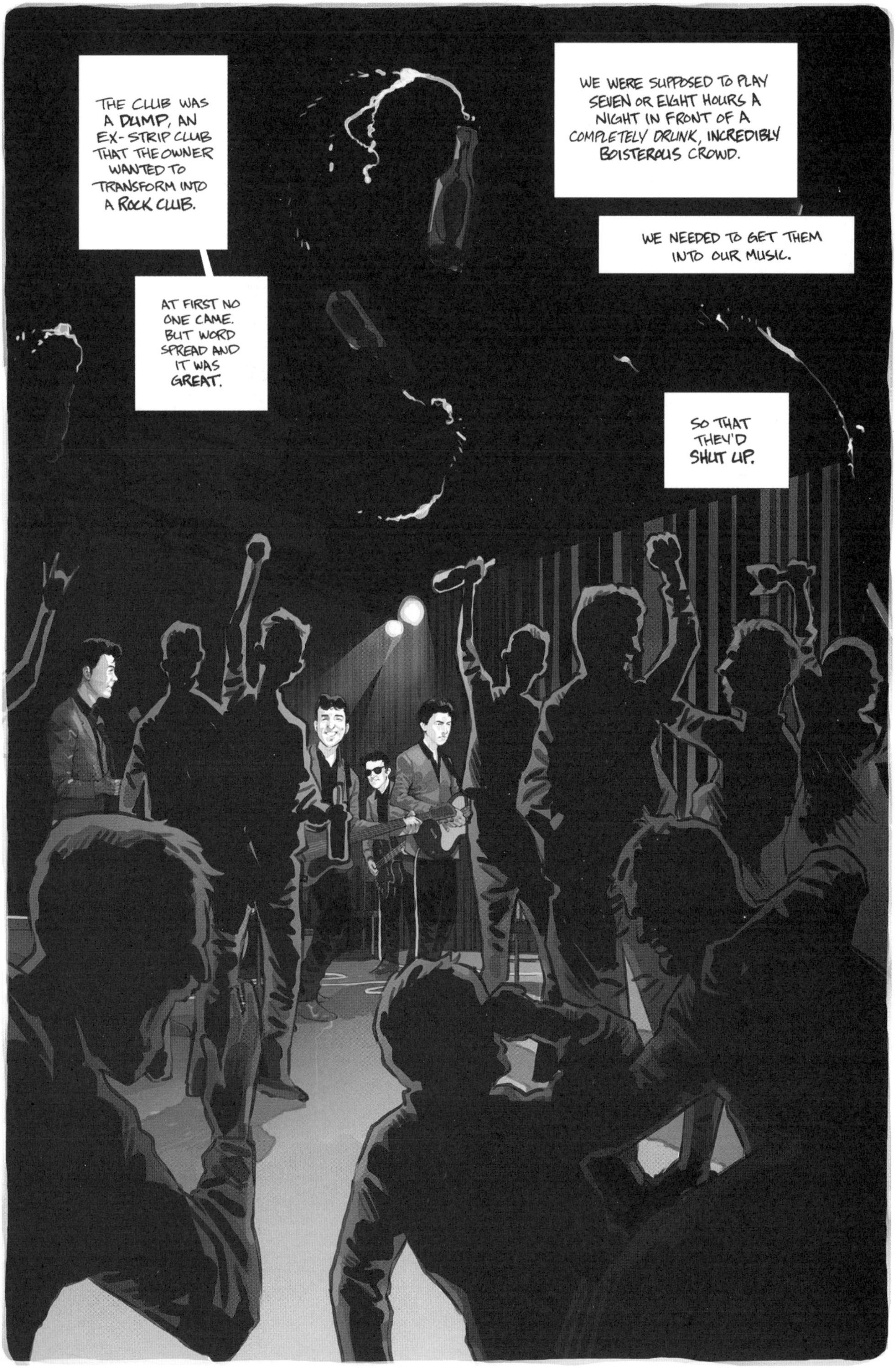
THE CLUB WAS A DUMP, AN EX-STRIP CLUB THAT THE OWNER WANTED TO TRANSFORM INTO A ROCK CLUB.
AT FIRST NO ONE CAME. BUT WORD SPREAD AND IT WAS GREAT.
WE WERE SUPPOSED TO PLAY SEVEN OR EIGHT HOURS A NIGHT IN FRONT OF A COMPLETELY DRUNK, INCREDIBLY BOISTEROUS CROWD.
WE NEEDED TO GET THEM INTO OUR MUSIC.
SO THAT THEY'D SHUT UP.

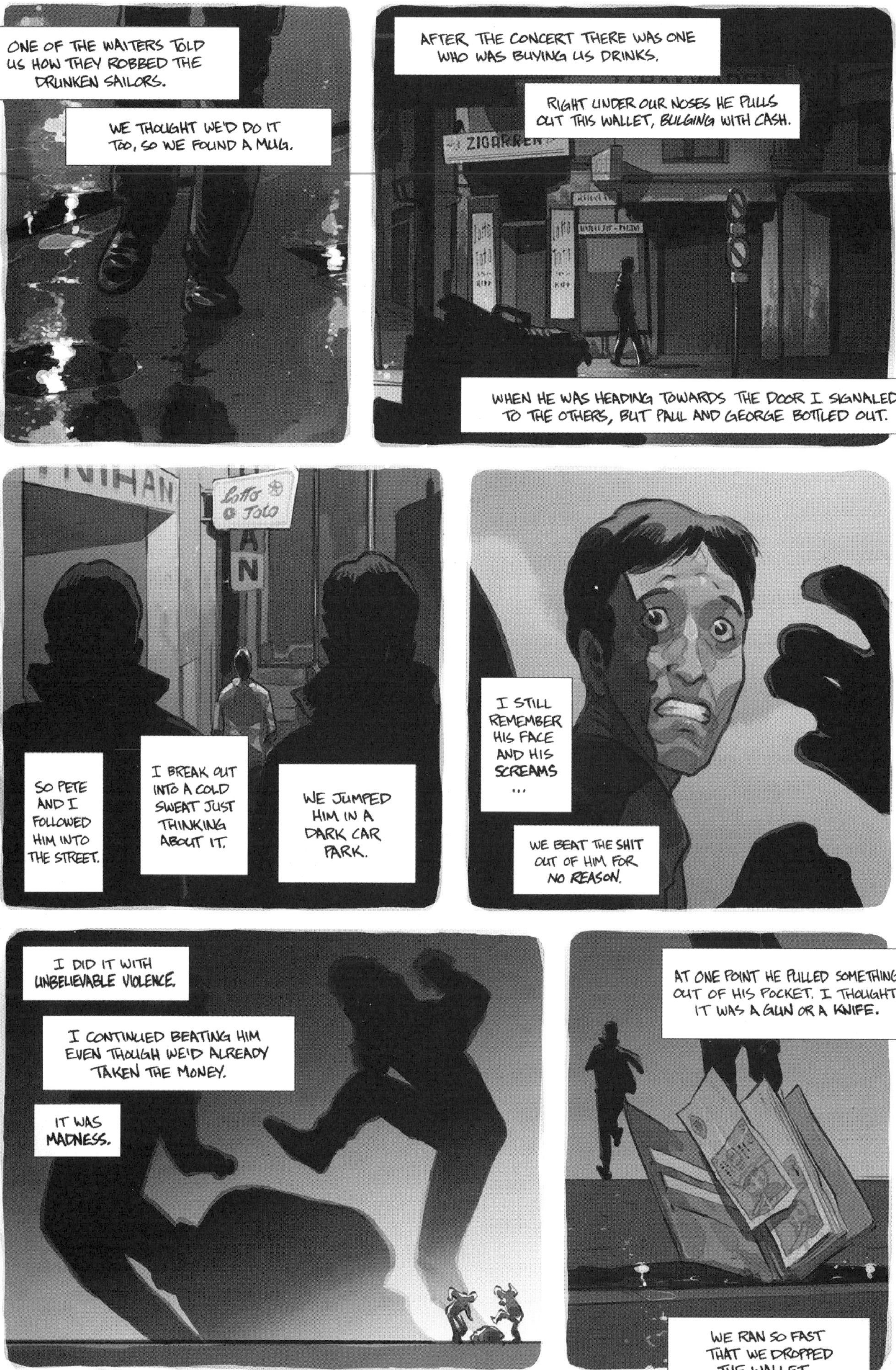
ONE OF THE WAITERS TOLD US HOW THEY ROBBED THE DRUNKEN SAILORS.
WE THOUGHT WE'D DO IT TOO, SO WE FOUND A MUG.
AFTER THE CONCERT THERE WAS ONE WHO WAS BUYING US DRINKS.
RIGHT UNDER OUR NOSES HE PULLS OUT THIS WALLET, BULGING WITH CASH.
ZIGARREN
Lotto Toto
WHEN HE WAS HEADING TOWARDS THE DOOR I SIGNALED TO THE OTHERS, BUT PAUL AND GEORGE BOTTLED OUT.
Lotto Toto
SO PETE AND I FOLLOWED HIM INTO THE STREET.
I BREAK OUT INTO A COLD SWEAT JUST THINKING ABOUT IT.
WE JUMPED HIM IN A DARK CAR PARK.
I STILL REMEMBER HIS FACE AND HIS SCREAMS ...
WE BEAT THE SHIT OUT OF HIM FOR NO REASON.
I DID IT WITH UNBELIEVABLE VIOLENCE.
I CONTINUED BEATING HIM EVEN THOUGH WE'D ALREADY TAKEN THE MONEY.
IT WAS MADNESS.
AT ONE POINT HE PULLED SOMETHING OUT OF HIS POCKET. I THOUGHT IT WAS A GUN OR A KNIFE.
WE RAN SO FAST THAT WE DROPPED THE WALLET.

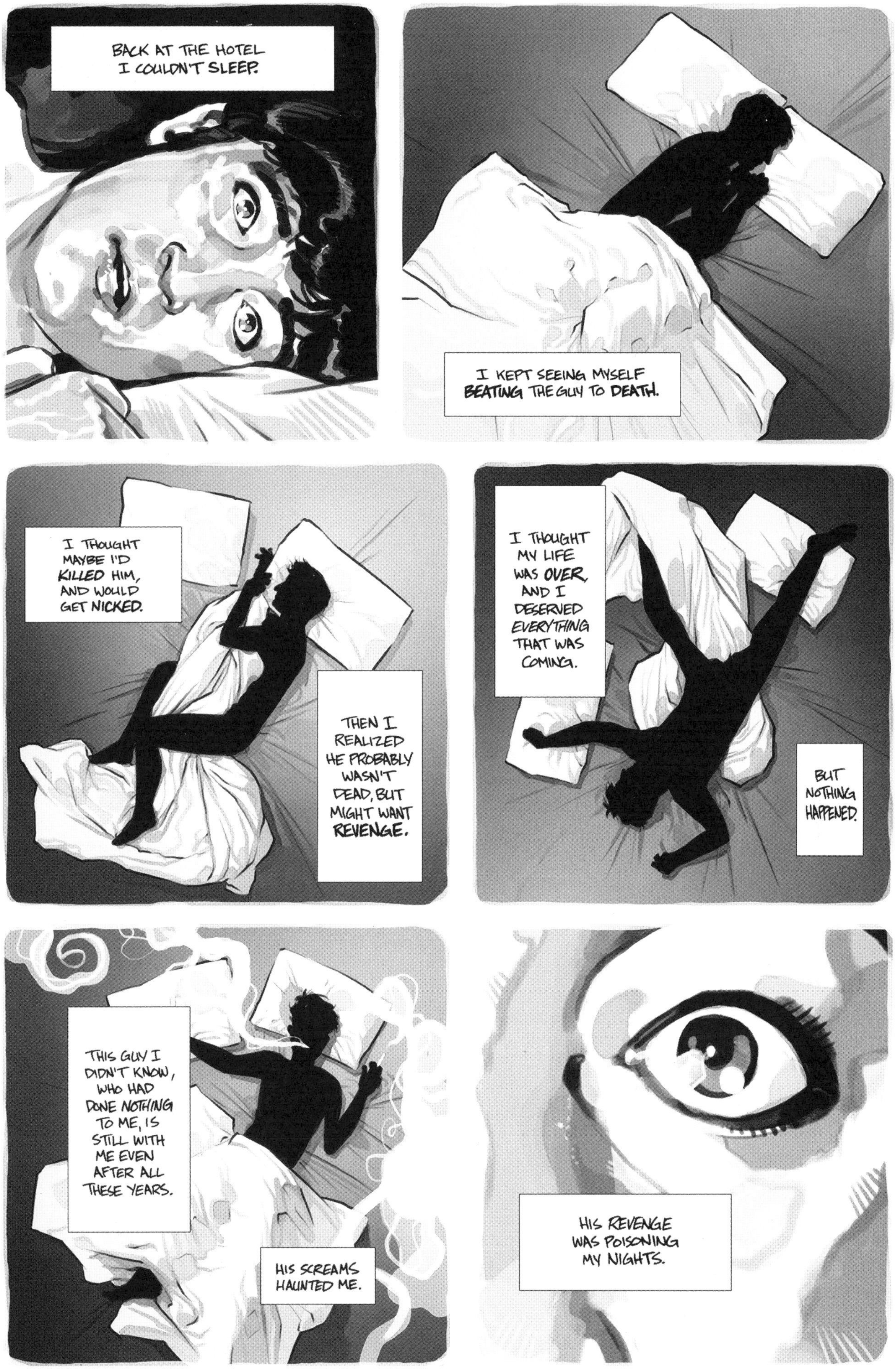
BACK AT THE HOTEL I COULDN'T SLEEP.
I KEPT SEEING MYSELF BEATING THE GUY TO DEATH.
I THOUGHT MAYBE I'D KILLED HIM, AND WOULD GET NICKED.
THEN I REALIZED HE PROBABLY WASN'T DEAD, BUT MIGHT WANT REVENGE.
I THOUGHT MY LIFE WAS OVER, AND I DESERVED EVERYTHING THAT WAS COMING.
BUT NOTHING HAPPENED.
THIS GUY I DIDN'T KNOW, WHO HAD DONE NOTHING TO ME, IS STILL WITH ME EVEN AFTER ALL THESE YEARS.
HIS SCREAMS HAUNTED ME.
HIS REVENGE WAS POISONING MY NIGHTS.

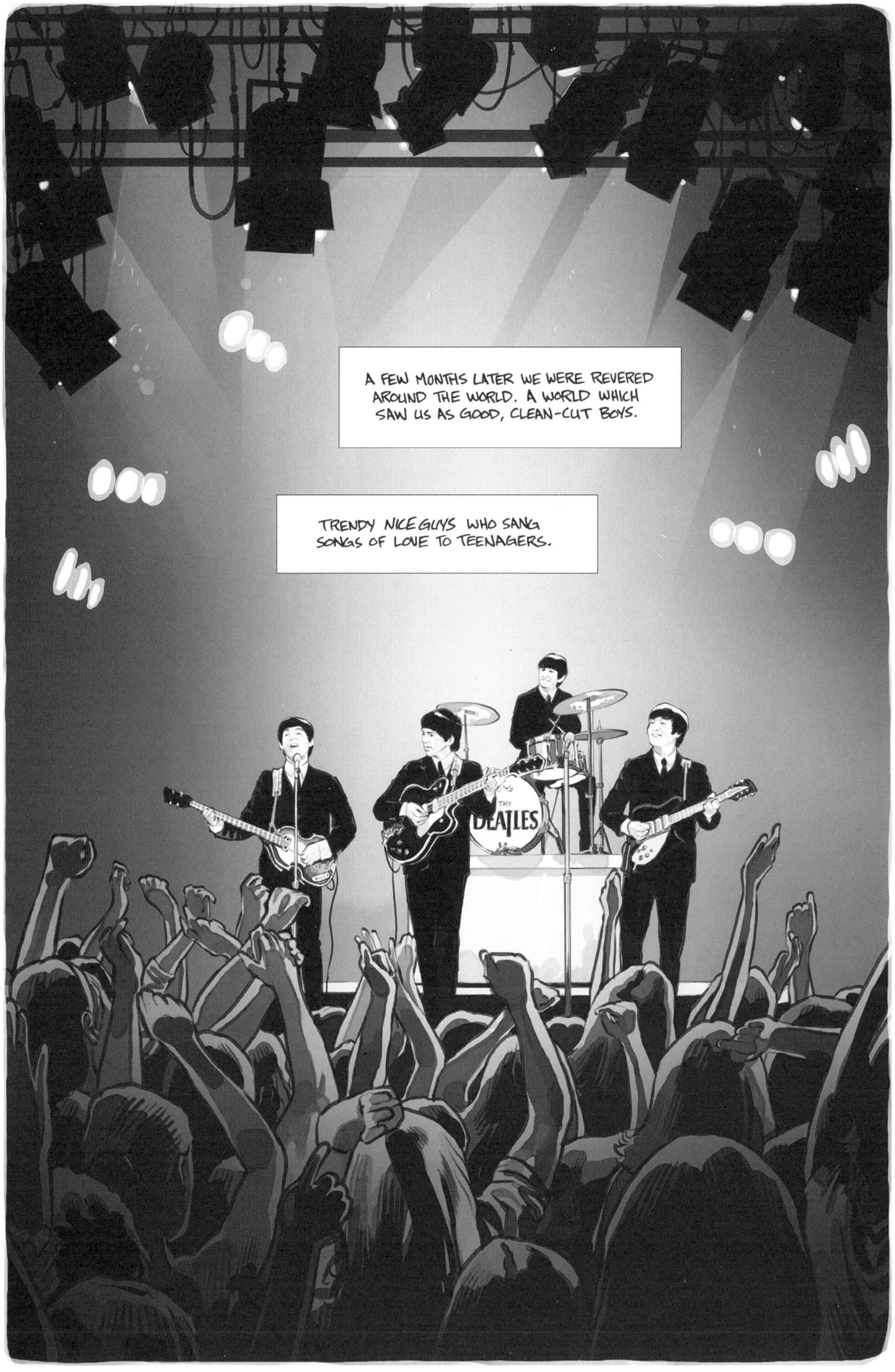
A FEW MONTHS LATER WE WERE REVERED AROUND THE WORLD. A WORLD WHICH SAW US AS GOOD, CLEAN-CUT BOYS.
TRENDY NICE GUYS WHO SANG SONGS OF LOVE TO TEENAGERS.
THE BEATLES

ninth session

I WAS LOOKING FOR INNER PEACE

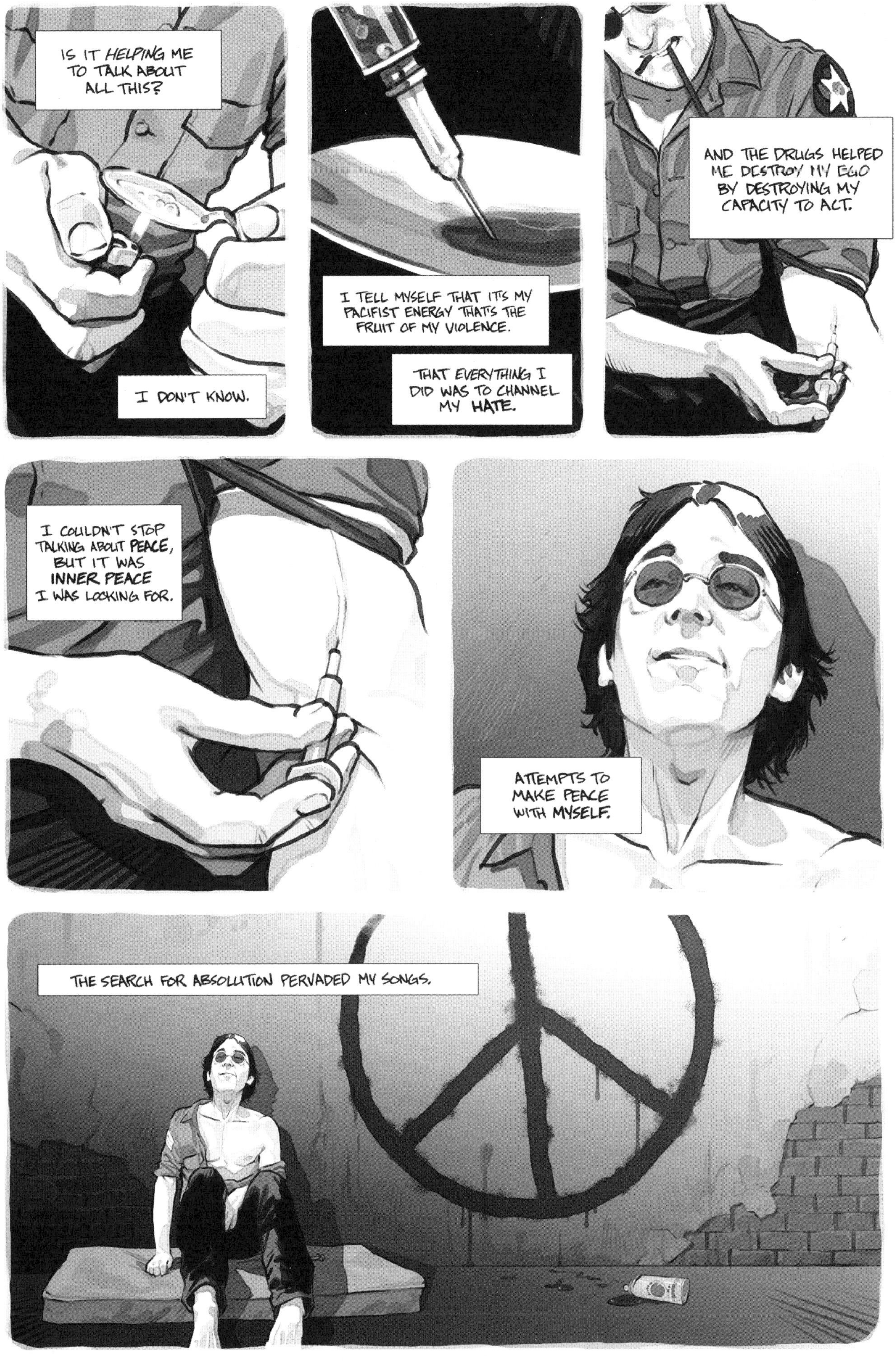
IS IT *HELPING* ME TO TALK ABOUT ALL THIS?
I DON'T KNOW.
I TELL MYSELF THAT IT'S MY PACIFIST ENERGY THAT'S THE FRUIT OF MY VIOLENCE.
THAT *EVERYTHING* I DID WAS TO CHANNEL MY **HATE.**
AND THE DRUGS HELPED ME DESTROY MY EGO BY DESTROYING MY CAPACITY TO ACT.
I COULDN'T STOP TALKING ABOUT **PEACE,** BUT IT WAS **INNER PEACE** I WAS LOOKING FOR.
ATTEMPTS TO MAKE PEACE WITH **MYSELF.**
THE SEARCH FOR ABSOLUTION PERVADED MY SONGS.

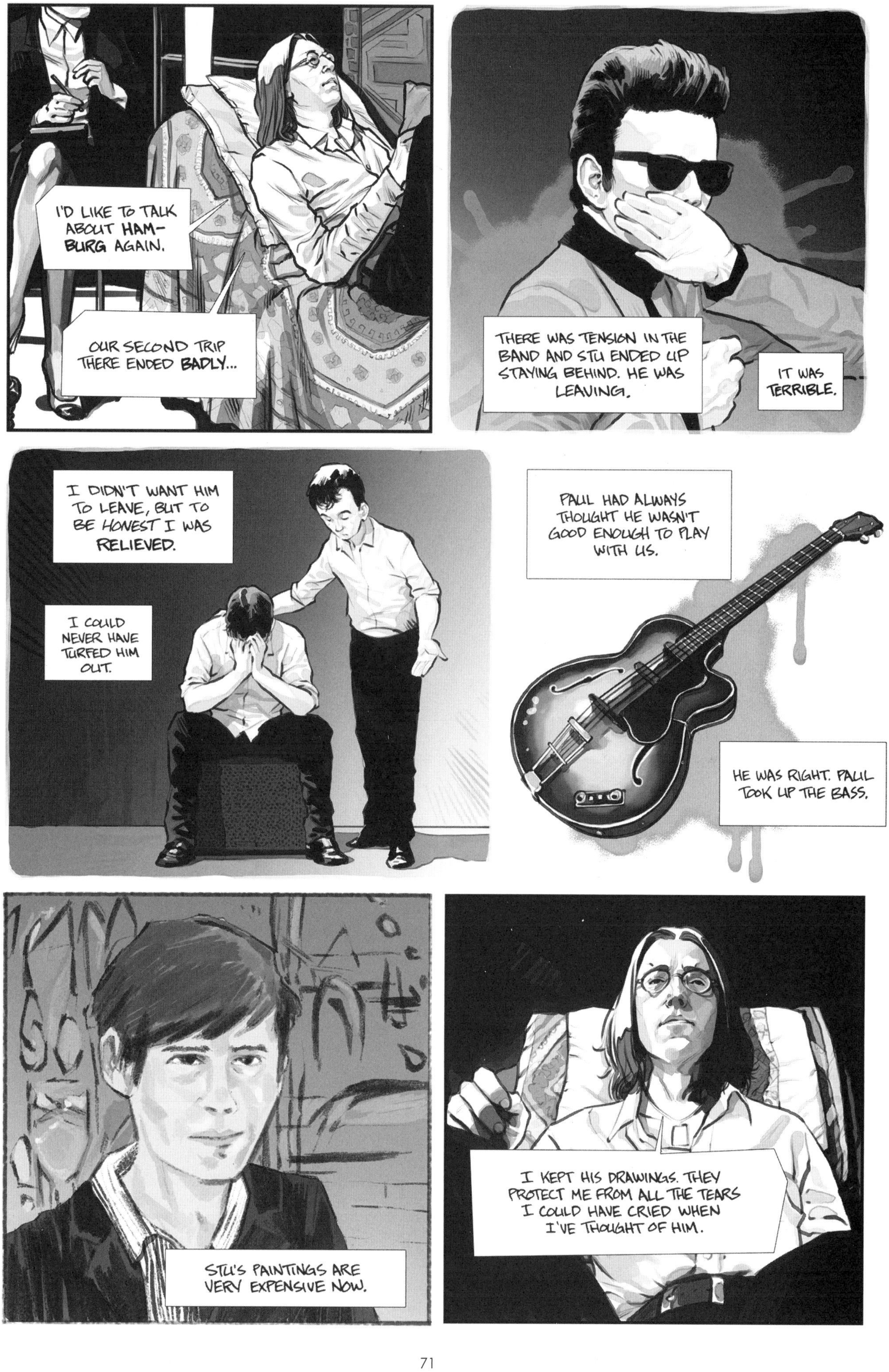
I'D LIKE TO TALK ABOUT HAMBURG AGAIN.
OUR SECOND TRIP THERE ENDED BADLY...
THERE WAS TENSION IN THE BAND AND STU ENDED UP STAYING BEHIND. HE WAS LEAVING.
IT WAS TERRIBLE.
I DIDN'T WANT HIM TO LEAVE, BUT TO BE HONEST I WAS RELIEVED.
I COULD NEVER HAVE TURFED HIM OUT.
PAUL HAD ALWAYS THOUGHT HE WASN'T GOOD ENOUGH TO PLAY WITH US.
HE WAS RIGHT. PAUL TOOK UP THE BASS.
STU'S PAINTINGS ARE VERY EXPENSIVE NOW.
I KEPT HIS DRAWINGS. THEY PROTECT ME FROM ALL THE TEARS I COULD HAVE CRIED WHEN I'VE THOUGHT OF HIM.

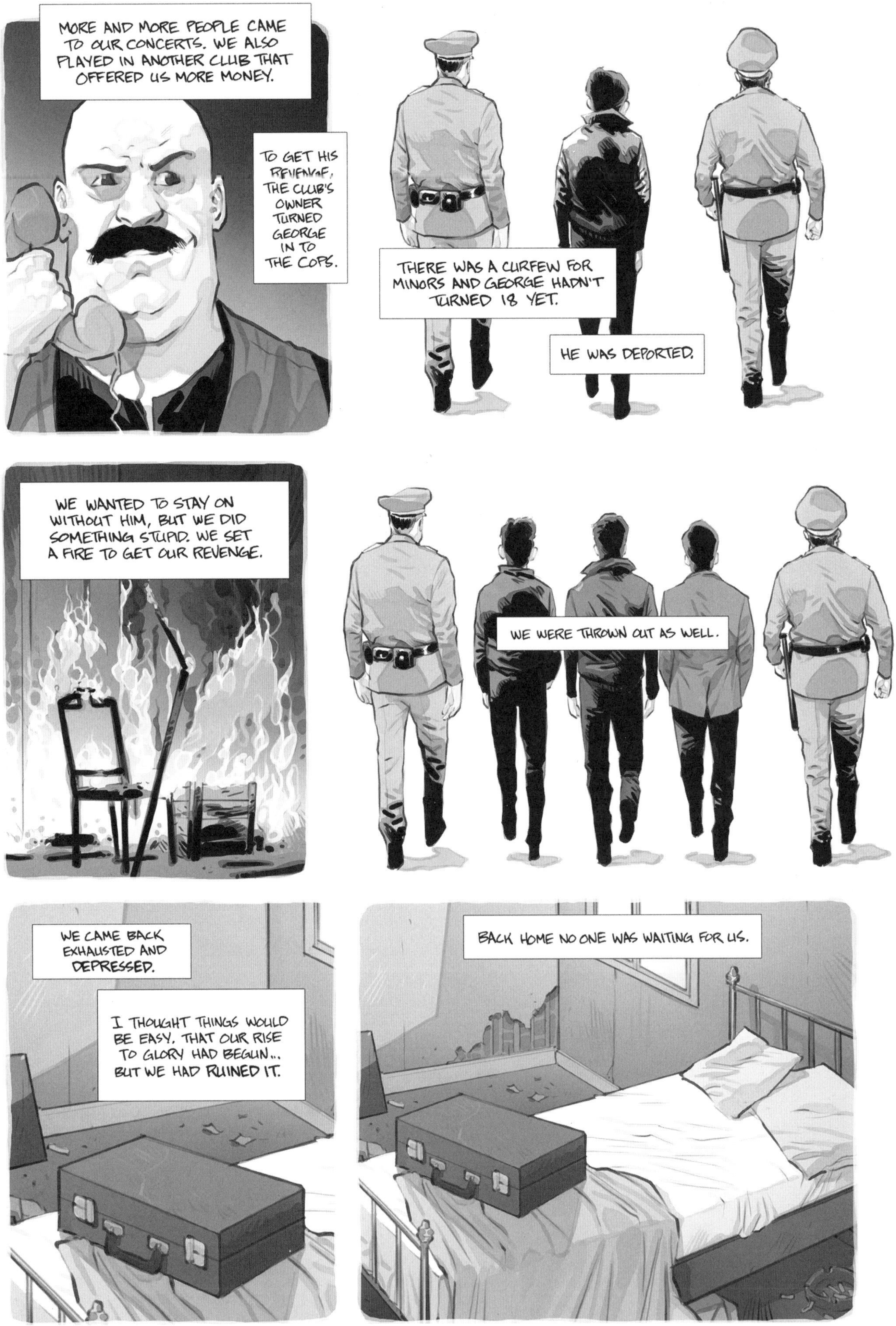
MORE AND MORE PEOPLE CAME TO OUR CONCERTS. WE ALSO PLAYED IN ANOTHER CLUB THAT OFFERED US MORE MONEY.
TO GET HIS REVENGE, THE CLUB'S OWNER TURNED GEORGE IN TO THE COPS.
THERE WAS A CURFEW FOR MINORS AND GEORGE HADN'T TURNED 18 YET.
HE WAS DEPORTED.
WE WANTED TO STAY ON WITHOUT HIM, BUT WE DID SOMETHING STUPID. WE SET A FIRE TO GET OUR REVENGE.
WE WERE THROWN OUT AS WELL.
WE CAME BACK EXHAUSTED AND DEPRESSED.
I THOUGHT THINGS WOULD BE EASY. THAT OUR RISE TO GLORY HAD BEGUN... BUT WE HAD RUINED IT.
BACK HOME NO ONE WAS WAITING FOR US.

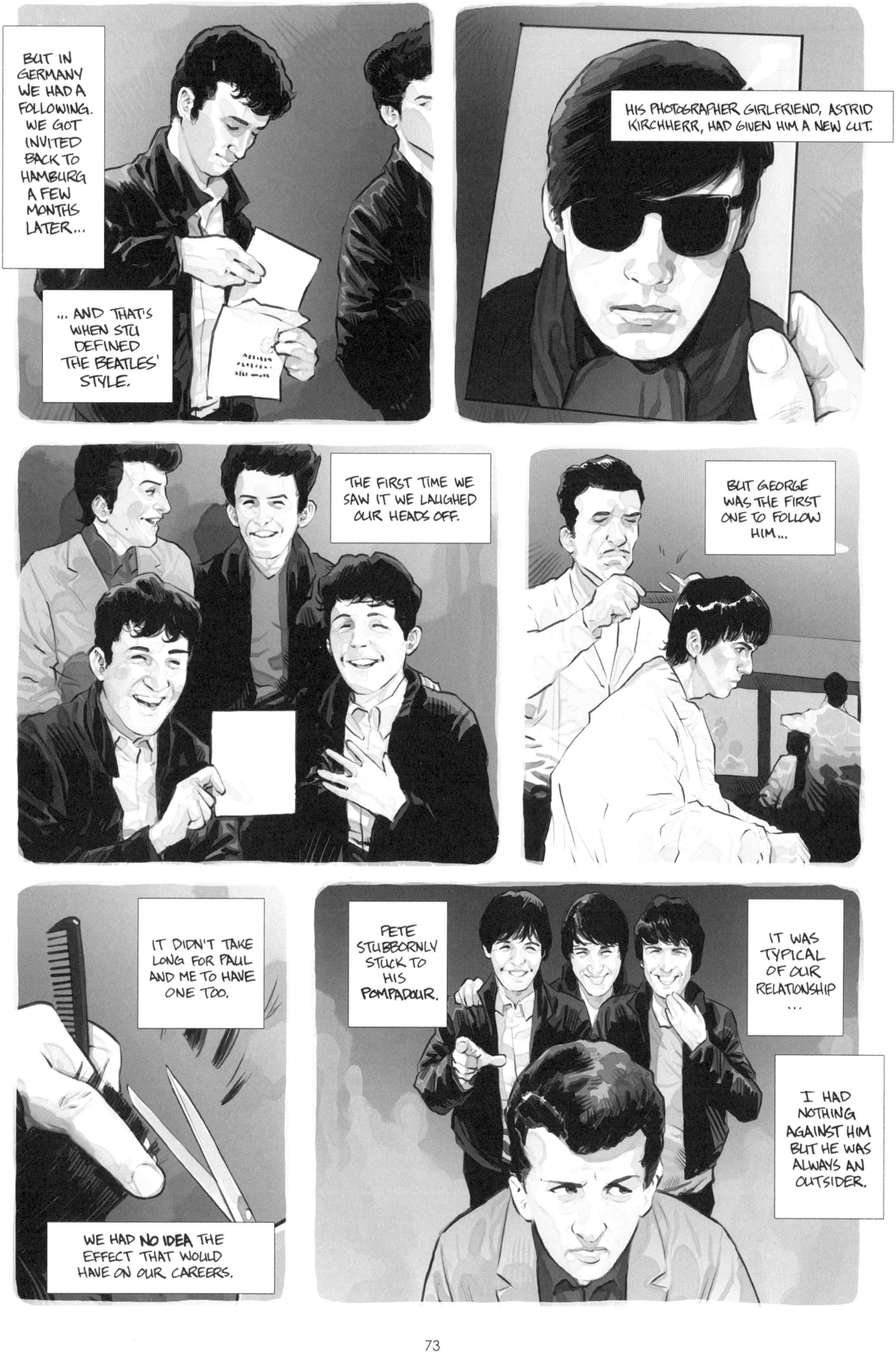

BUT IN GERMANY WE HAD A FOLLOWING. WE GOT INVITED BACK TO HAMBURG A FEW MONTHS LATER...
... AND THAT'S WHEN STU DEFINED THE BEATLES' STYLE.
HIS PHOTOGRAPHER GIRLFRIEND, ASTRID KIRCHHERR, HAD GIVEN HIM A NEW CUT.
THE FIRST TIME WE SAW IT WE LAUGHED OUR HEADS OFF.
BUT GEORGE WAS THE FIRST ONE TO FOLLOW HIM...
IT DIDN'T TAKE LONG FOR PAUL AND ME TO HAVE ONE TOO.
WE HAD **NO IDEA** THE EFFECT THAT WOULD HAVE ON OUR CAREERS.
PETE STUBBORNLY STUCK TO HIS **POMPADOUR.**
IT WAS TYPICAL OF OUR RELATIONSHIP ...
I HAD NOTHING AGAINST HIM BUT HE WAS ALWAYS AN OUTSIDER.

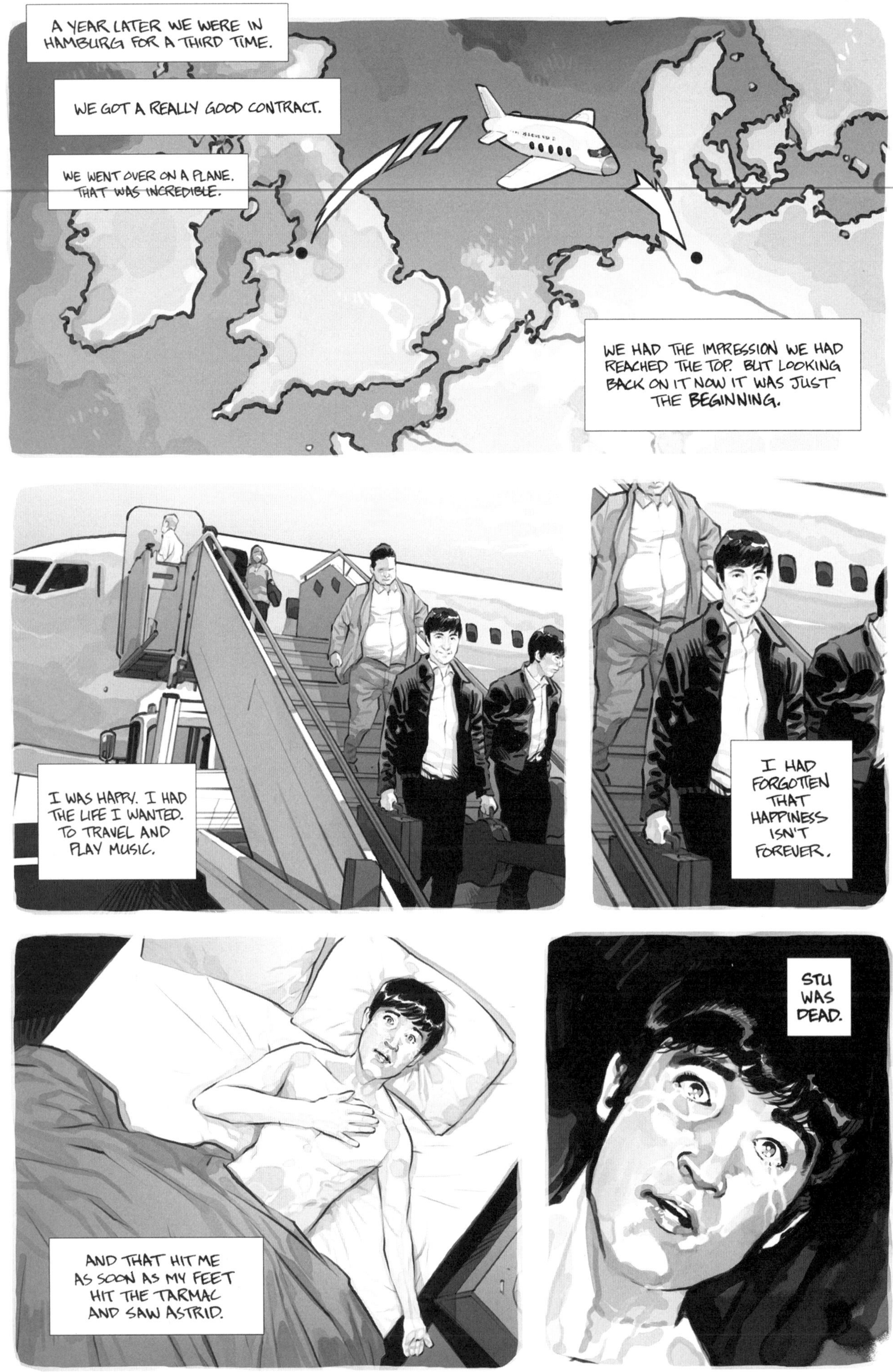
A YEAR LATER WE WERE IN HAMBURG FOR A THIRD TIME.
WE GOT A REALLY GOOD CONTRACT.
WE WENT OVER ON A PLANE. THAT WAS INCREDIBLE.
WE HAD THE IMPRESSION WE HAD REACHED THE TOP. BUT LOOKING BACK ON IT NOW IT WAS JUST THE BEGINNING.
I WAS HAPPY. I HAD THE LIFE I WANTED. TO TRAVEL AND PLAY MUSIC.
I HAD FORGOTTEN THAT HAPPINESS ISN'T FOREVER.
AND THAT HIT ME AS SOON AS MY FEET HIT THE TARMAC AND SAW ASTRID.
STU WAS DEAD.

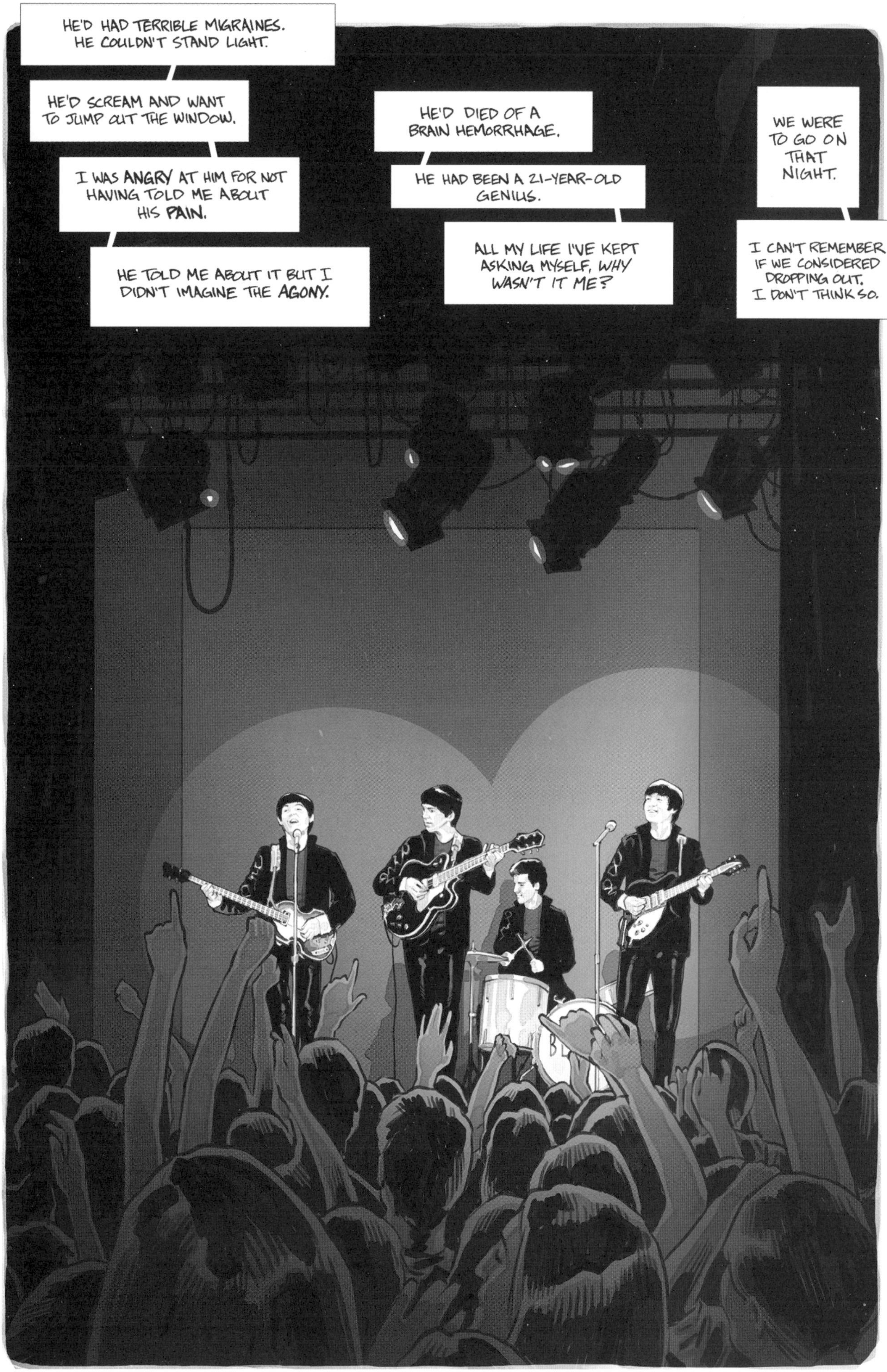
HE'D HAD TERRIBLE MIGRAINES. HE COULDN'T STAND LIGHT.
HE'D SCREAM AND WANT TO JUMP OUT THE WINDOW.
I WAS ANGRY AT HIM FOR NOT HAVING TOLD ME ABOUT HIS PAIN.
HE TOLD ME ABOUT IT BUT I DIDN'T IMAGINE THE AGONY.
HE'D DIED OF A BRAIN HEMORRHAGE.
HE HAD BEEN A 21-YEAR-OLD GENIUS.
ALL MY LIFE I'VE KEPT ASKING MYSELF, WHY WASN'T IT ME?
WE WERE TO GO ON THAT NIGHT.
I CAN'T REMEMBER IF WE CONSIDERED DROPPING OUT. I DON'T THINK SO.

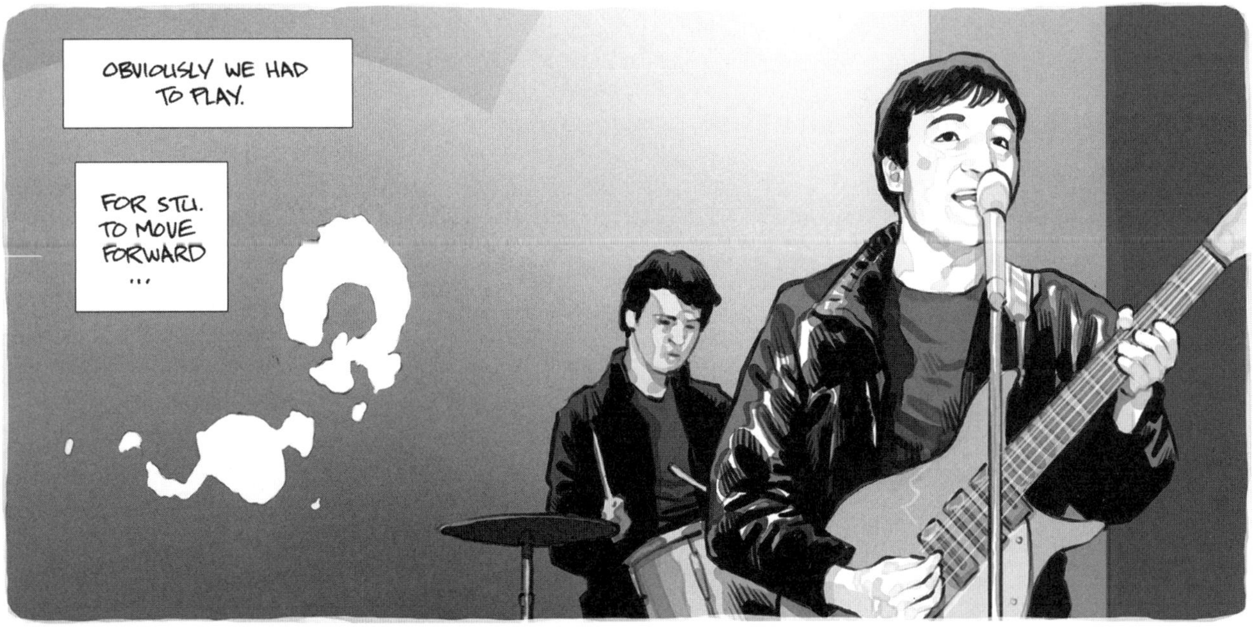
OBVIOUSLY WE HAD TO PLAY.
FOR STU. TO MOVE FORWARD ...

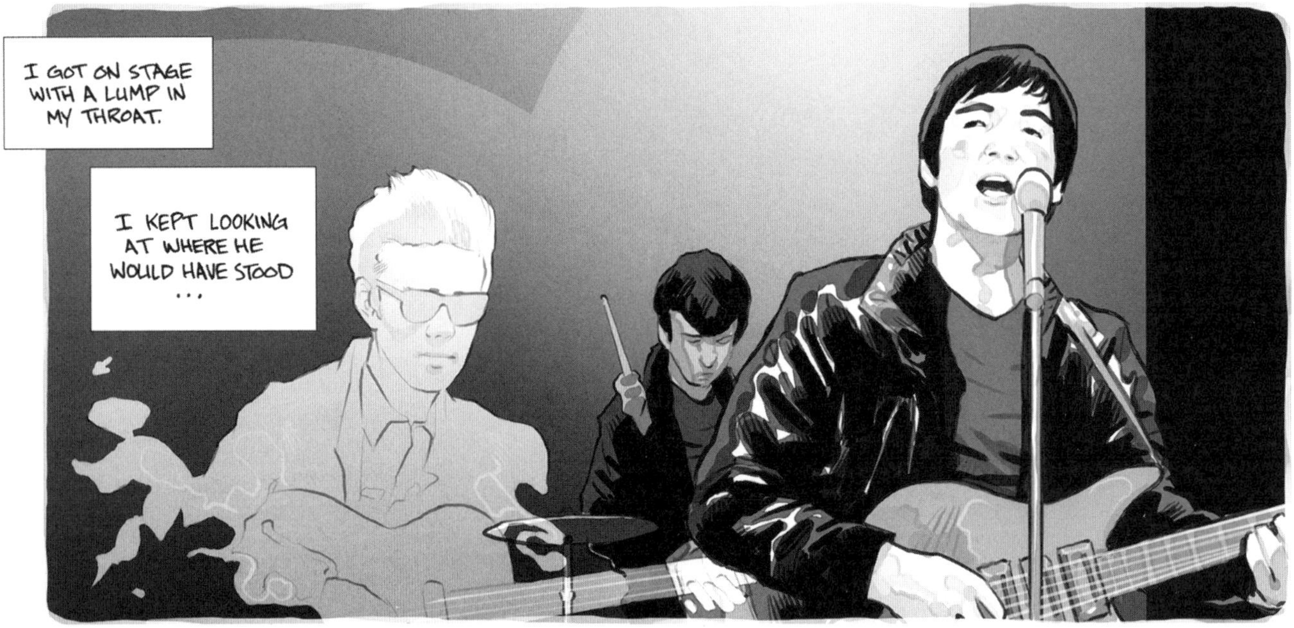
I GOT ON STAGE WITH A LUMP IN MY THROAT.
I KEPT LOOKING AT WHERE HE WOULD HAVE STOOD ...

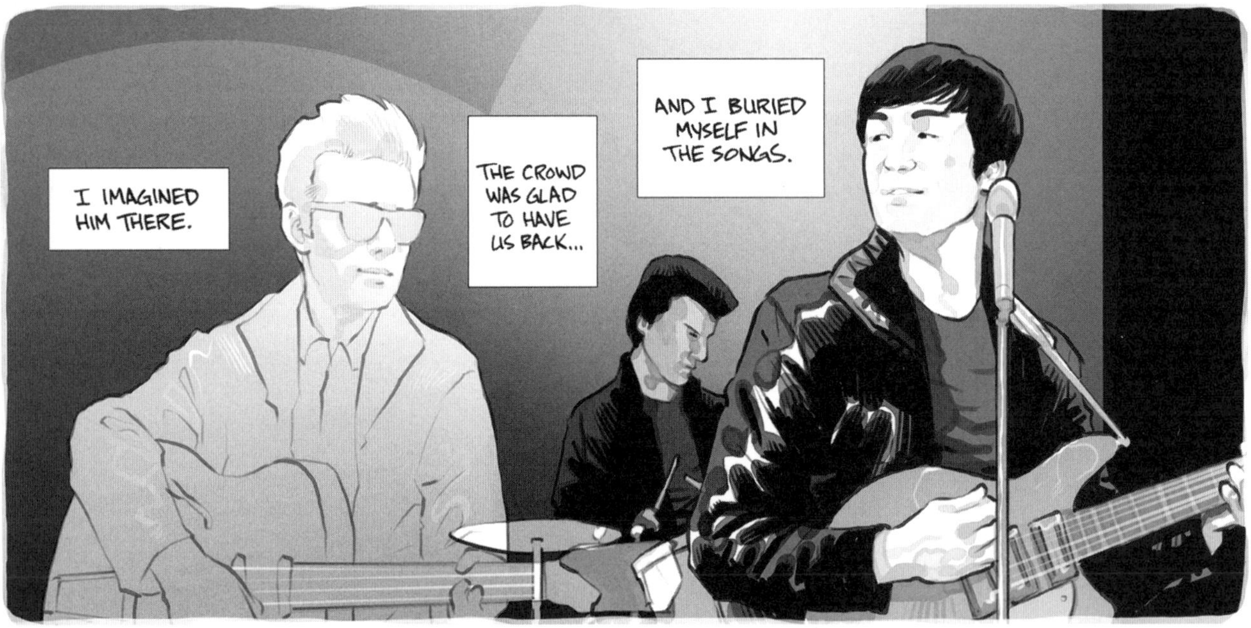
I IMAGINED HIM THERE.
THE CROWD WAS GLAD TO HAVE US BACK...
AND I BURIED MYSELF IN THE SONGS.

tenth session
WE BECAME HUGE

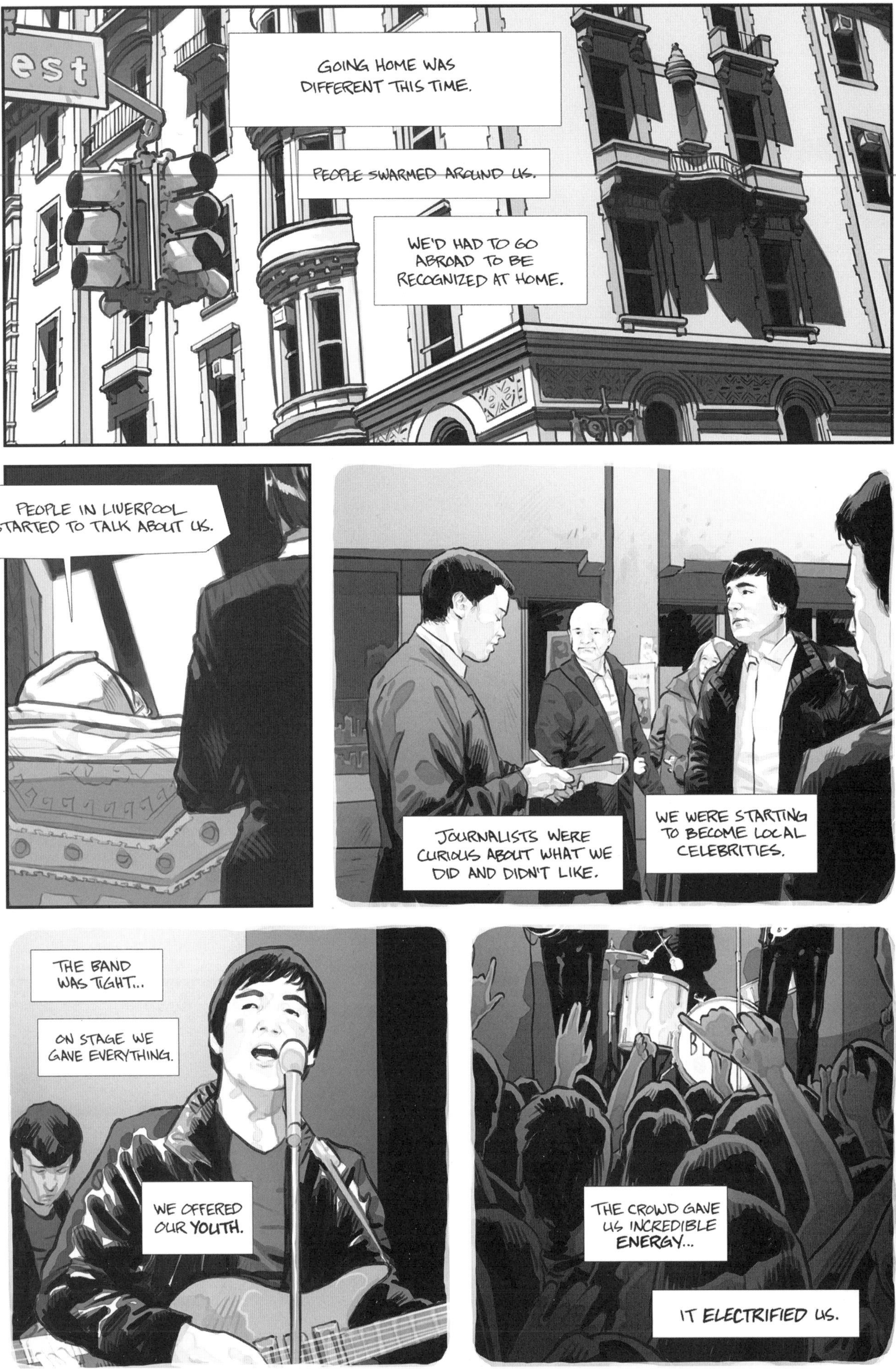
est
GOING HOME WAS DIFFERENT THIS TIME.
PEOPLE SWARMED AROUND US.
WE'D HAD TO GO ABROAD TO BE RECOGNIZED AT HOME.
PEOPLE IN LIVERPOOL STARTED TO TALK ABOUT US.
JOURNALISTS WERE CURIOUS ABOUT WHAT WE DID AND DIDN'T LIKE.
WE WERE STARTING TO BECOME LOCAL CELEBRITIES.
THE BAND WAS TIGHT...
ON STAGE WE GAVE EVERYTHING.
WE OFFERED OUR **YOUTH**.
THE CROWD GAVE US INCREDIBLE **ENERGY**...
IT **ELECTRIFIED** US.

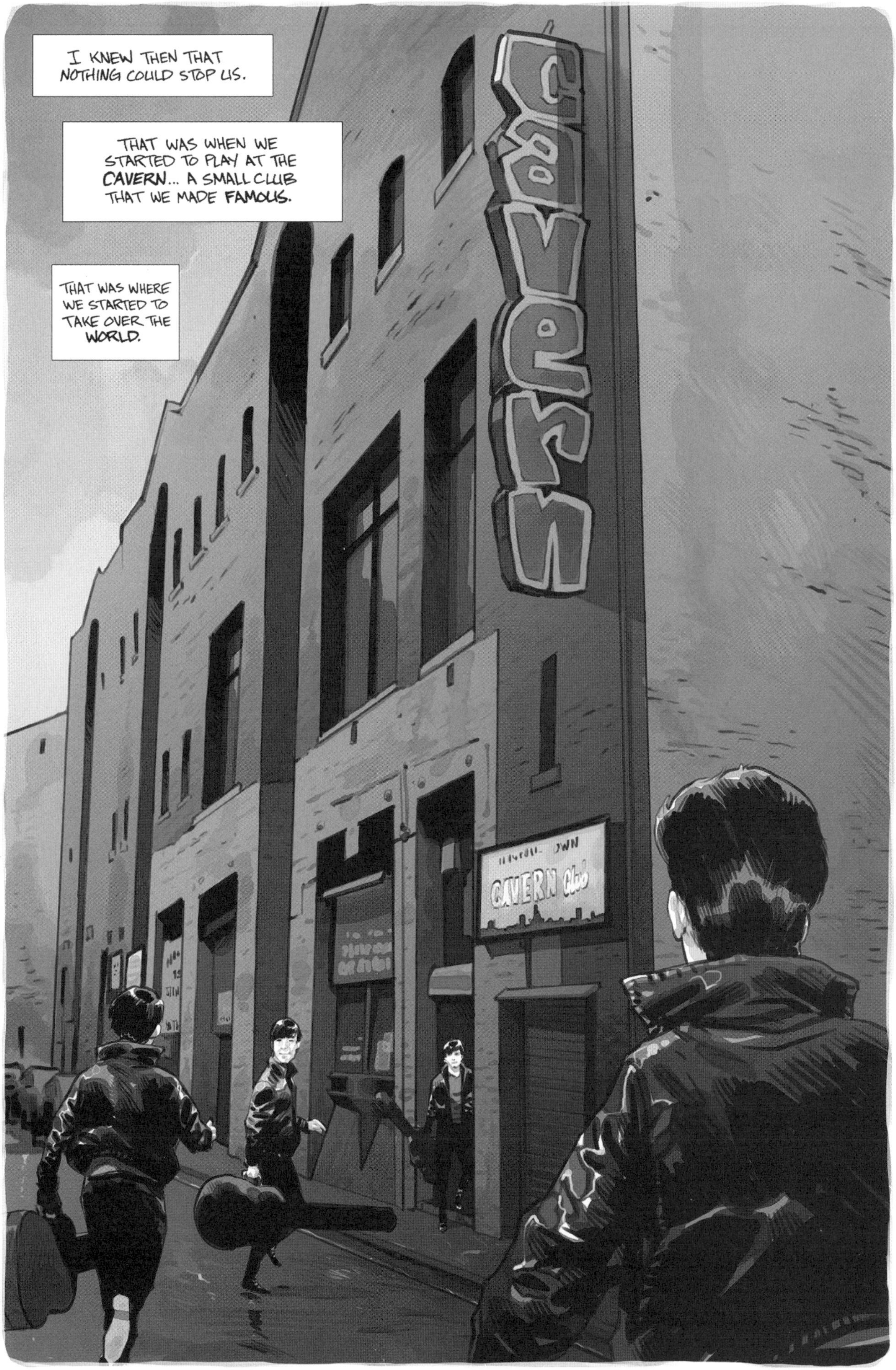
I KNEW THEN THAT NOTHING COULD STOP US.
THAT WAS WHEN WE STARTED TO PLAY AT THE CAVERN... A SMALL CLUB THAT WE MADE FAMOUS.
THAT WAS WHERE WE STARTED TO TAKE OVER THE WORLD.
Cavern
CAVERN Club

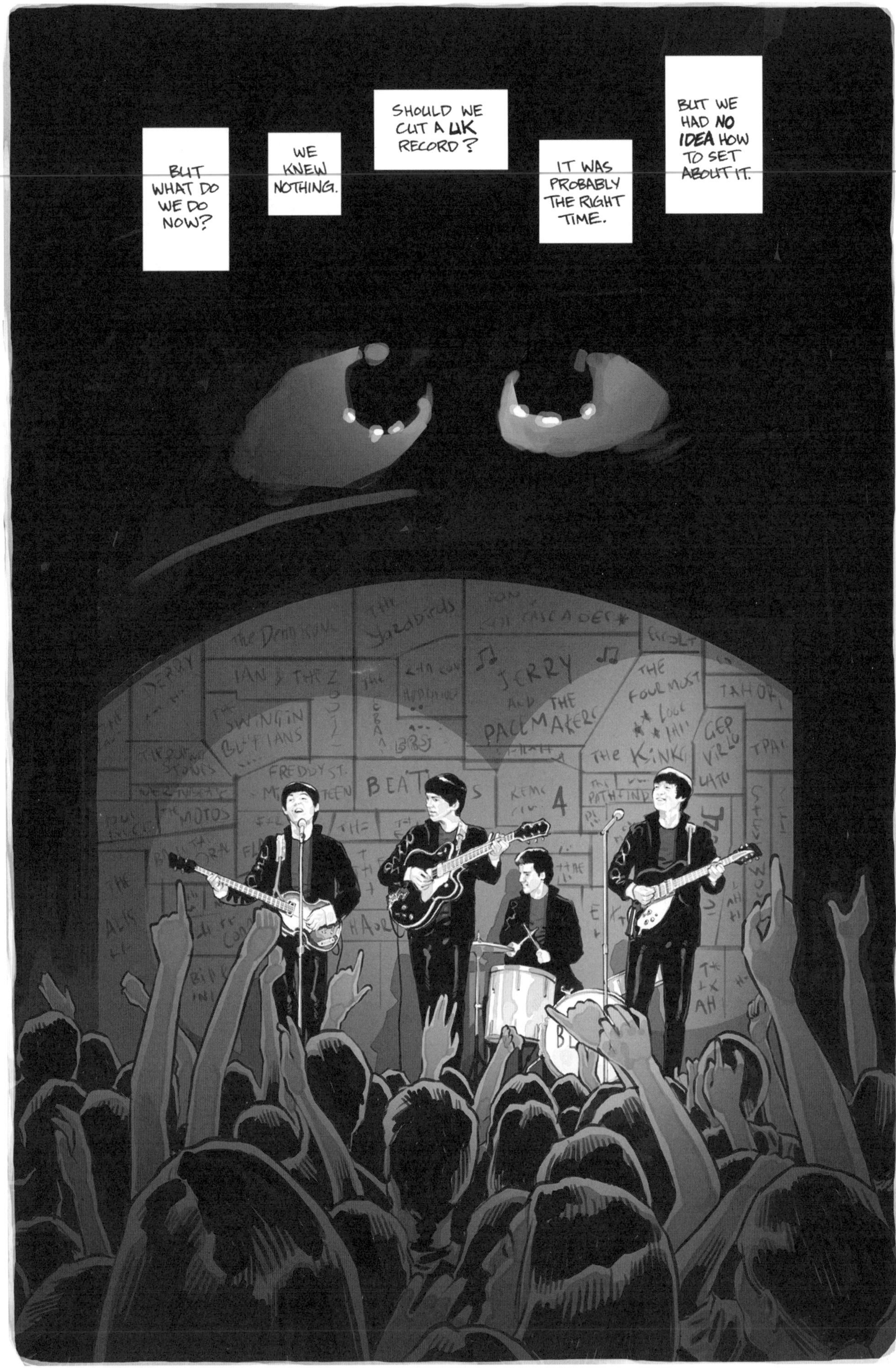
BUT WHAT DO WE DO NOW?
WE KNEW NOTHING.
SHOULD WE CUT A UK RECORD?
IT WAS PROBABLY THE RIGHT TIME.
BUT WE HAD NO IDEA HOW TO SET ABOUT IT.

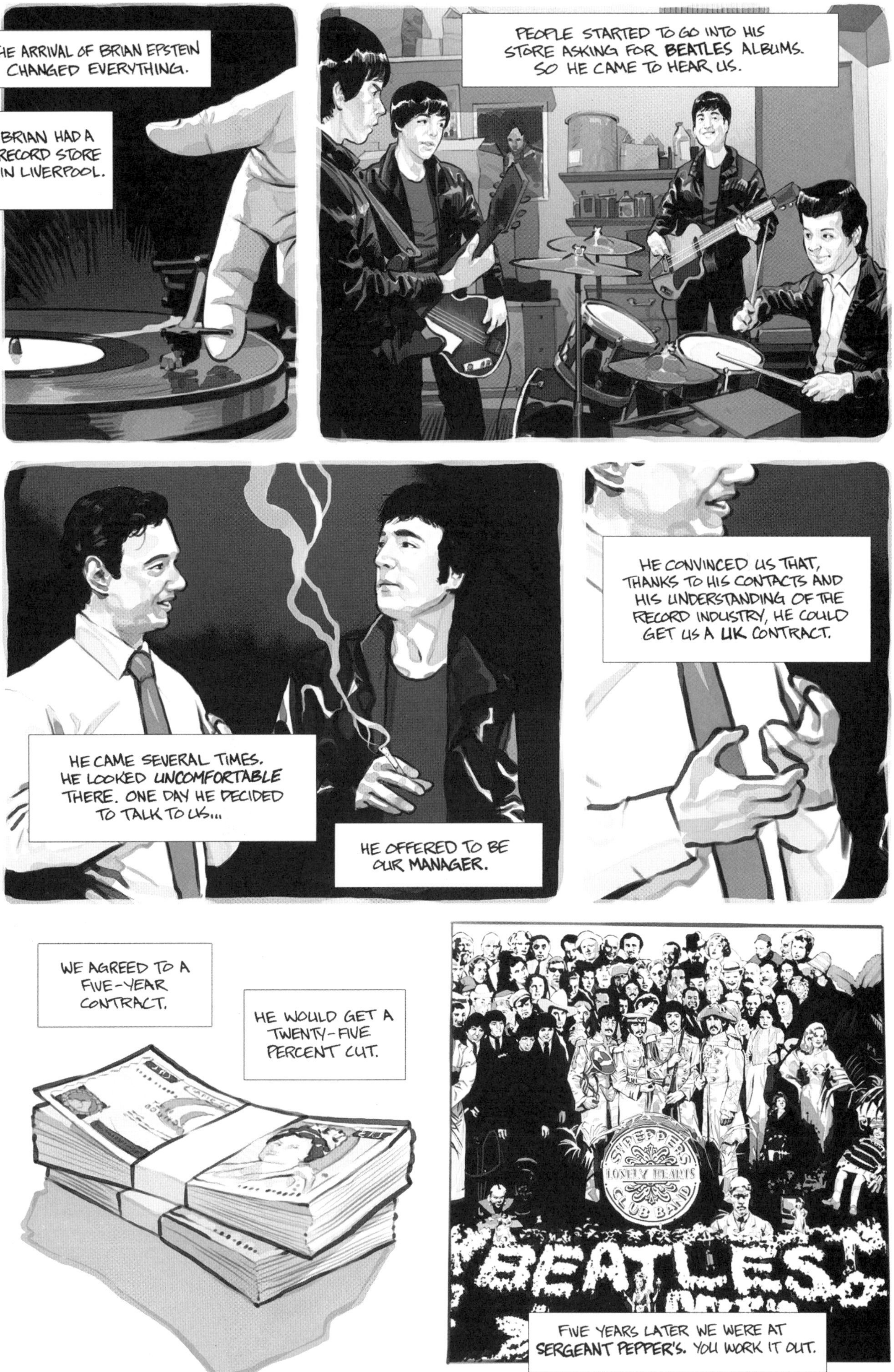

THE ARRIVAL OF BRIAN EPSTEIN CHANGED EVERYTHING.
BRIAN HAD A RECORD STORE IN LIVERPOOL.
PEOPLE STARTED TO GO INTO HIS STORE ASKING FOR **BEATLES** ALBUMS. SO HE CAME TO HEAR US.
HE CAME SEVERAL TIMES. HE LOOKED **UNCOMFORTABLE** THERE. ONE DAY HE DECIDED TO TALK TO US...
HE OFFERED TO BE OUR **MANAGER**.
HE CONVINCED US THAT, THANKS TO HIS CONTACTS AND HIS UNDERSTANDING OF THE RECORD INDUSTRY, HE COULD GET US A **UK** CONTRACT.
WE AGREED TO A FIVE-YEAR CONTRACT.
HE WOULD GET A TWENTY-FIVE PERCENT CUT.
SGT. PEPPER'S LONELY HEARTS CLUB BAND
BEATLES
FIVE YEARS LATER WE WERE AT **SERGEANT PEPPER'S**. YOU WORK IT OUT.

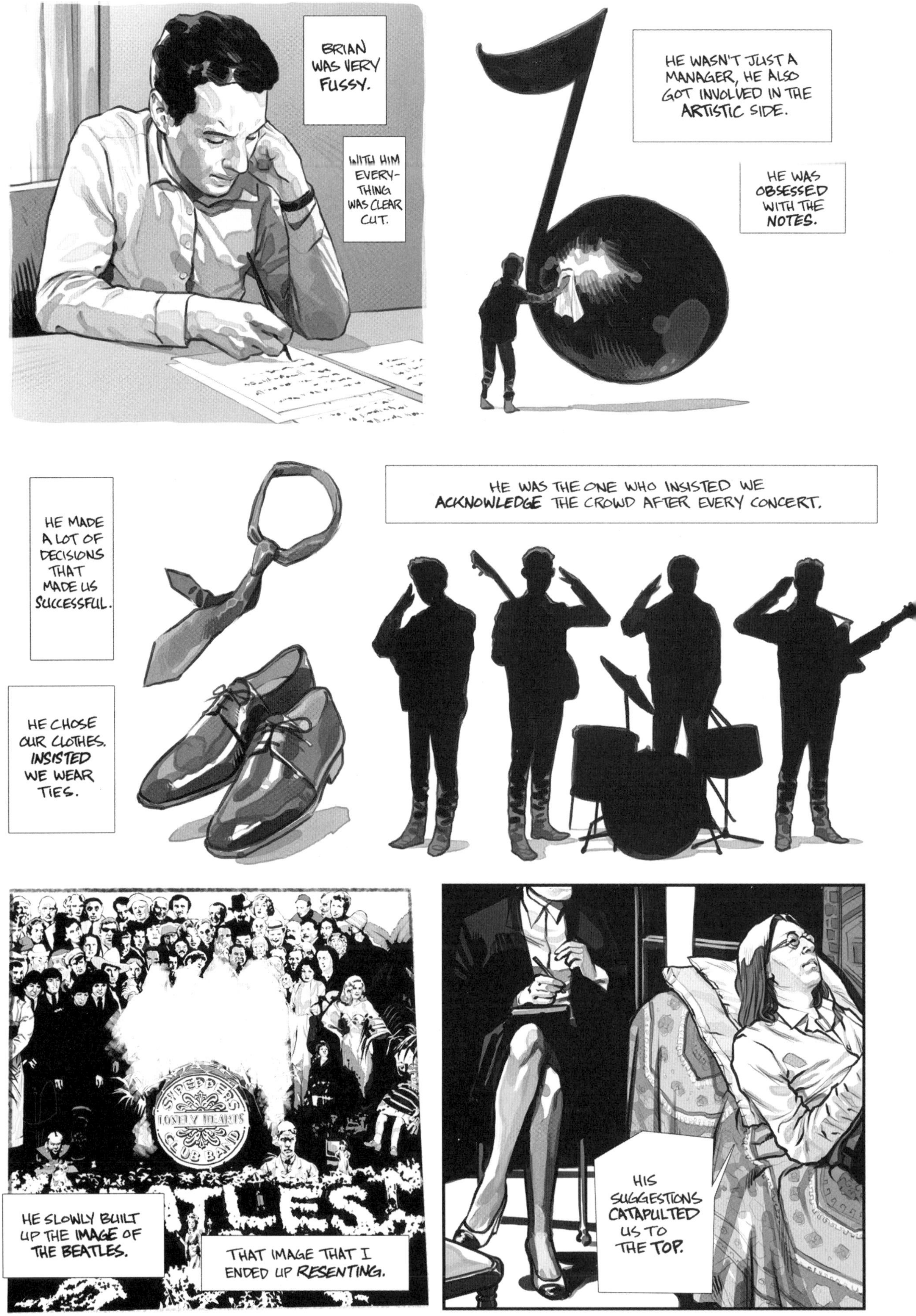
BRIAN WAS VERY FUSSY.
WITH HIM EVERY-THING WAS CLEAR CUT.
HE WASN'T JUST A MANAGER, HE ALSO GOT INVOLVED IN THE ARTISTIC SIDE.
HE WAS OBSESSED WITH THE NOTES.
HE MADE A LOT OF DECISIONS THAT MADE US SUCCESSFUL.
HE CHOSE OUR CLOTHES. INSISTED WE WEAR TIES.
HE WAS THE ONE WHO INSISTED WE ACKNOWLEDGE THE CROWD AFTER EVERY CONCERT.
HE SLOWLY BUILT UP THE IMAGE OF THE BEATLES.
THAT IMAGE THAT I ENDED UP RESENTING.
HIS SUGGESTIONS CATAPULTED US TO THE TOP.

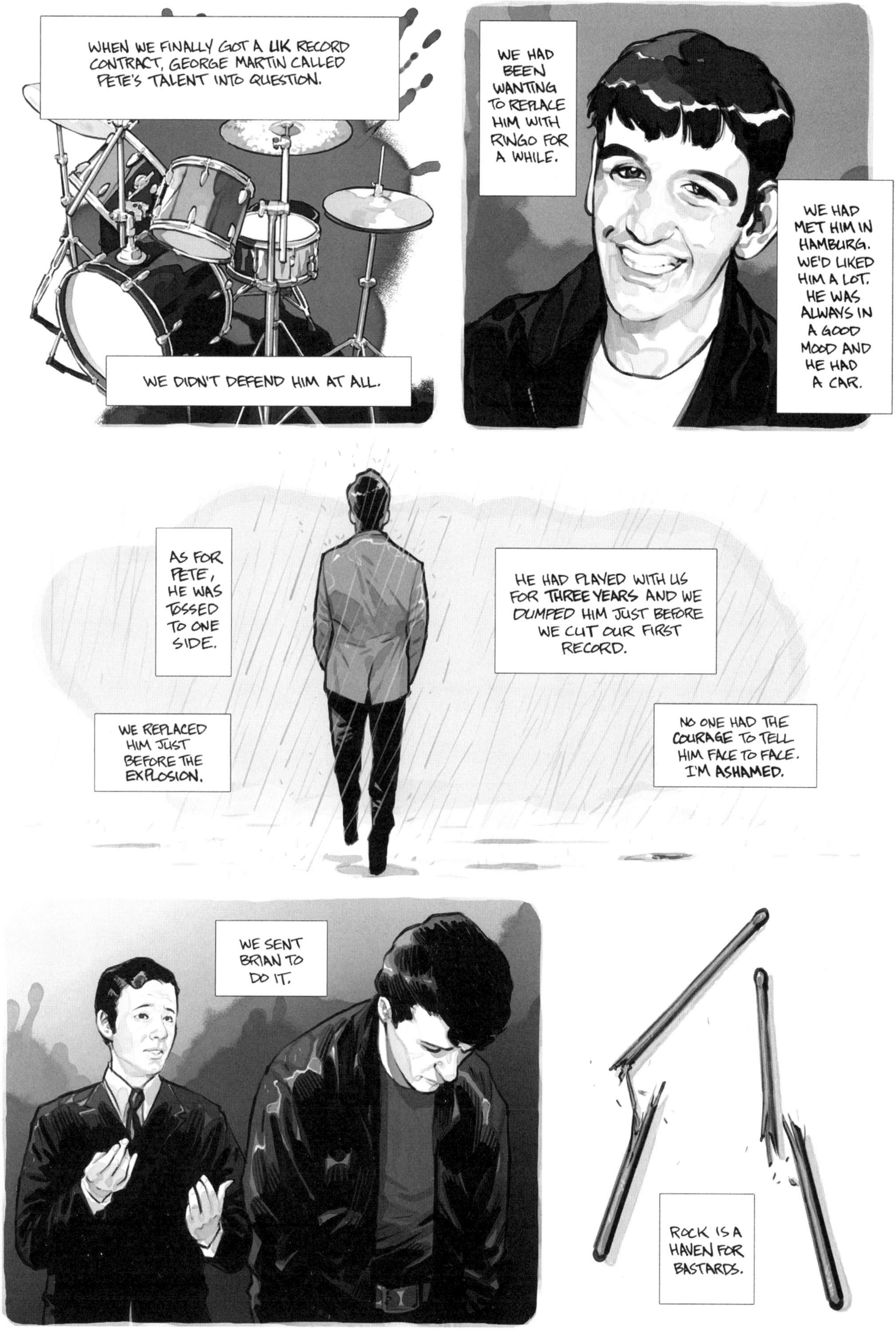
WHEN WE FINALLY GOT A UK RECORD CONTRACT, GEORGE MARTIN CALLED PETE'S TALENT INTO QUESTION.
WE DIDN'T DEFEND HIM AT ALL.
WE HAD BEEN WANTING TO REPLACE HIM WITH RINGO FOR A WHILE.
WE HAD MET HIM IN HAMBURG. WE'D LIKED HIM A LOT. HE WAS ALWAYS IN A GOOD MOOD AND HE HAD A CAR.
AS FOR PETE, HE WAS TOSSED TO ONE SIDE.
HE HAD PLAYED WITH US FOR THREE YEARS AND WE DUMPED HIM JUST BEFORE WE CUT OUR FIRST RECORD.
WE REPLACED HIM JUST BEFORE THE EXPLOSION.
NO ONE HAD THE COURAGE TO TELL HIM FACE TO FACE. I'M ASHAMED.
WE SENT BRIAN TO DO IT.
ROCK IS A HAVEN FOR BASTARDS.

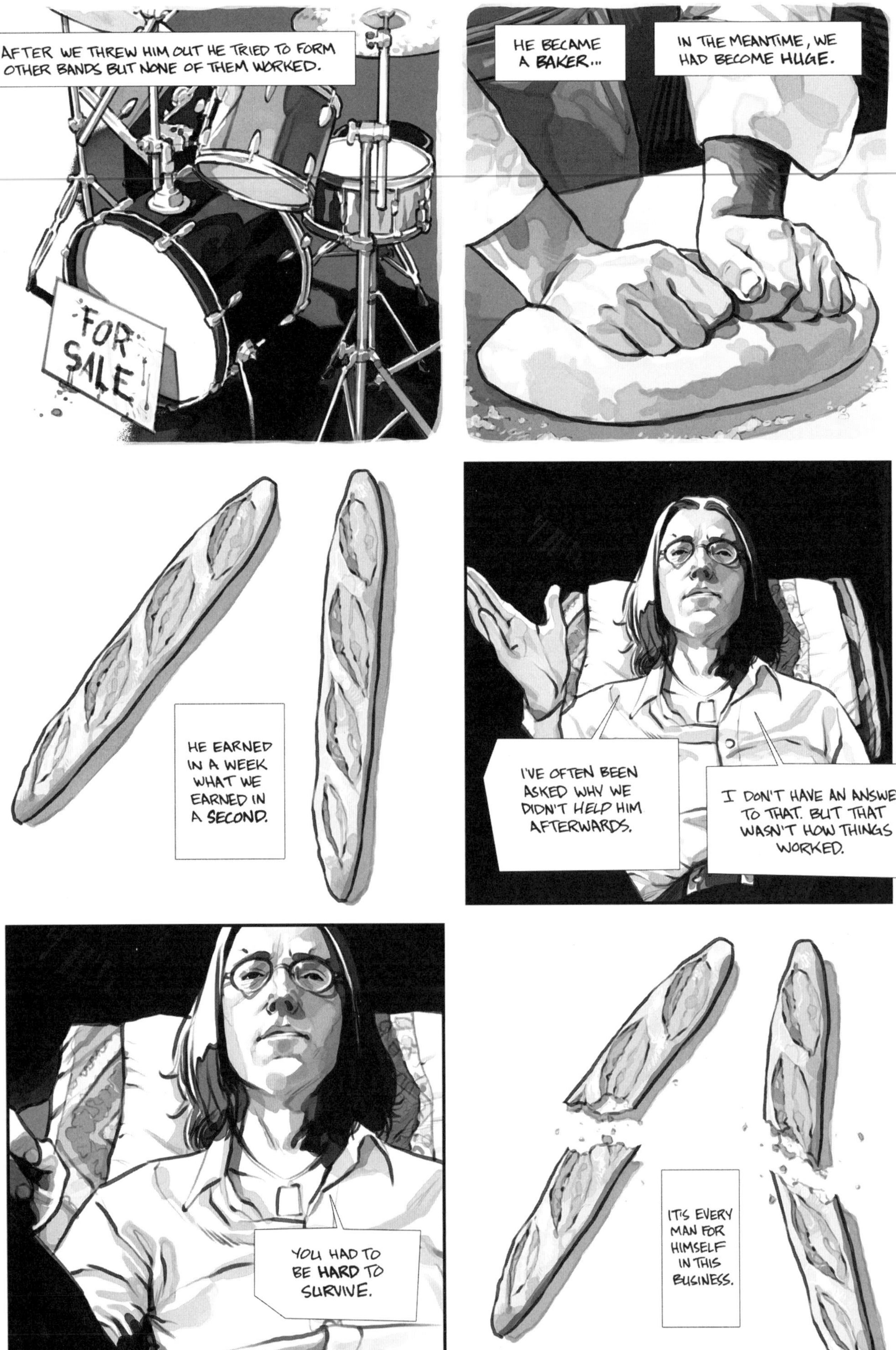
AFTER WE THREW HIM OUT HE TRIED TO FORM OTHER BANDS BUT NONE OF THEM WORKED.
FOR SALE
HE BECAME A BAKER...
IN THE MEANTIME, WE HAD BECOME HUGE.
HE EARNED IN A WEEK WHAT WE EARNED IN A SECOND.
I'VE OFTEN BEEN ASKED WHY WE DIDN'T HELP HIM AFTERWARDS.
I DON'T HAVE AN ANSWER TO THAT. BUT THAT WASN'T HOW THINGS WORKED.
YOU HAD TO BE HARD TO SURVIVE.
IT'S EVERY MAN FOR HIMSELF IN THIS BUSINESS.

eleventh session

MY CAREER WAS OVER

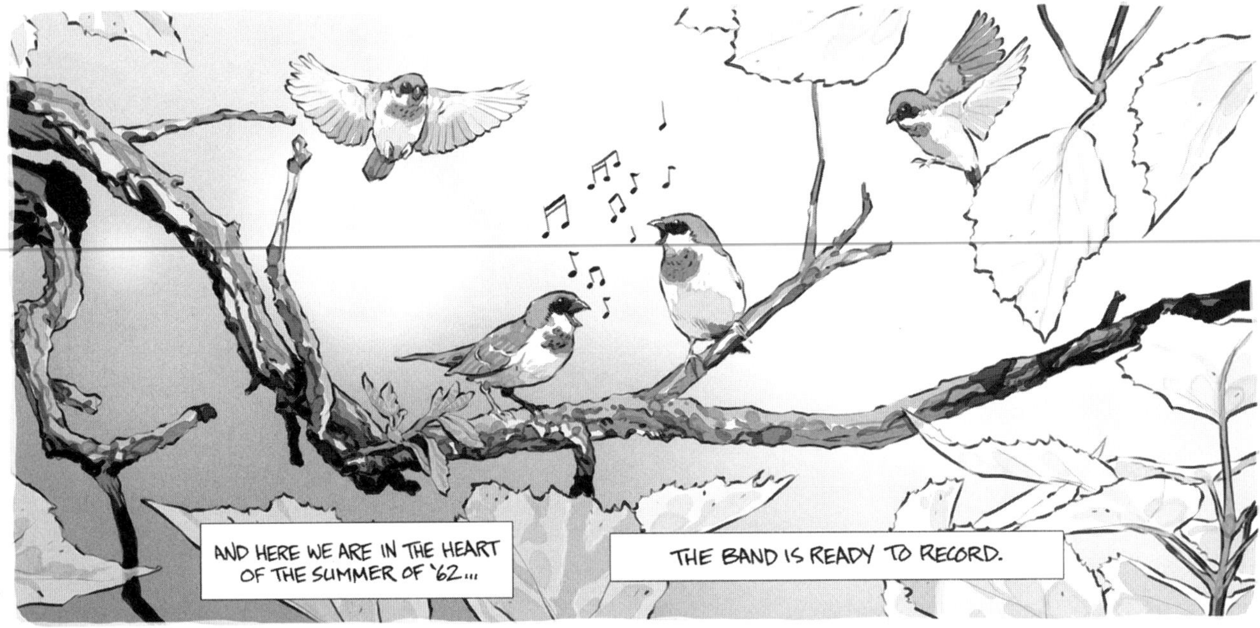
AND HERE WE ARE IN THE HEART OF THE SUMMER OF '62...
THE BAND IS READY TO RECORD.

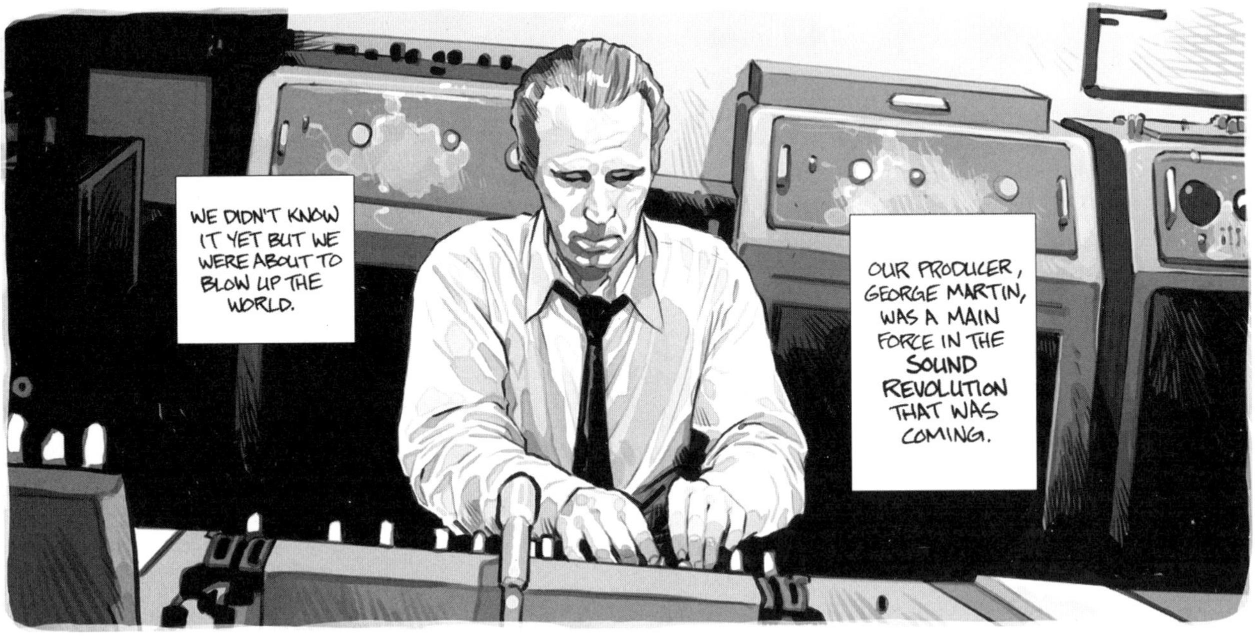
WE DIDN'T KNOW IT YET BUT WE WERE ABOUT TO BLOW UP THE WORLD.
OUR PRODUCER, GEORGE MARTIN, WAS A MAIN FORCE IN THE SOUND REVOLUTION THAT WAS COMING.

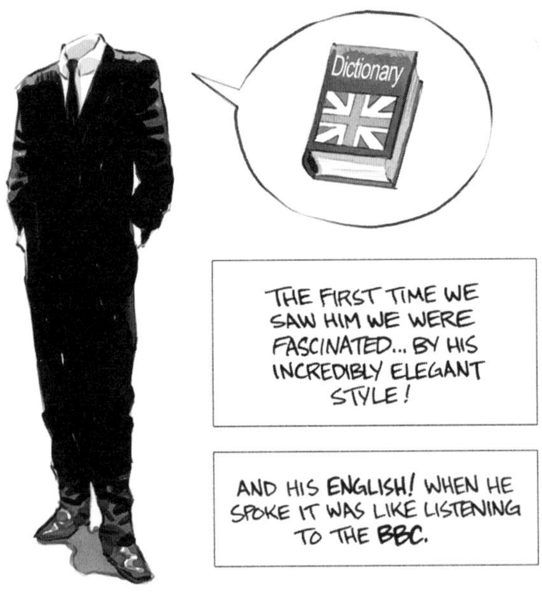
Dictionary
THE FIRST TIME WE SAW HIM WE WERE FASCINATED... BY HIS INCREDIBLY ELEGANT STYLE!
AND HIS ENGLISH! WHEN HE SPOKE IT WAS LIKE LISTENING TO THE BBC.

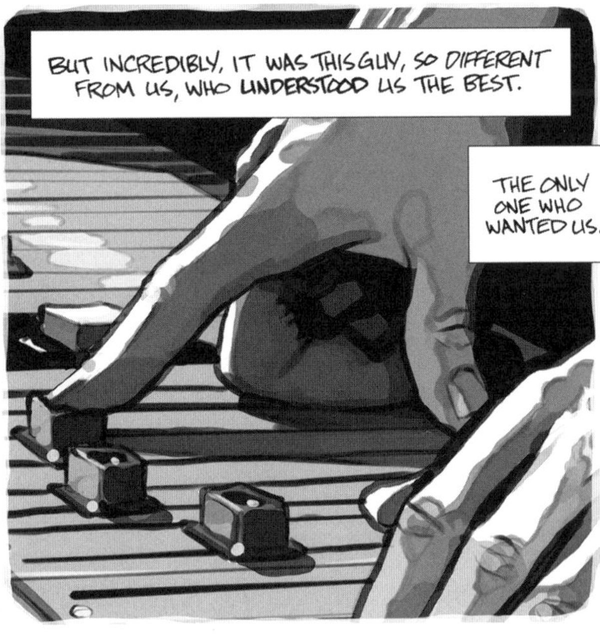
BUT INCREDIBLY, IT WAS THIS GUY, SO DIFFERENT FROM US, WHO UNDERSTOOD US THE BEST.
THE ONLY ONE WHO WANTED US.

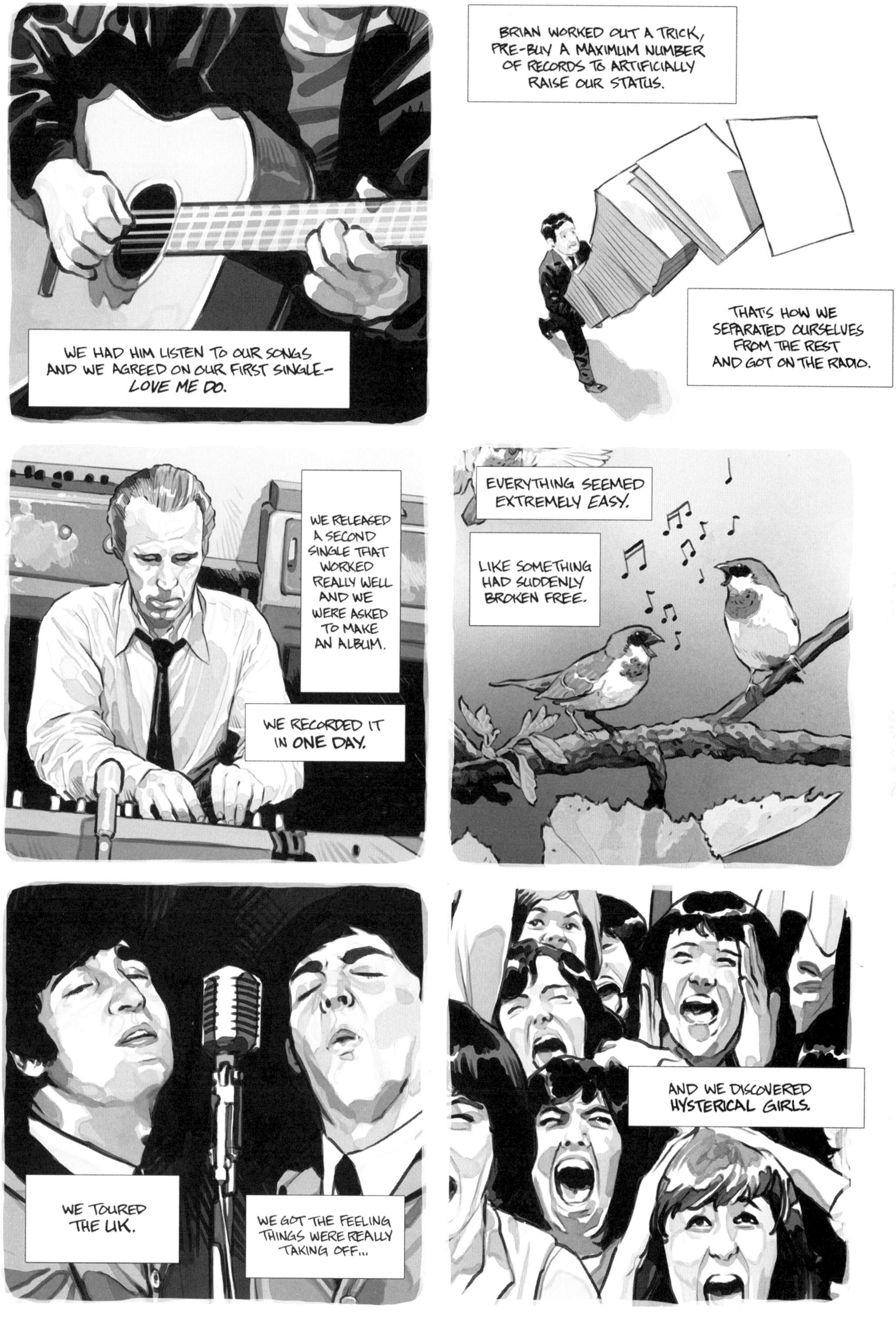
WE HAD HIM LISTEN TO OUR SONGS AND WE AGREED ON OUR FIRST SINGLE- LOVE ME DO.
BRIAN WORKED OUT A TRICK, PRE-BUY A MAXIMUM NUMBER OF RECORDS TO ARTIFICIALLY RAISE OUR STATUS.
THAT'S HOW WE SEPARATED OURSELVES FROM THE REST AND GOT ON THE RADIO.
WE RELEASED A SECOND SINGLE THAT WORKED REALLY WELL AND WE WERE ASKED TO MAKE AN ALBUM.
WE RECORDED IT IN ONE DAY.
EVERYTHING SEEMED EXTREMELY EASY.
LIKE SOMETHING HAD SUDDENLY BROKEN FREE.
WE TOURED THE UK.
WE GOT THE FEELING THINGS WERE REALLY TAKING OFF...
AND WE DISCOVERED HYSTERICAL GIRLS.

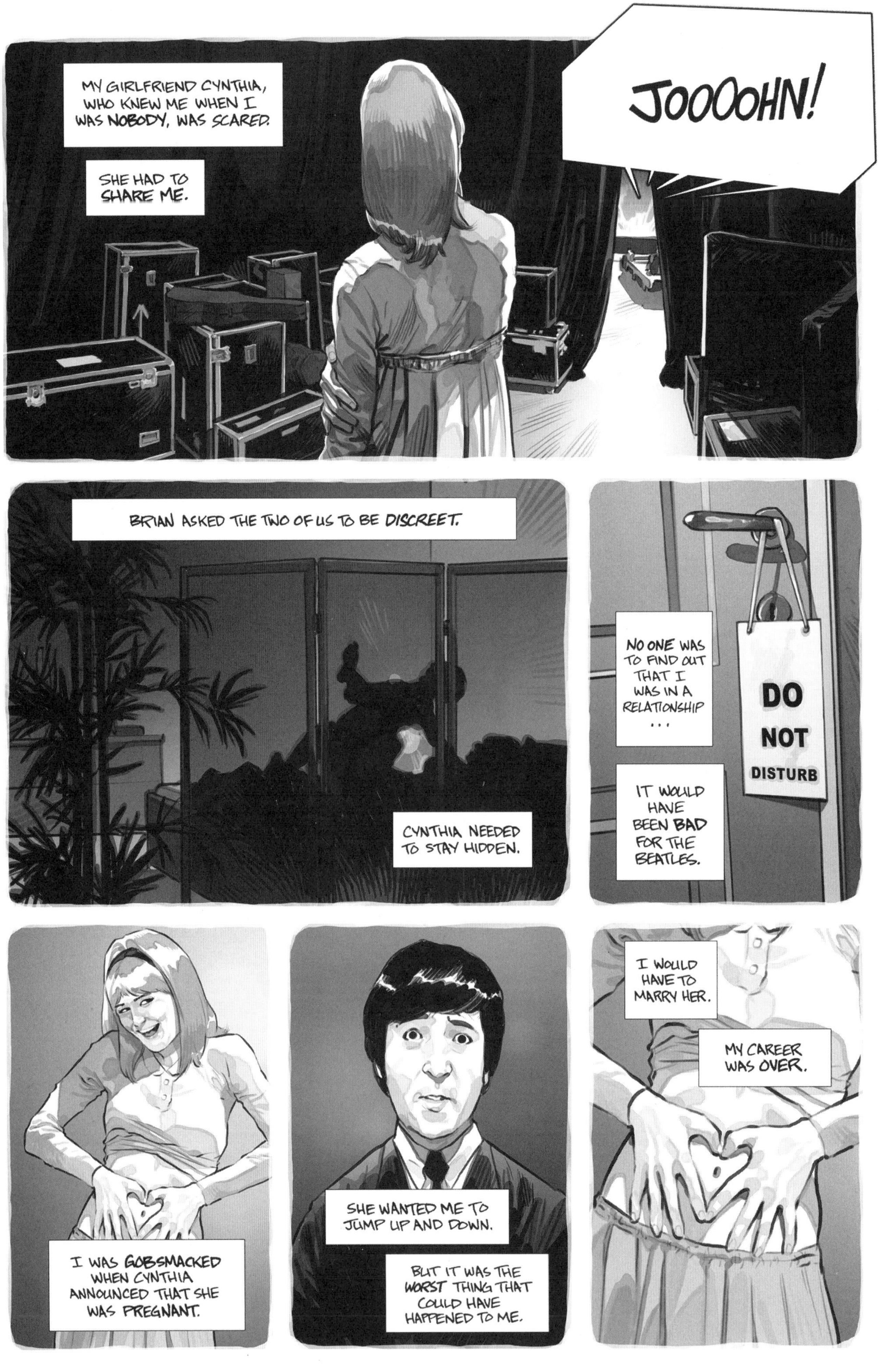
MY GIRLFRIEND CYNTHIA, WHO KNEW ME WHEN I WAS NOBODY, WAS SCARED.
SHE HAD TO SHARE ME.
JOOOOHN!
BRIAN ASKED THE TWO OF US TO BE DISCREET.
CYNTHIA NEEDED TO STAY HIDDEN.
NO ONE WAS TO FIND OUT THAT I WAS IN A RELATIONSHIP . . .
DO NOT DISTURB
IT WOULD HAVE BEEN BAD FOR THE BEATLES.
I WAS GOBSMACKED WHEN CYNTHIA ANNOUNCED THAT SHE WAS PREGNANT.
SHE WANTED ME TO JUMP UP AND DOWN.
BUT IT WAS THE WORST THING THAT COULD HAVE HAPPENED TO ME.
I WOULD HAVE TO MARRY HER.
MY CAREER WAS OVER.

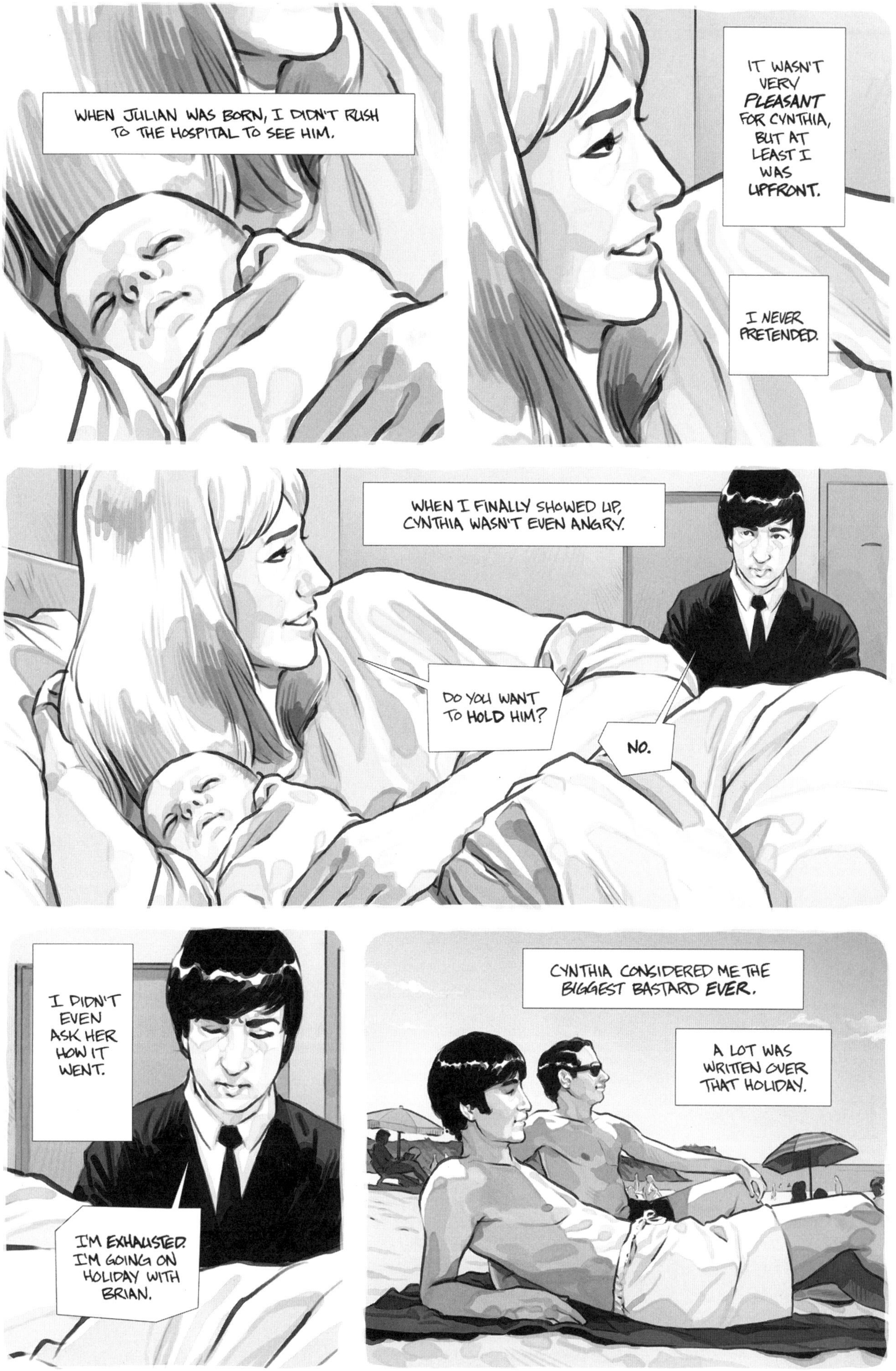
WHEN JULIAN WAS BORN, I DIDN'T RUSH TO THE HOSPITAL TO SEE HIM.
IT WASN'T VERY PLEASANT FOR CYNTHIA, BUT AT LEAST I WAS UPFRONT.
I NEVER PRETENDED.
WHEN I FINALLY SHOWED UP, CYNTHIA WASN'T EVEN ANGRY.
DO YOU WANT TO HOLD HIM?
NO.
I DIDN'T EVEN ASK HER HOW IT WENT.
I'M EXHAUSTED. I'M GOING ON HOLIDAY WITH BRIAN.
CYNTHIA CONSIDERED ME THE BIGGEST BASTARD EVER.
A LOT WAS WRITTEN OVER THAT HOLIDAY.

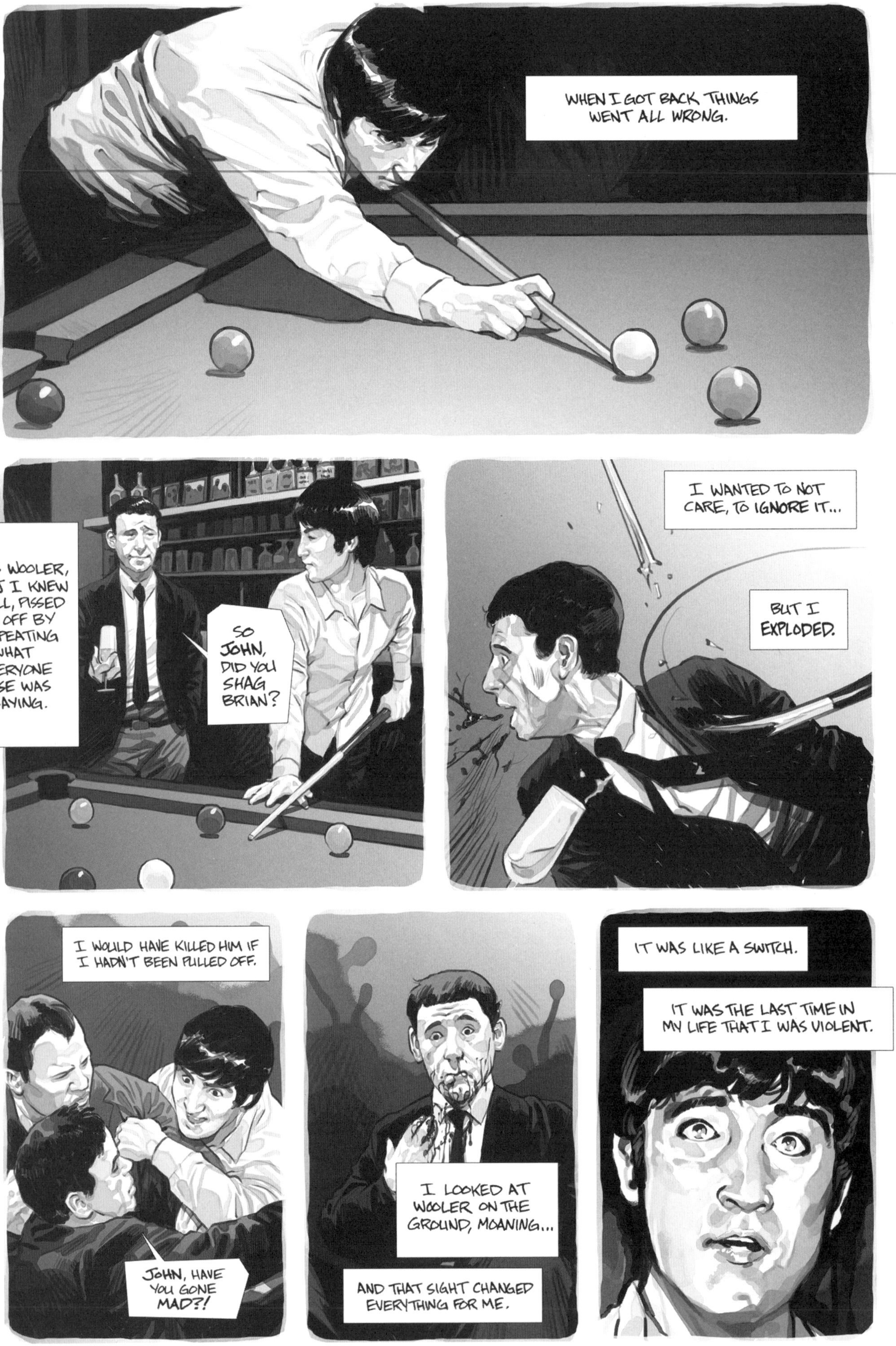
WHEN I GOT BACK THINGS WENT ALL WRONG.
BOB WOOLER, A DJ I KNEW WELL, PISSED ME OFF BY REPEATING WHAT EVERYONE ELSE WAS SAYING.
SO JOHN, DID YOU SHAG BRIAN?
I WANTED TO NOT CARE, TO IGNORE IT...
BUT I EXPLODED.
I WOULD HAVE KILLED HIM IF I HADN'T BEEN PULLED OFF.
JOHN, HAVE YOU GONE MAD?!
I LOOKED AT WOOLER ON THE GROUND, MOANING...
AND THAT SIGHT CHANGED EVERYTHING FOR ME.
IT WAS LIKE A SWITCH.
IT WAS THE LAST TIME IN MY LIFE THAT I WAS VIOLENT.

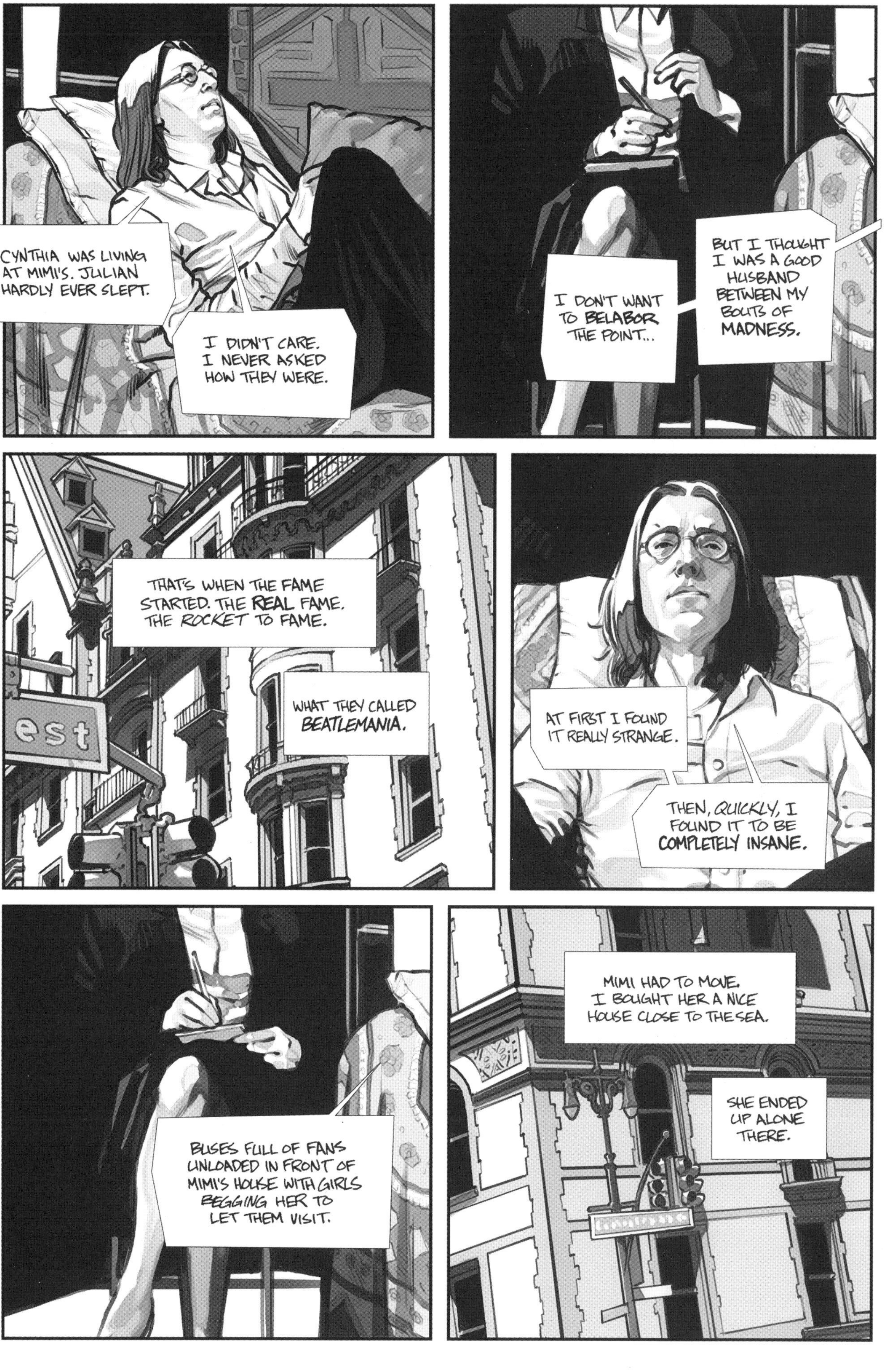
CYNTHIA WAS LIVING AT MIMI'S. JULIAN HARDLY EVER SLEPT.
I DIDN'T CARE. I NEVER ASKED HOW THEY WERE.
I DON'T WANT TO BELABOR THE POINT...
BUT I THOUGHT I WAS A GOOD HUSBAND BETWEEN MY BOUTS OF MADNESS.
THAT'S WHEN THE FAME STARTED. THE REAL FAME. THE ROCKET TO FAME.
WHAT THEY CALLED BEATLEMANIA.
est
AT FIRST I FOUND IT REALLY STRANGE.
THEN, QUICKLY, I FOUND IT TO BE COMPLETELY INSANE.
BUSES FULL OF FANS UNLOADED IN FRONT OF MIMI'S HOUSE WITH GIRLS BEGGING HER TO LET THEM VISIT.
MIMI HAD TO MOVE. I BOUGHT HER A NICE HOUSE CLOSE TO THE SEA.
SHE ENDED UP ALONE THERE.

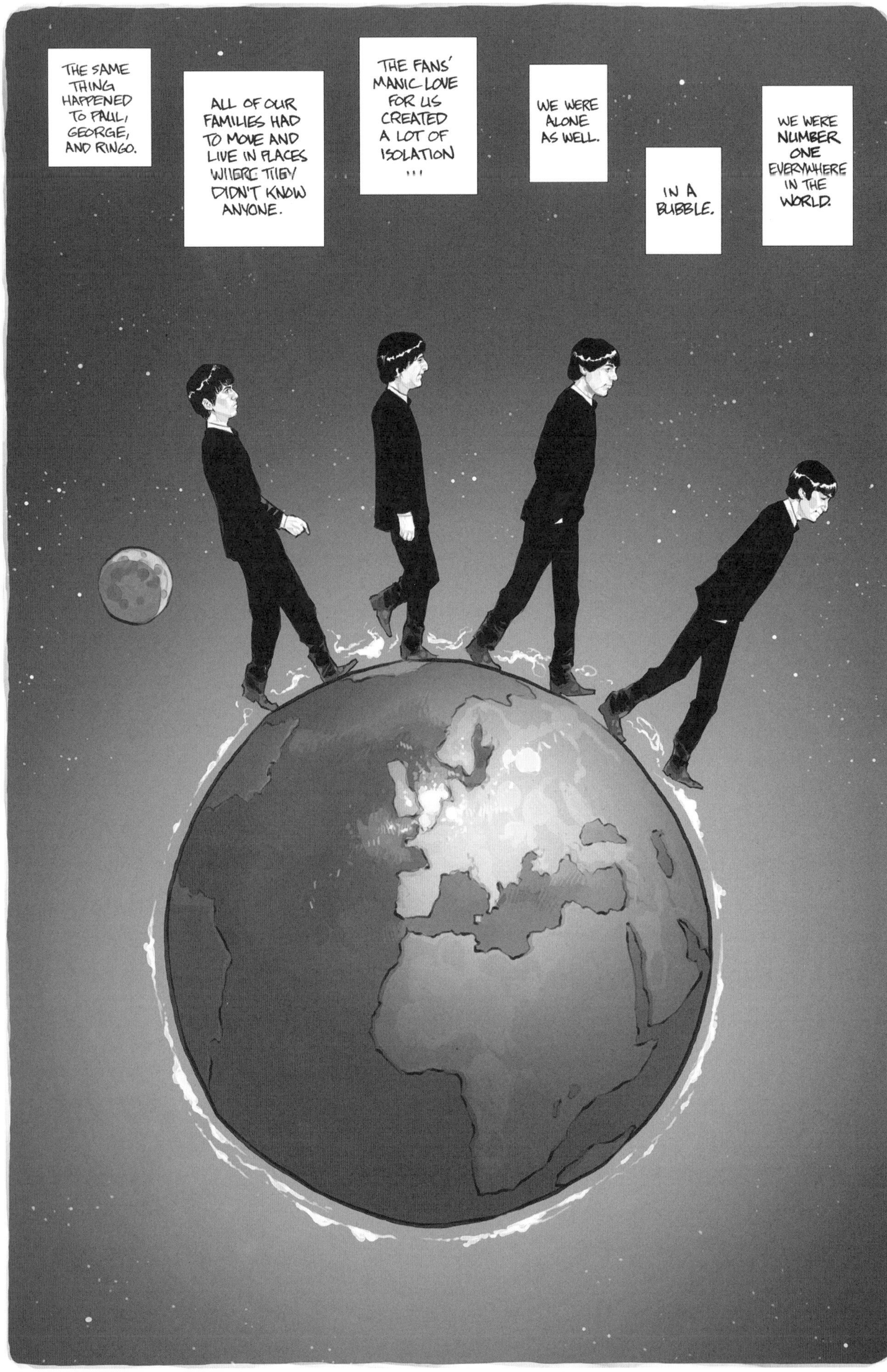
THE SAME THING HAPPENED TO PAUL, GEORGE, AND RINGO.
ALL OF OUR FAMILIES HAD TO MOVE AND LIVE IN PLACES WHERE THEY DIDN'T KNOW ANYONE.
THE FANS' MANIC LOVE FOR US CREATED A LOT OF ISOLATION ...
WE WERE ALONE AS WELL.
IN A BUBBLE.
WE WERE NUMBER ONE EVERYWHERE IN THE WORLD.

twelfth session

IT'S THAT, WELL... I'M JESUS!

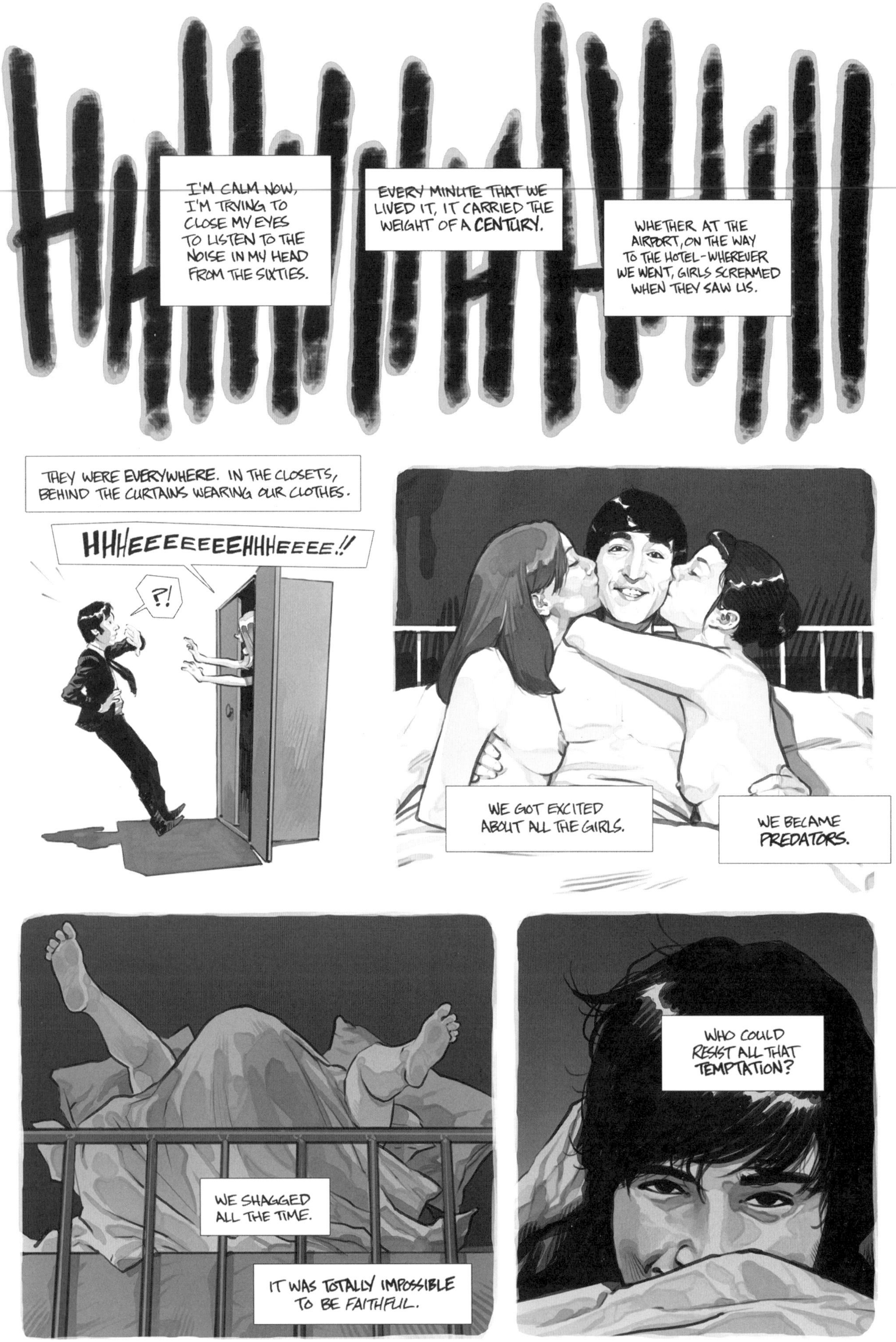
I'M CALM NOW, I'M TRYING TO CLOSE MY EYES TO LISTEN TO THE NOISE IN MY HEAD FROM THE SIXTIES.
EVERY MINUTE THAT WE LIVED IT, IT CARRIED THE WEIGHT OF A **CENTURY**.
WHETHER AT THE AIRPORT, ON THE WAY TO THE HOTEL-WHEREVER WE WENT, GIRLS SCREAMED WHEN THEY SAW US.
THEY WERE **EVERYWHERE**. IN THE CLOSETS, BEHIND THE CURTAINS WEARING OUR CLOTHES.
HHHEEEEEEEEHHHEEEE.!!
?!
WE GOT EXCITED ABOUT ALL THE GIRLS.
WE BECAME **PREDATORS.**
WE SHAGGED ALL THE TIME.
IT WAS **TOTALLY** IMPOSSIBLE TO BE FAITHFUL.
WHO COULD RESIST ALL THAT **TEMPTATION?**

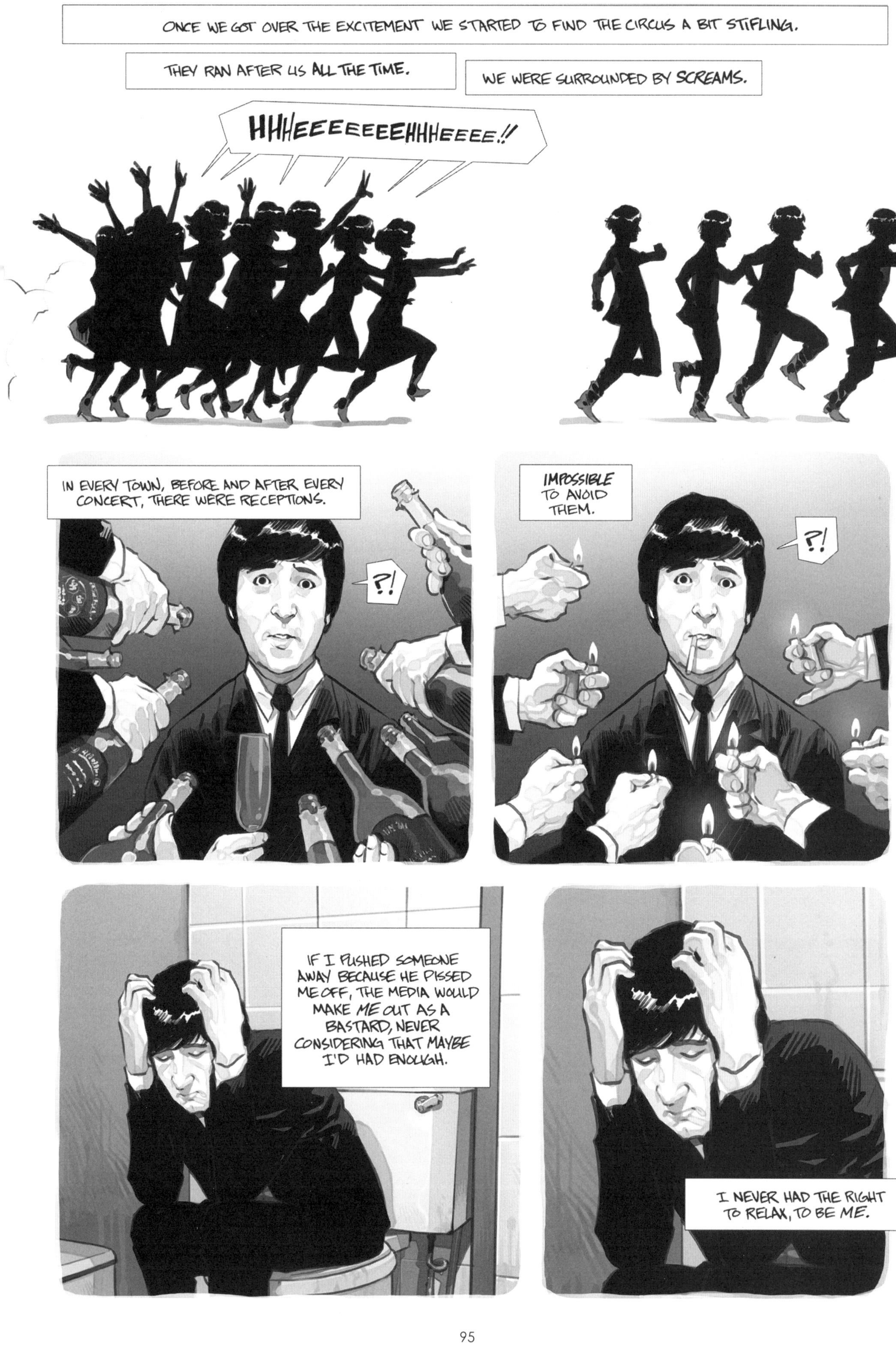

ONCE WE GOT OVER THE EXCITEMENT WE STARTED TO FIND THE CIRCUS A BIT STIFLING.
THEY RAN AFTER US ALL THE TIME.
WE WERE SURROUNDED BY SCREAMS.
HHHEEEEEEEHHHEEEE.!!
IN EVERY TOWN, BEFORE AND AFTER EVERY CONCERT, THERE WERE RECEPTIONS.
?!
IMPOSSIBLE TO AVOID THEM.
?!
IF I PUSHED SOMEONE AWAY BECAUSE HE PISSED ME OFF, THE MEDIA WOULD MAKE ME OUT AS A BASTARD, NEVER CONSIDERING THAT MAYBE I'D HAD ENOUGH.
I NEVER HAD THE RIGHT TO RELAX, TO BE ME.

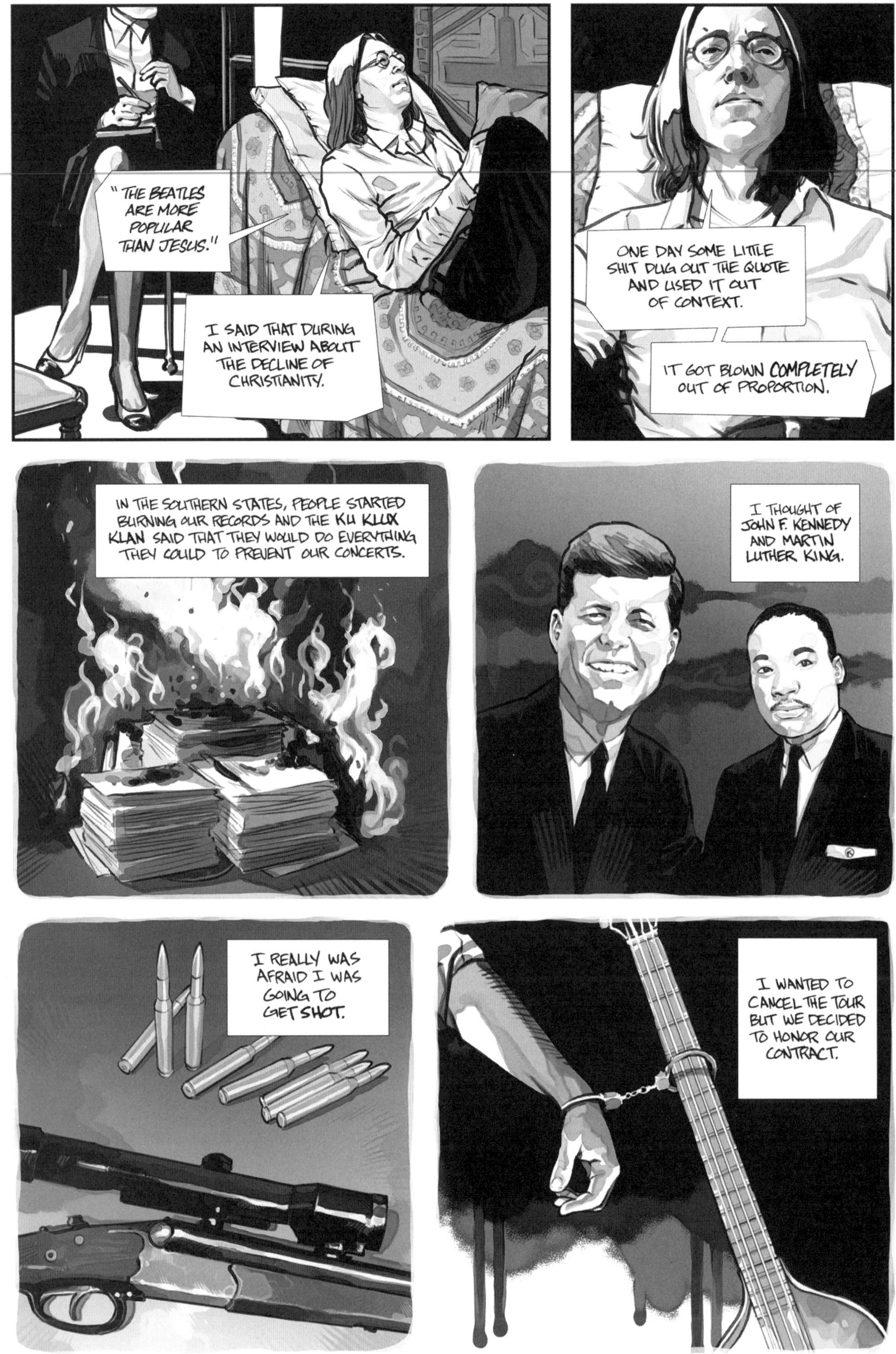
"THE BEATLES ARE MORE POPULAR THAN JESUS."
I SAID THAT DURING AN INTERVIEW ABOUT THE DECLINE OF CHRISTIANITY.
ONE DAY SOME LITTLE SHIT DUG OUT THE QUOTE AND USED IT OUT OF CONTEXT.
IT GOT BLOWN COMPLETELY OUT OF PROPORTION.
IN THE SOUTHERN STATES, PEOPLE STARTED BURNING OUR RECORDS AND THE KU KLUX KLAN SAID THAT THEY WOULD DO EVERYTHING THEY COULD TO PREVENT OUR CONCERTS.
I THOUGHT OF JOHN F. KENNEDY AND MARTIN LUTHER KING.
I REALLY WAS AFRAID I WAS GOING TO GET SHOT.
I WANTED TO CANCEL THE TOUR BUT WE DECIDED TO HONOR OUR CONTRACT.

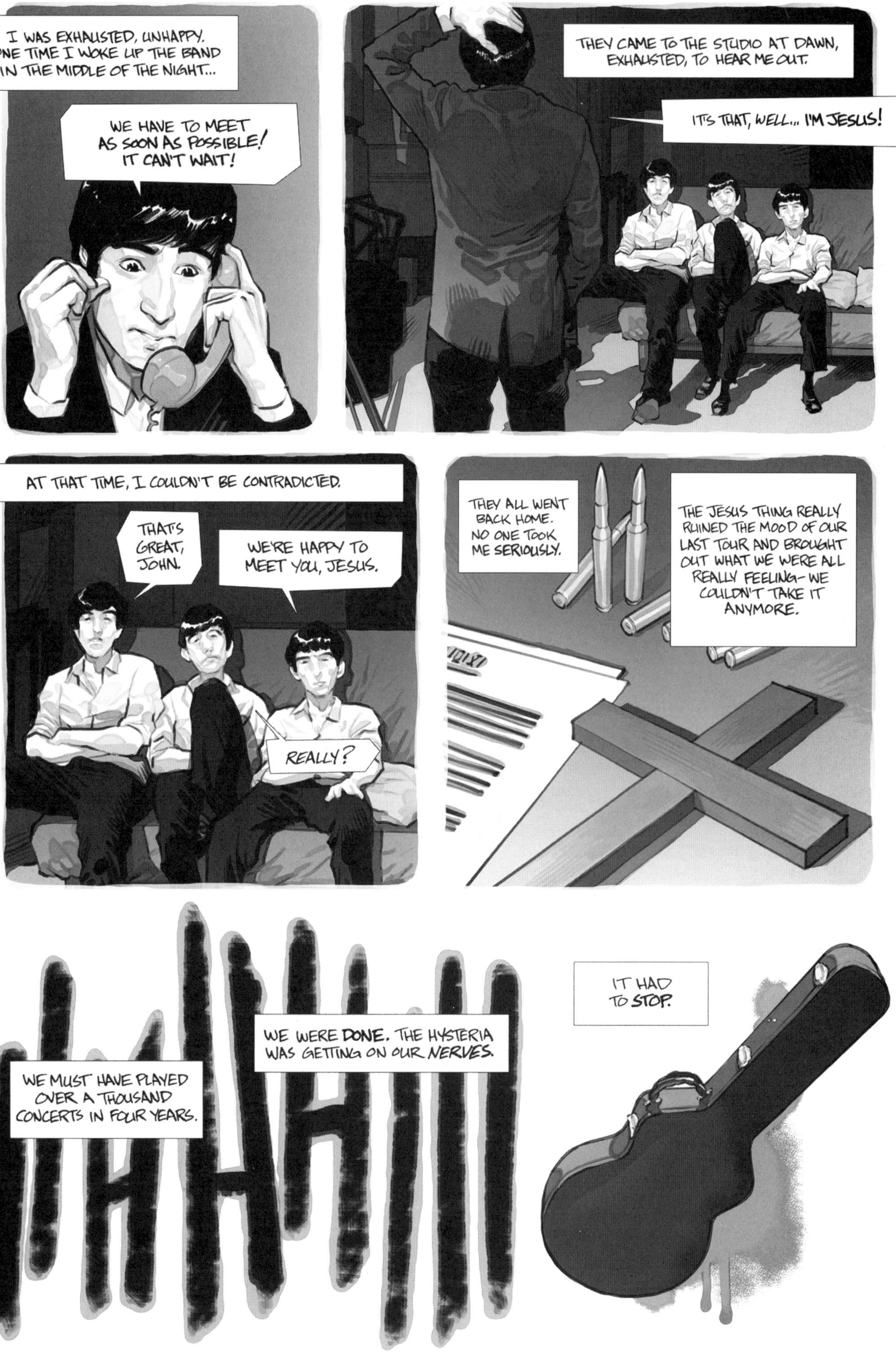
I WAS EXHAUSTED, UNHAPPY. ONE TIME I WOKE UP THE BAND IN THE MIDDLE OF THE NIGHT...
WE HAVE TO MEET AS SOON AS POSSIBLE! IT CAN'T WAIT!
THEY CAME TO THE STUDIO AT DAWN, EXHAUSTED, TO HEAR ME OUT.
IT'S THAT, WELL... I'M JESUS!
AT THAT TIME, I COULDN'T BE CONTRADICTED.
THAT'S GREAT, JOHN.
WE'RE HAPPY TO MEET YOU, JESUS.
REALLY?
THEY ALL WENT BACK HOME. NO ONE TOOK ME SERIOUSLY.
THE JESUS THING REALLY RUINED THE MOOD OF OUR LAST TOUR AND BROUGHT OUT WHAT WE WERE ALL REALLY FEELING- WE COULDN'T TAKE IT ANYMORE.
WE MUST HAVE PLAYED OVER A THOUSAND CONCERTS IN FOUR YEARS.
WE WERE DONE. THE HYSTERIA WAS GETTING ON OUR NERVES.
IT HAD TO STOP.

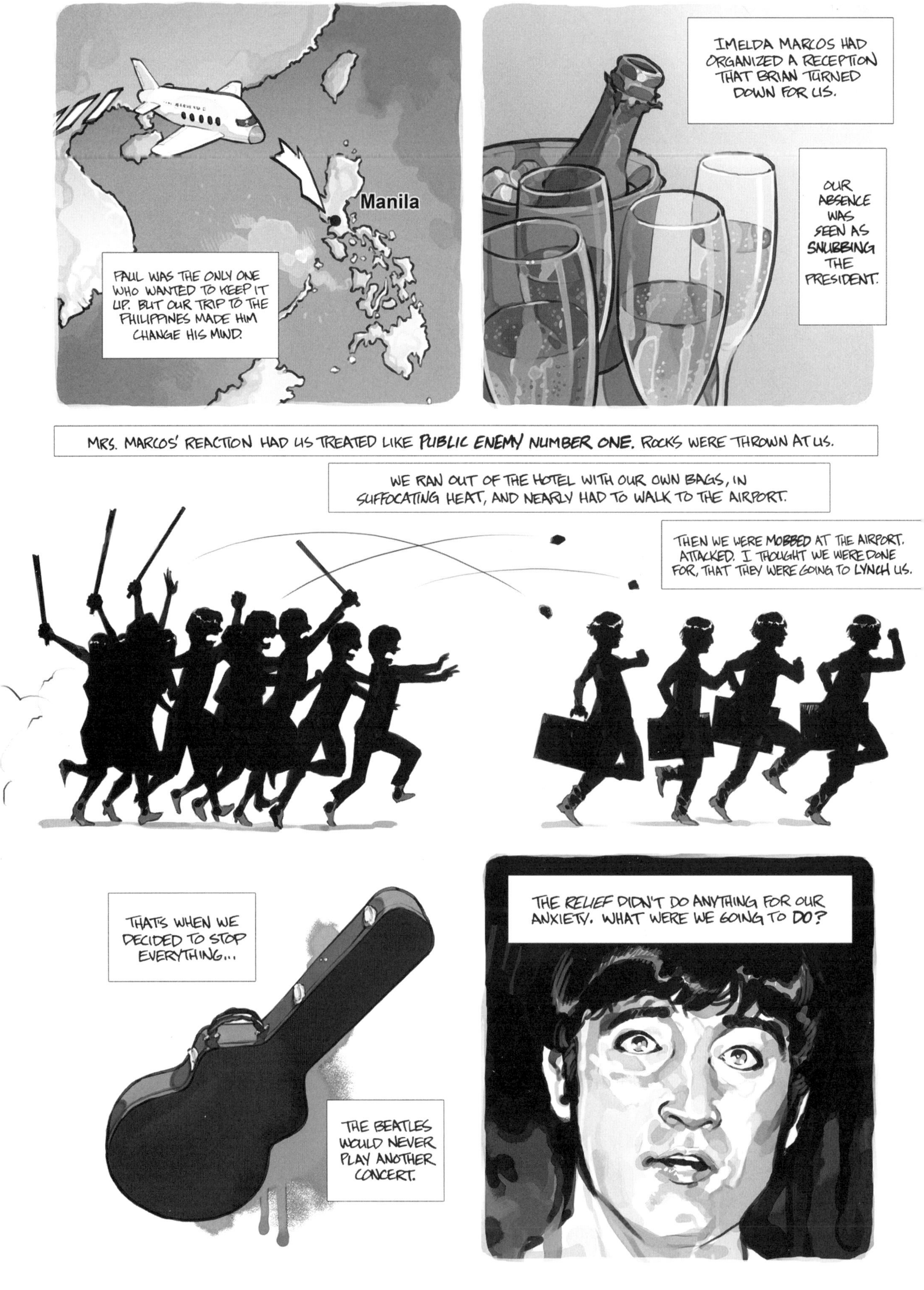
Manila
PAUL WAS THE ONLY ONE WHO WANTED TO KEEP IT UP. BUT OUR TRIP TO THE PHILIPPINES MADE HIM CHANGE HIS MIND.
IMELDA MARCOS HAD ORGANIZED A RECEPTION THAT BRIAN TURNED DOWN FOR US.
OUR ABSENCE WAS SEEN AS SNUBBING THE PRESIDENT.
MRS. MARCOS' REACTION HAD US TREATED LIKE PUBLIC ENEMY NUMBER ONE. ROCKS WERE THROWN AT US.
WE RAN OUT OF THE HOTEL WITH OUR OWN BAGS, IN SUFFOCATING HEAT, AND NEARLY HAD TO WALK TO THE AIRPORT.
THEN WE WERE MOBBED AT THE AIRPORT. ATTACKED. I THOUGHT WE WERE DONE FOR, THAT THEY WERE GOING TO LYNCH US.
THAT'S WHEN WE DECIDED TO STOP EVERYTHING...
THE BEATLES WOULD NEVER PLAY ANOTHER CONCERT.
THE RELIEF DIDN'T DO ANYTHING FOR OUR ANXIETY. WHAT WERE WE GOING TO DO?

thirteenth session

THE PART I PLAYED
WORE GLASSES

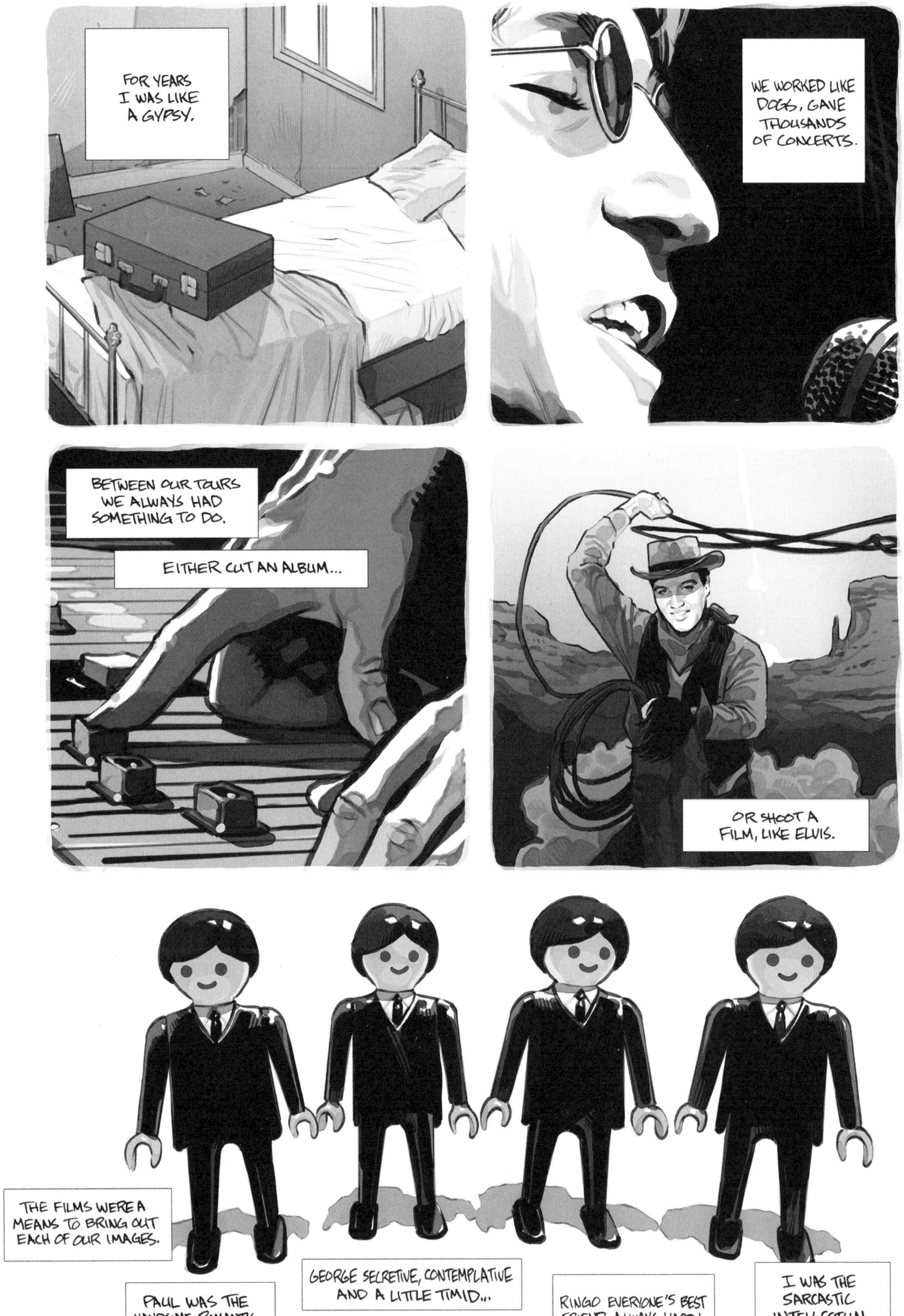
FOR YEARS I WAS LIKE A GYPSY.
WE WORKED LIKE DOGS, GAVE THOUSANDS OF CONCERTS.
BETWEEN OUR TOURS WE ALWAYS HAD SOMETHING TO DO.
EITHER CUT AN ALBUM...
OR SHOOT A FILM, LIKE ELVIS.
THE FILMS WERE A MEANS TO BRING OUT EACH OF OUR IMAGES.
PAUL WAS THE HANDSOME ROMANTIC...
GEORGE SECRETIVE, CONTEMPLATIVE AND A LITTLE TIMID...
RINGO EVERYONE'S BEST FRIEND, ALWAYS HAPPY...
I WAS THE SARCASTIC INTELLECTUAL.

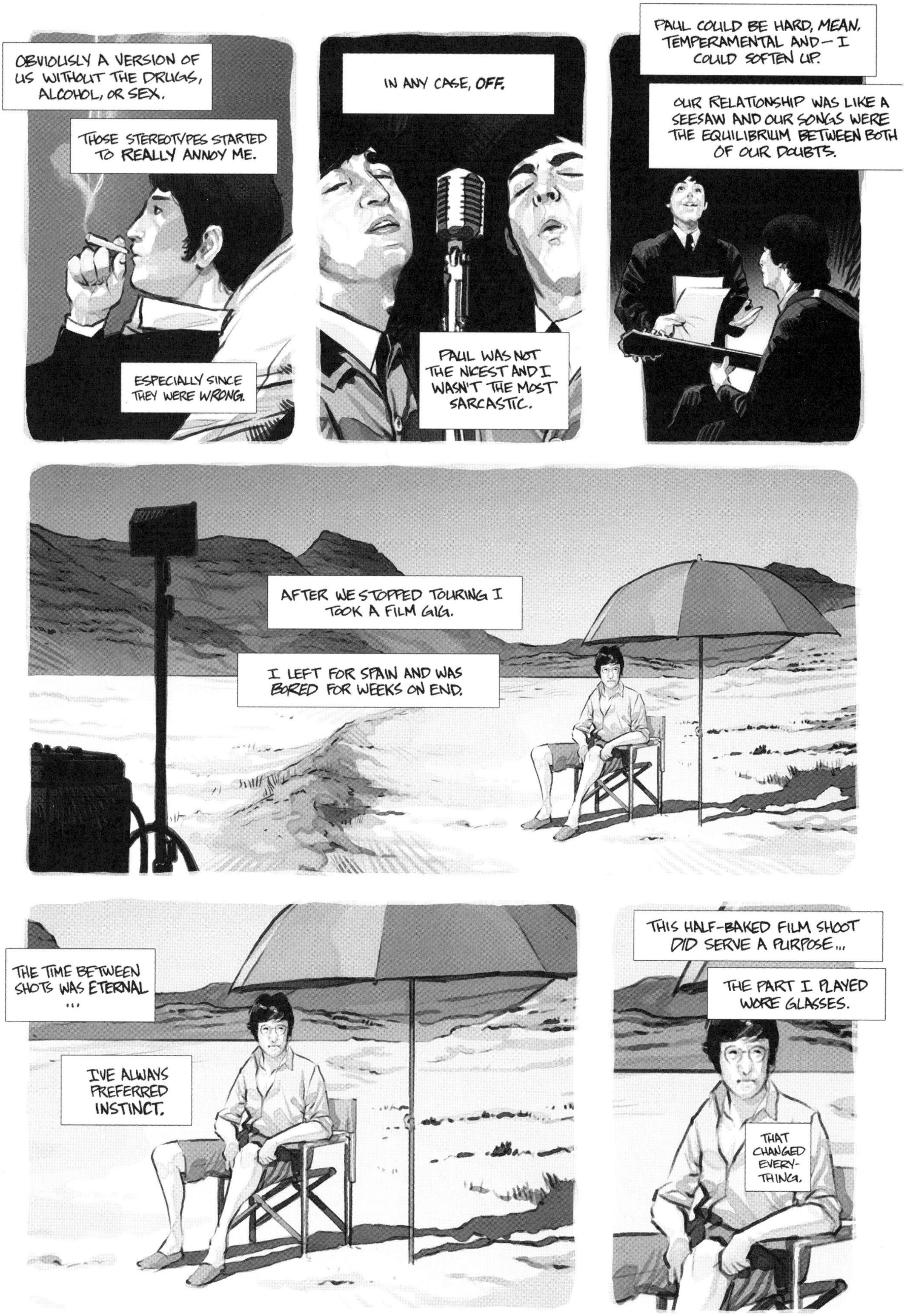
OBVIOUSLY A VERSION OF US WITHOUT THE DRUGS, ALCOHOL, OR SEX.
THOSE STEREOTYPES STARTED TO REALLY ANNOY ME.
ESPECIALLY SINCE THEY WERE WRONG.
IN ANY CASE, OFF.
PAUL WAS NOT THE NICEST AND I WASN'T THE MOST SARCASTIC.
PAUL COULD BE HARD, MEAN, TEMPERAMENTAL AND— I COULD SOFTEN UP.
OUR RELATIONSHIP WAS LIKE A SEESAW AND OUR SONGS WERE THE EQUILIBRIUM BETWEEN BOTH OF OUR DOUBTS.
AFTER WE STOPPED TOURING I TOOK A FILM GIG.
I LEFT FOR SPAIN AND WAS BORED FOR WEEKS ON END.
THE TIME BETWEEN SHOTS WAS ETERNAL ...
I'VE ALWAYS PREFERRED INSTINCT.
THIS HALF-BAKED FILM SHOOT DID SERVE A PURPOSE...
THE PART I PLAYED WORE GLASSES.
THAT CHANGED EVERY-THING.

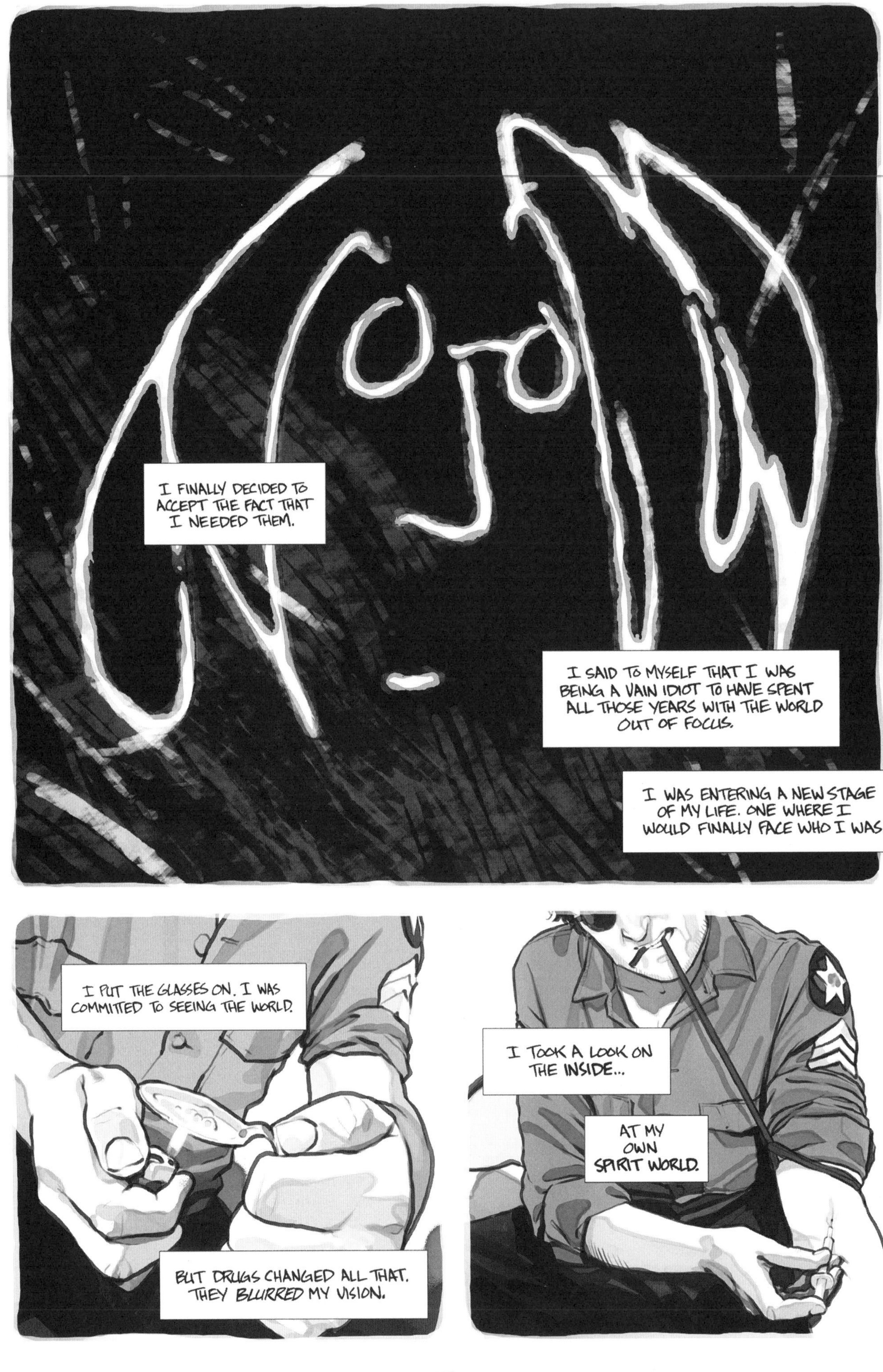

I FINALLY DECIDED TO ACCEPT THE FACT THAT I NEEDED THEM.
I SAID TO MYSELF THAT I WAS BEING A VAIN IDIOT TO HAVE SPENT ALL THOSE YEARS WITH THE WORLD OUT OF FOCUS.
I WAS ENTERING A NEW STAGE OF MY LIFE. ONE WHERE I WOULD FINALLY FACE WHO I WAS.
I PUT THE GLASSES ON. I WAS COMMITTED TO SEEING THE WORLD.
BUT DRUGS CHANGED ALL THAT. THEY BLURRED MY VISION.
I TOOK A LOOK ON THE INSIDE...
AT MY OWN SPIRIT WORLD.

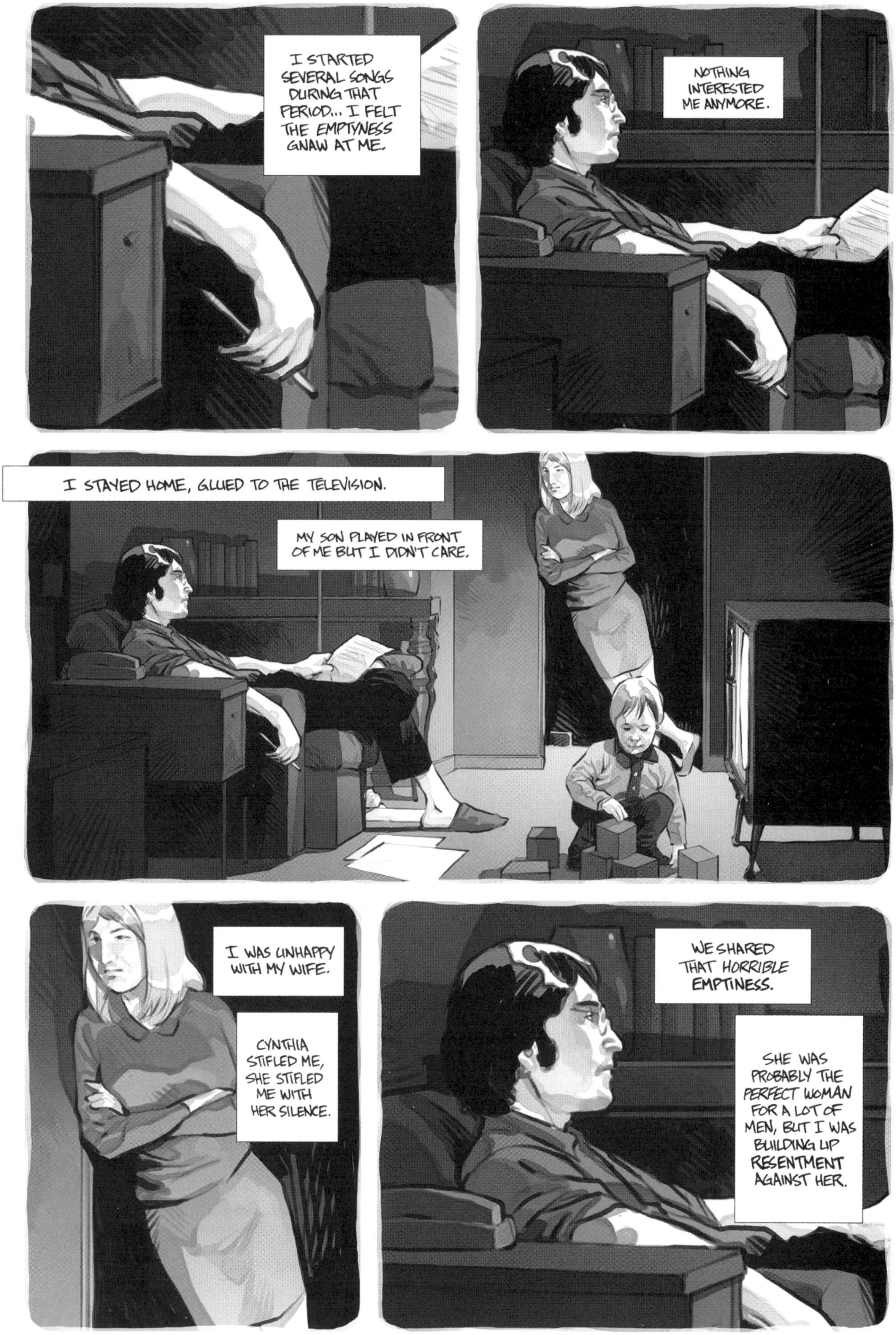
I STARTED SEVERAL SONGS DURING THAT PERIOD... I FELT THE EMPTYNESS GNAW AT ME.
NOTHING INTERESTED ME ANYMORE.
I STAYED HOME, GLUED TO THE TELEVISION.
MY SON PLAYED IN FRONT OF ME BUT I DIDN'T CARE.
I WAS UNHAPPY WITH MY WIFE.
CYNTHIA STIFLED ME, SHE STIFLED ME WITH HER SILENCE.
WE SHARED THAT HORRIBLE EMPTINESS.
SHE WAS PROBABLY THE PERFECT WOMAN FOR A LOT OF MEN, BUT I WAS BUILDING UP RESENTMENT AGAINST HER.

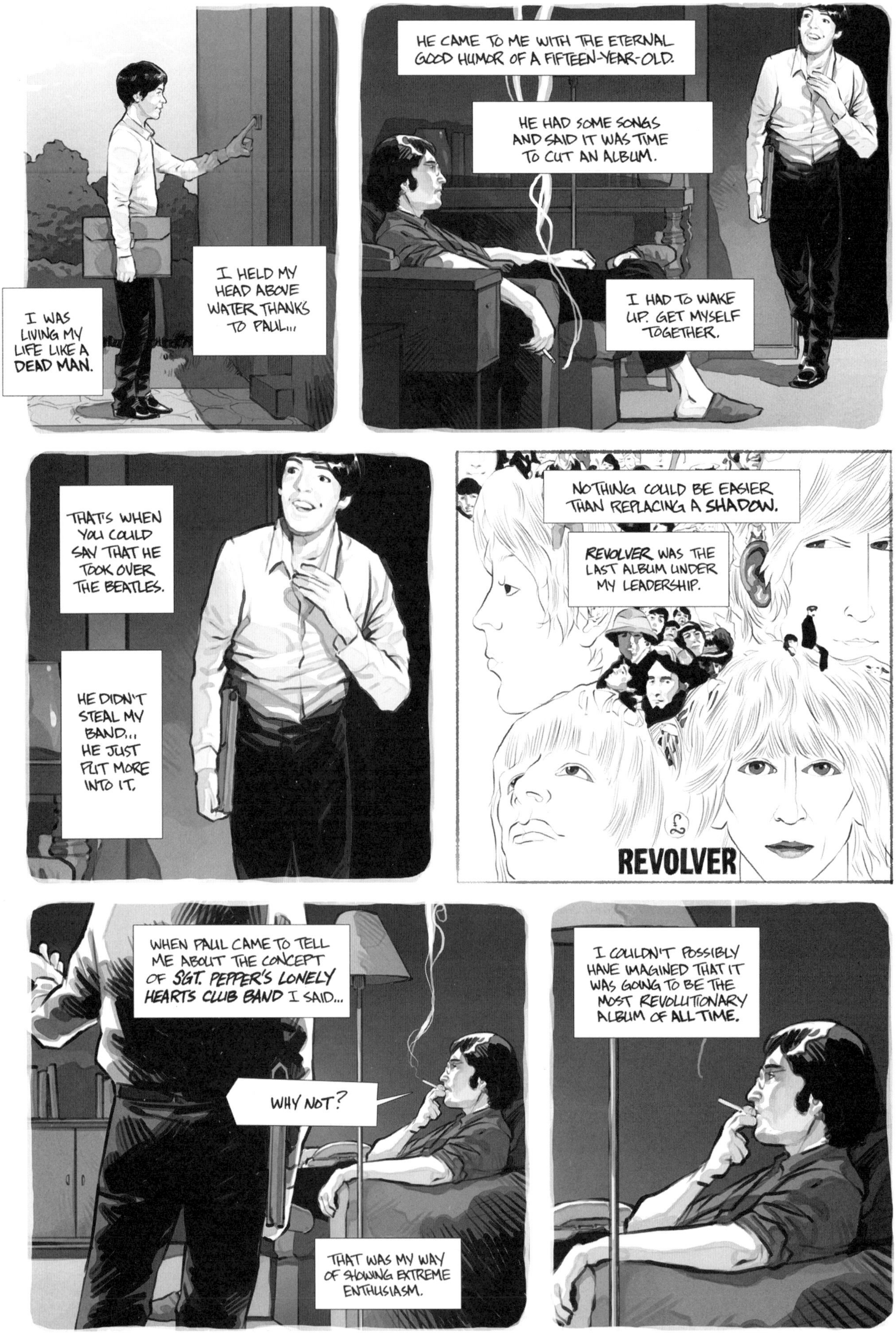

I WAS LIVING MY LIFE LIKE A DEAD MAN.
I HELD MY HEAD ABOVE WATER THANKS TO PAUL...
HE CAME TO ME WITH THE ETERNAL GOOD HUMOR OF A FIFTEEN-YEAR-OLD.
HE HAD SOME SONGS AND SAID IT WAS TIME TO CUT AN ALBUM.
I HAD TO WAKE UP. GET MYSELF TOGETHER.
THAT'S WHEN YOU COULD SAY THAT HE TOOK OVER THE BEATLES.
HE DIDN'T STEAL MY BAND... HE JUST PUT MORE INTO IT.
NOTHING COULD BE EASIER THAN REPLACING A SHADOW.
REVOLVER WAS THE LAST ALBUM UNDER MY LEADERSHIP.
REVOLVER
WHEN PAUL CAME TO TELL ME ABOUT THE CONCEPT OF SGT. PEPPER'S LONELY HEARTS CLUB BAND I SAID...
WHY NOT?
THAT WAS MY WAY OF SHOWING EXTREME ENTHUSIASM.
I COULDN'T POSSIBLY HAVE IMAGINED THAT IT WAS GOING TO BE THE MOST REVOLUTIONARY ALBUM OF ALL TIME.

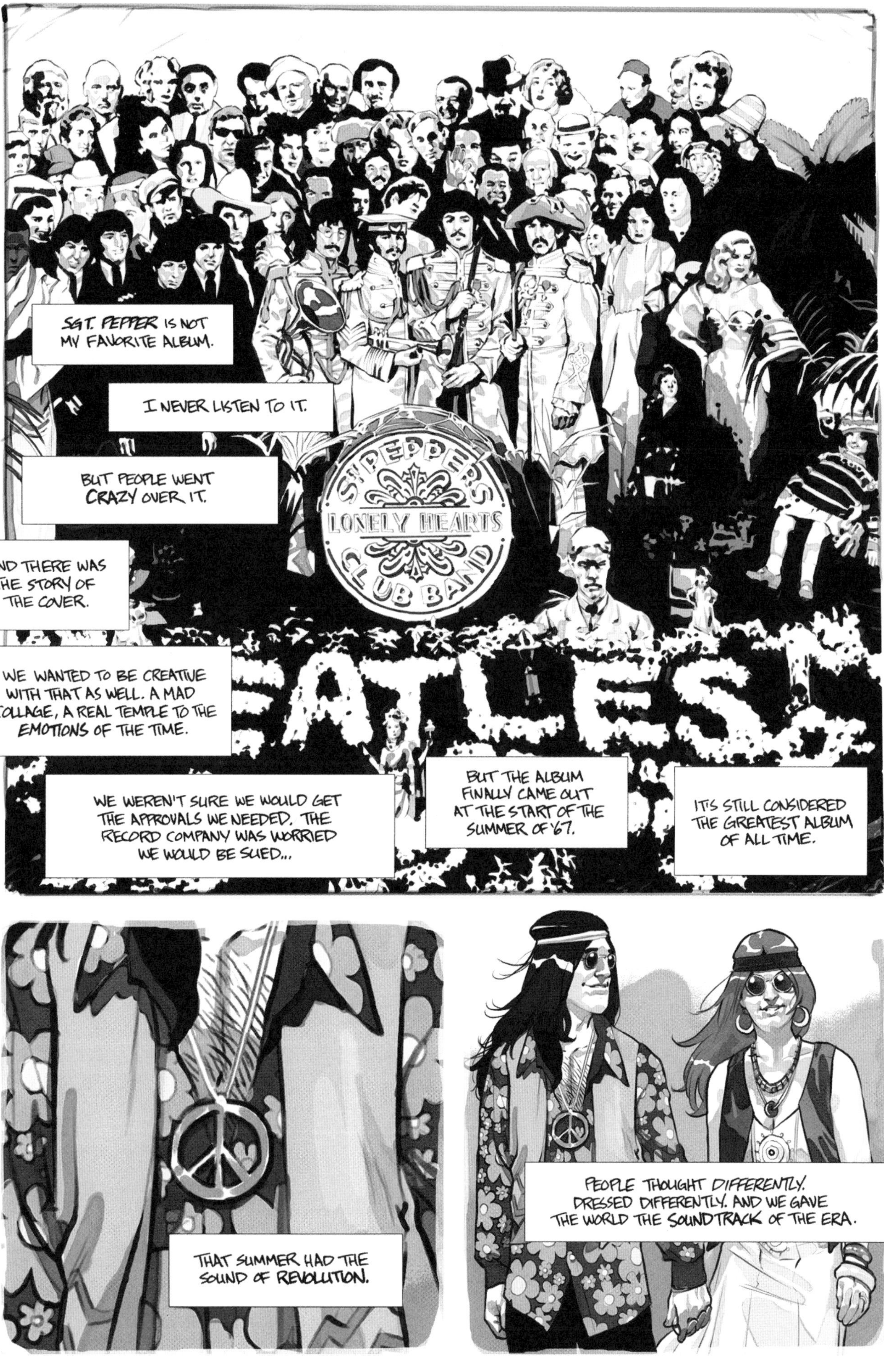
SGT. PEPPER IS NOT MY FAVORITE ALBUM.
I NEVER LISTEN TO IT.
BUT PEOPLE WENT CRAZY OVER IT.
ST PEPPERS LONELY HEARTS CLUB BAND
AND THERE WAS THE STORY OF THE COVER.
WE WANTED TO BE CREATIVE WITH THAT AS WELL. A MAD COLLAGE, A REAL TEMPLE TO THE EMOTIONS OF THE TIME.
WE WEREN'T SURE WE WOULD GET THE APPROVALS WE NEEDED. THE RECORD COMPANY WAS WORRIED WE WOULD BE SUED...
BUT THE ALBUM FINALLY CAME OUT AT THE START OF THE SUMMER OF '67.
IT'S STILL CONSIDERED THE GREATEST ALBUM OF ALL TIME.
THAT SUMMER HAD THE SOUND OF REVOLUTION.
PEOPLE THOUGHT DIFFERENTLY. DRESSED DIFFERENTLY. AND WE GAVE THE WORLD THE SOUNDTRACK OF THE ERA.

AND EVEN BETTER THAN A SONG, I WROTE AN ANTHEM.

ALL YOU NEED IS LOOOOVE!

BRIAN HAD BEEN ASKING US FOR A WHILE TO WRITE A SONG FOR A TV PROGRAM THAT WOULD BE BROADCAST AROUND THE WORLD.

I HAD THE OTHER BOYS LISTEN TO THE TUNE I HAD JUST WRITTEN AND THEY SAID IT WAS GREAT.

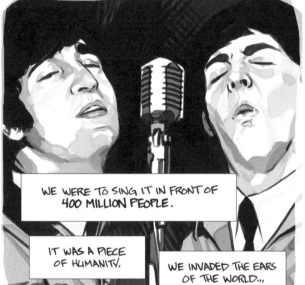

WE WERE TO SING IT IN FRONT OF 400 MILLION PEOPLE.

IT WAS A PIECE OF HUMANITY,

WE INVADED THE EARS OF THE WORLD...

AND IN THE MIDDLE OF ALL THOSE MILLIONS OF EARS THERE WAS ONE PERSON I WAS SINGING TO.

fourteenth session

I WAS SURROUNDED
BY THE DEAD

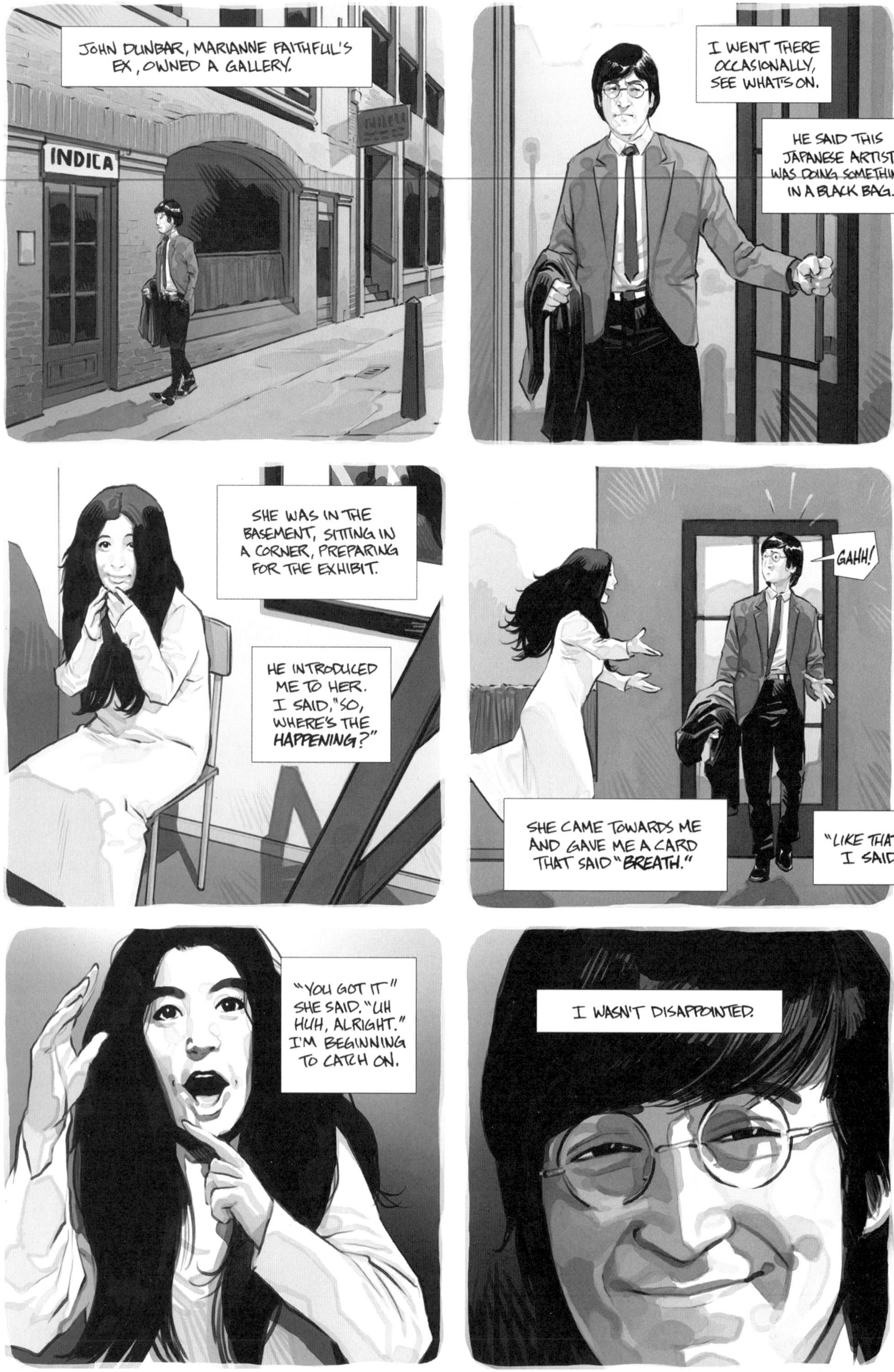
JOHN DUNBAR, MARIANNE FAITHFUL'S EX, OWNED A GALLERY.
INDICA
I WENT THERE OCCASIONALLY, SEE WHAT'S ON.
HE SAID THIS JAPANESE ARTIST WAS DOING SOMETHING IN A BLACK BAG.
SHE WAS IN THE BASEMENT, SITTING IN A CORNER, PREPARING FOR THE EXHIBIT.
HE INTRODUCED ME TO HER. I SAID, "SO, WHERE'S THE HAPPENING?"
GAHH!
SHE CAME TOWARDS ME AND GAVE ME A CARD THAT SAID "BREATH."
"LIKE THAT?" I SAID.
"YOU GOT IT" SHE SAID. "UH HUH, ALRIGHT." I'M BEGINNING TO CATCH ON.
I WASN'T DISAPPOINTED.

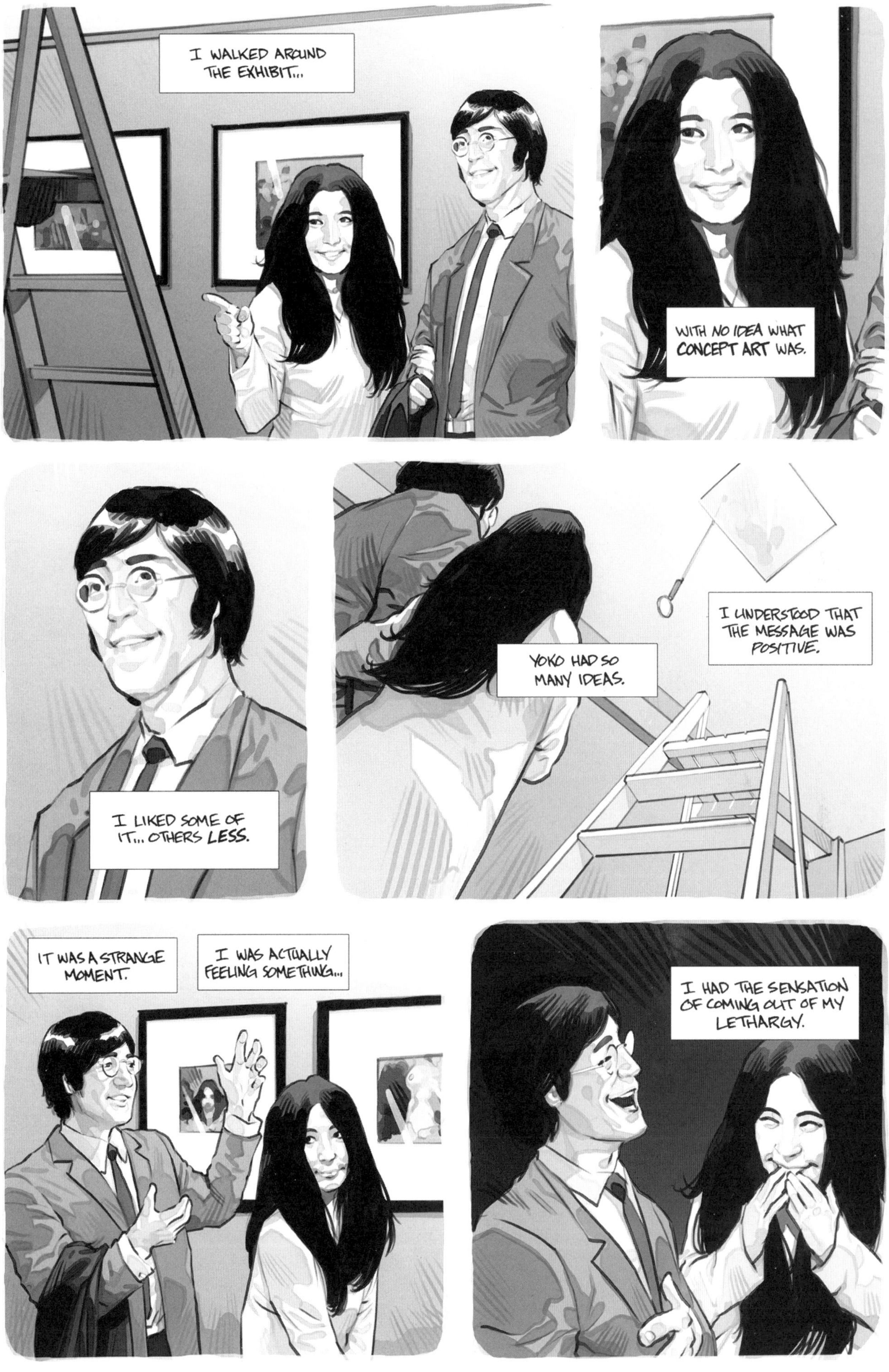
I WALKED AROUND THE EXHIBIT...
WITH NO IDEA WHAT CONCEPT ART WAS.
I LIKED SOME OF IT... OTHERS LESS.
YOKO HAD SO MANY IDEAS.
I UNDERSTOOD THAT THE MESSAGE WAS POSITIVE.
IT WAS A STRANGE MOMENT.
I WAS ACTUALLY FEELING SOMETHING...
I HAD THE SENSATION OF COMING OUT OF MY LETHARGY.

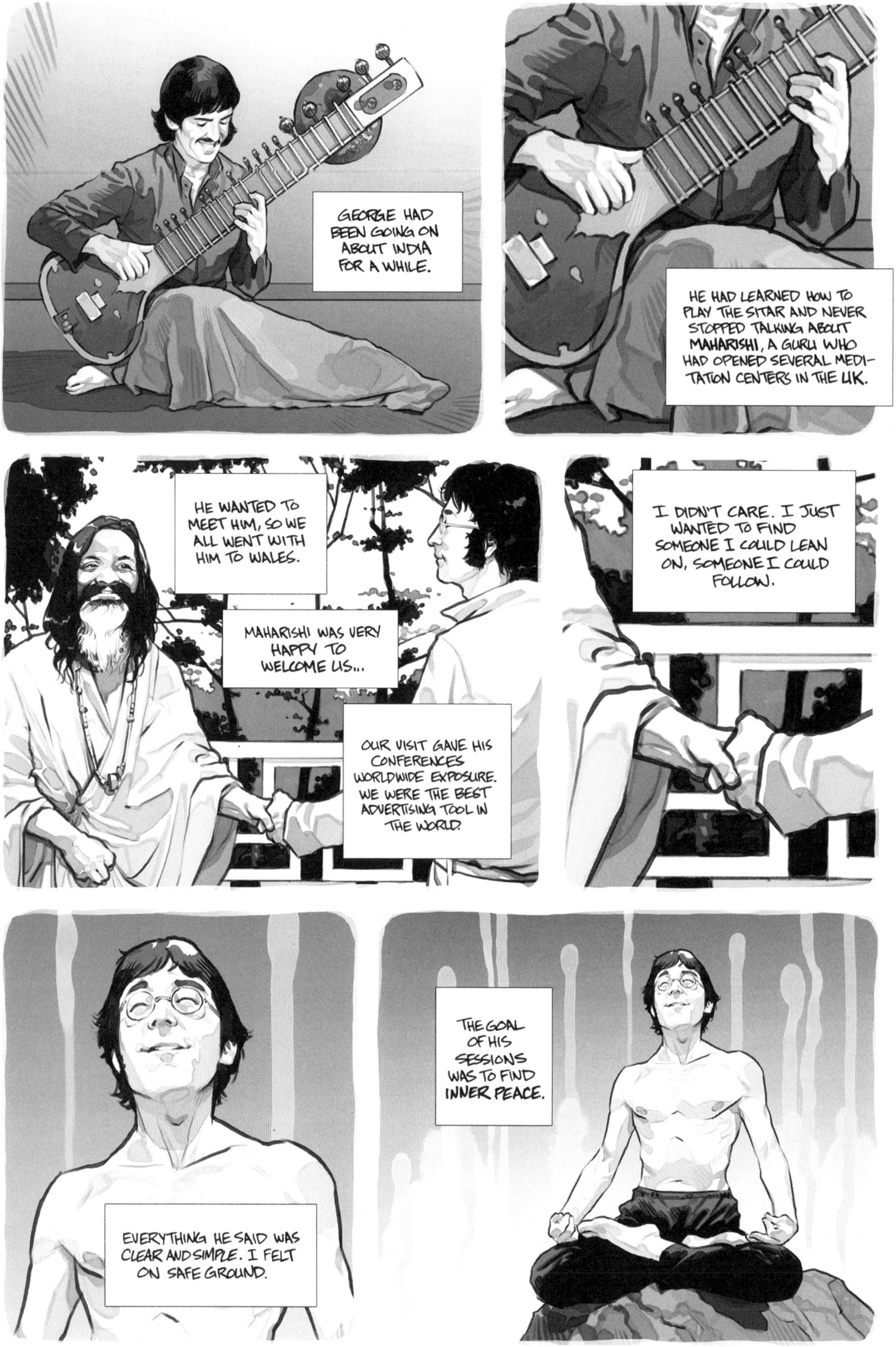
GEORGE HAD BEEN GOING ON ABOUT INDIA FOR A WHILE.
HE HAD LEARNED HOW TO PLAY THE SITAR AND NEVER STOPPED TALKING ABOUT MAHARISHI, A GURU WHO HAD OPENED SEVERAL MEDITATION CENTERS IN THE UK.
HE WANTED TO MEET HIM, SO WE ALL WENT WITH HIM TO WALES.
MAHARISHI WAS VERY HAPPY TO WELCOME US...
OUR VISIT GAVE HIS CONFERENCES WORLDWIDE EXPOSURE. WE WERE THE BEST ADVERTISING TOOL IN THE WORLD.
I DIDN'T CARE. I JUST WANTED TO FIND SOMEONE I COULD LEAN ON, SOMEONE I COULD FOLLOW.
EVERYTHING HE SAID WAS CLEAR AND SIMPLE. I FELT ON SAFE GROUND.
THE GOAL OF HIS SESSIONS WAS TO FIND INNER PEACE.

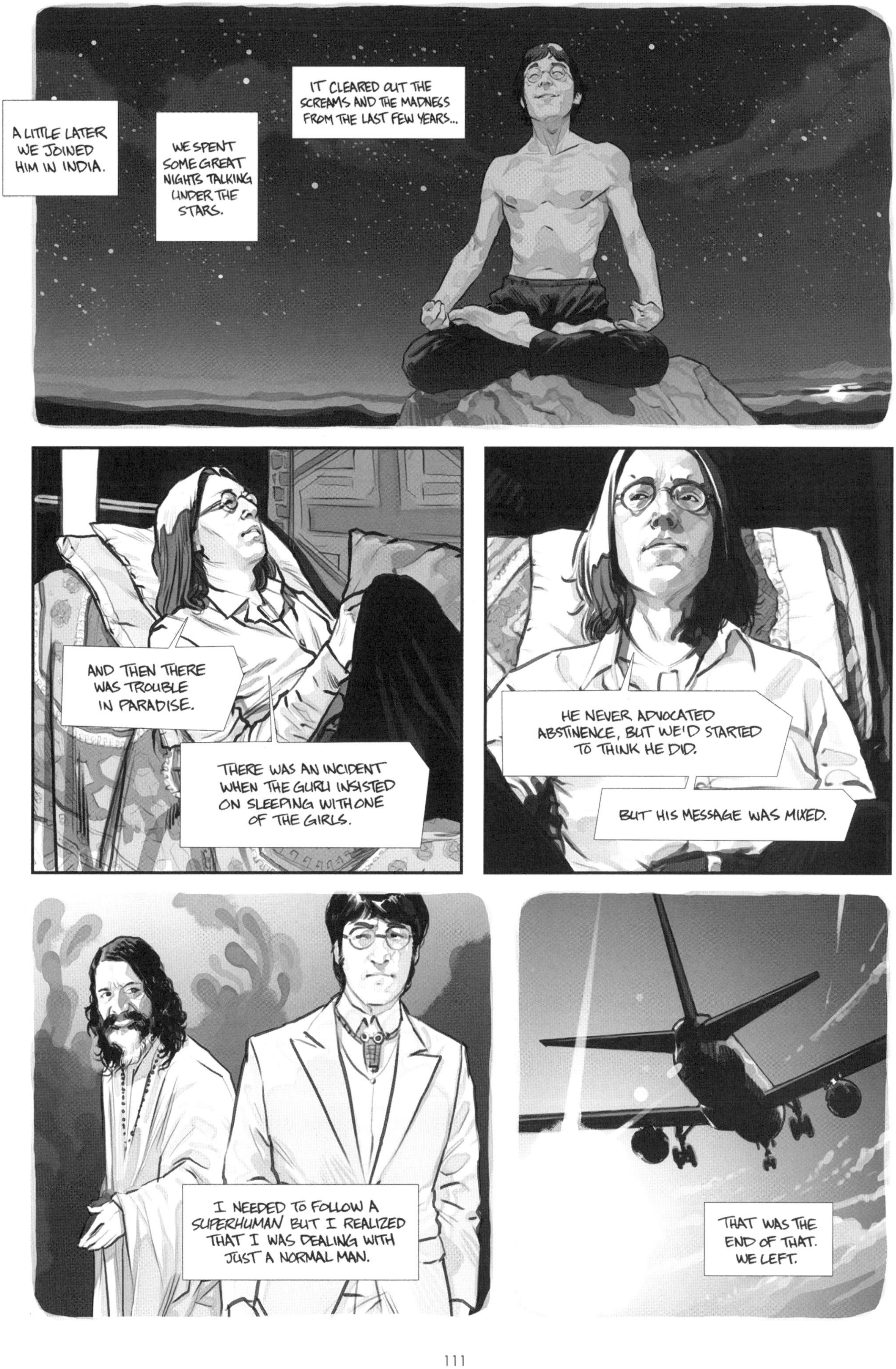
A LITTLE LATER WE JOINED HIM IN INDIA.
WE SPENT SOME GREAT NIGHTS TALKING UNDER THE STARS.
IT CLEARED OUT THE SCREAMS AND THE MADNESS FROM THE LAST FEW YEARS...
AND THEN THERE WAS TROUBLE IN PARADISE.
THERE WAS AN INCIDENT WHEN THE GURU INSISTED ON SLEEPING WITH ONE OF THE GIRLS.
HE NEVER ADVOCATED ABSTINENCE, BUT WE'D STARTED TO THINK HE DID.
BUT HIS MESSAGE WAS MIXED.
I NEEDED TO FOLLOW A SUPERHUMAN BUT I REALIZED THAT I WAS DEALING WITH JUST A NORMAL MAN.
THAT WAS THE END OF THAT. WE LEFT.

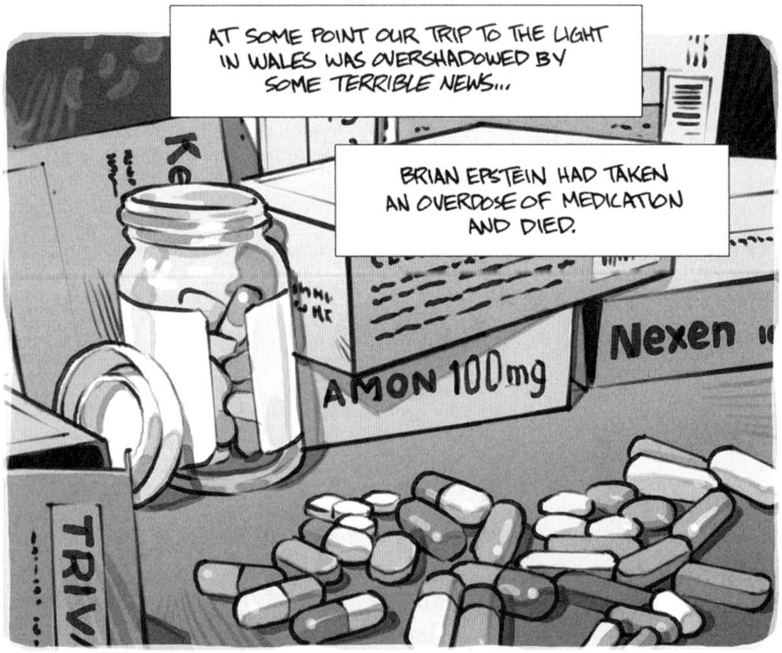
AT SOME POINT OUR TRIP TO THE LIGHT IN WALES WAS OVERSHADOWED BY SOME TERRIBLE NEWS...
BRIAN EPSTEIN HAD TAKEN AN OVERDOSE OF MEDICATION AND DIED.
Nexen
AMON 100mg
TRIV

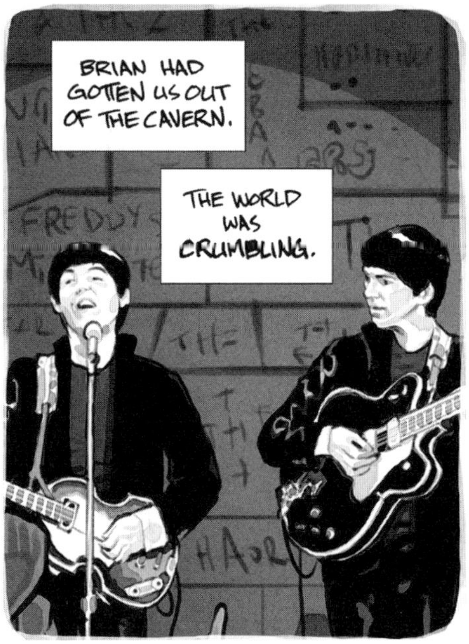
BRIAN HAD GOTTEN US OUT OF THE CAVERN.
THE WORLD WAS CRUMBLING.

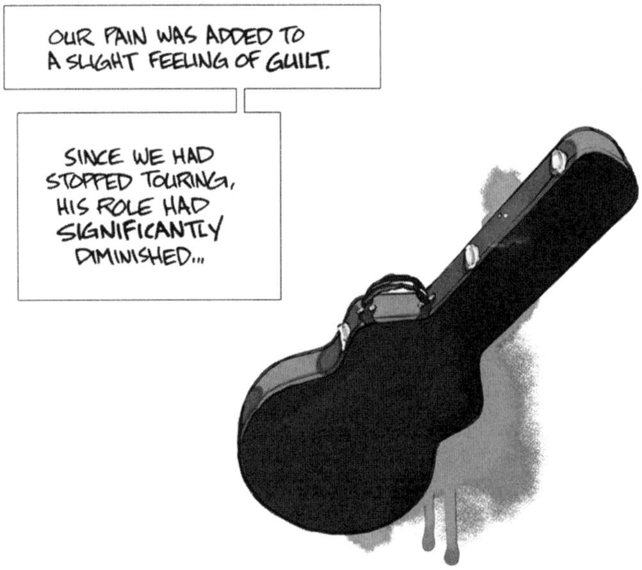
OUR PAIN WAS ADDED TO A SLIGHT FEELING OF GUILT.
SINCE WE HAD STOPPED TOURING, HIS ROLE HAD SIGNIFICANTLY DIMINISHED...

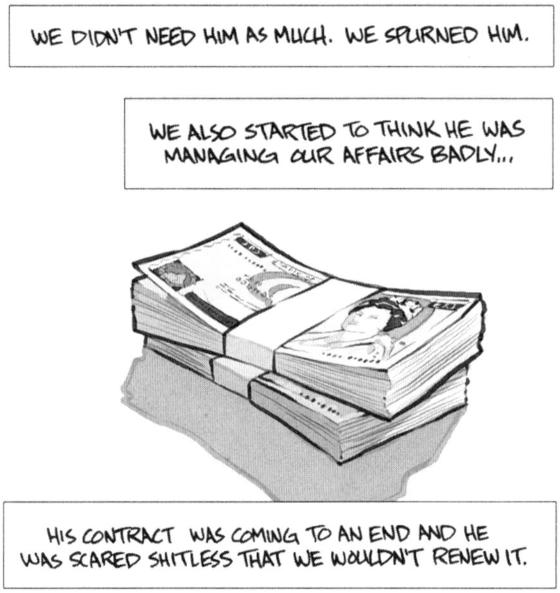
WE DIDN'T NEED HIM AS MUCH. WE SPURNED HIM.
WE ALSO STARTED TO THINK HE WAS MANAGING OUR AFFAIRS BADLY...
HIS CONTRACT WAS COMING TO AN END AND HE WAS SCARED SHITLESS THAT WE WOULDN'T RENEW IT.

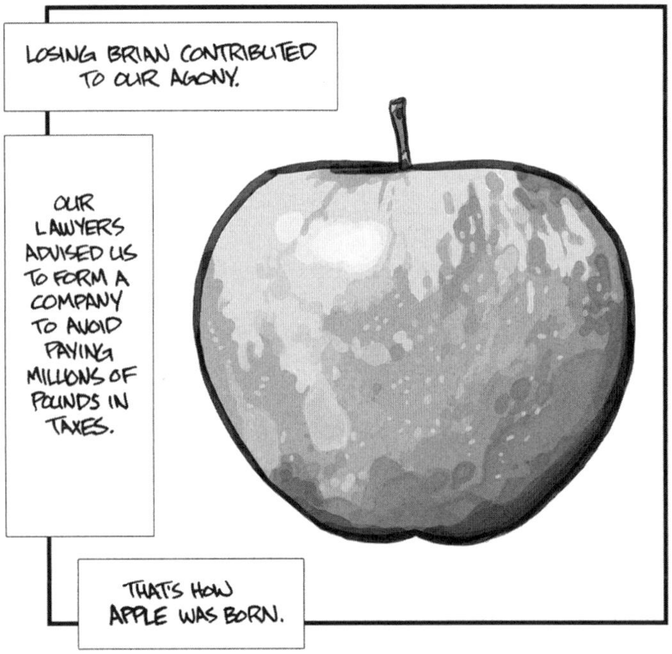
LOSING BRIAN CONTRIBUTED TO OUR AGONY.
OUR LAWYERS ADVISED US TO FORM A COMPANY TO AVOID PAYING MILLIONS OF POUNDS IN TAXES.
THAT'S HOW APPLE WAS BORN.

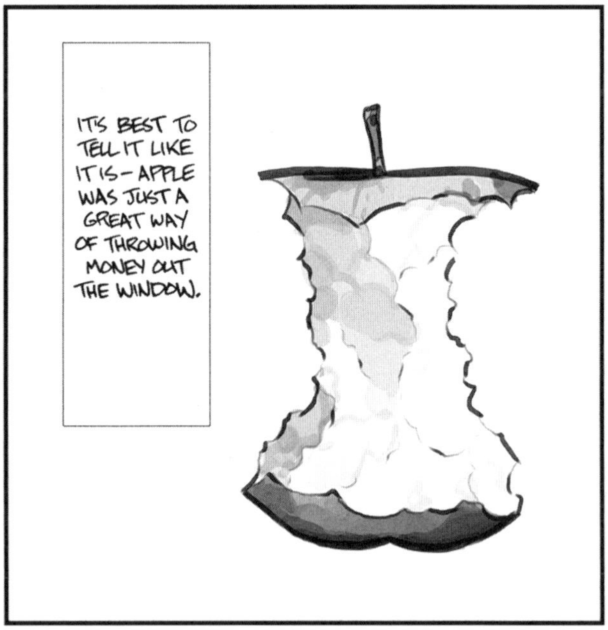
IT'S BEST TO TELL IT LIKE IT IS—APPLE WAS JUST A GREAT WAY OF THROWING MONEY OUT THE WINDOW.

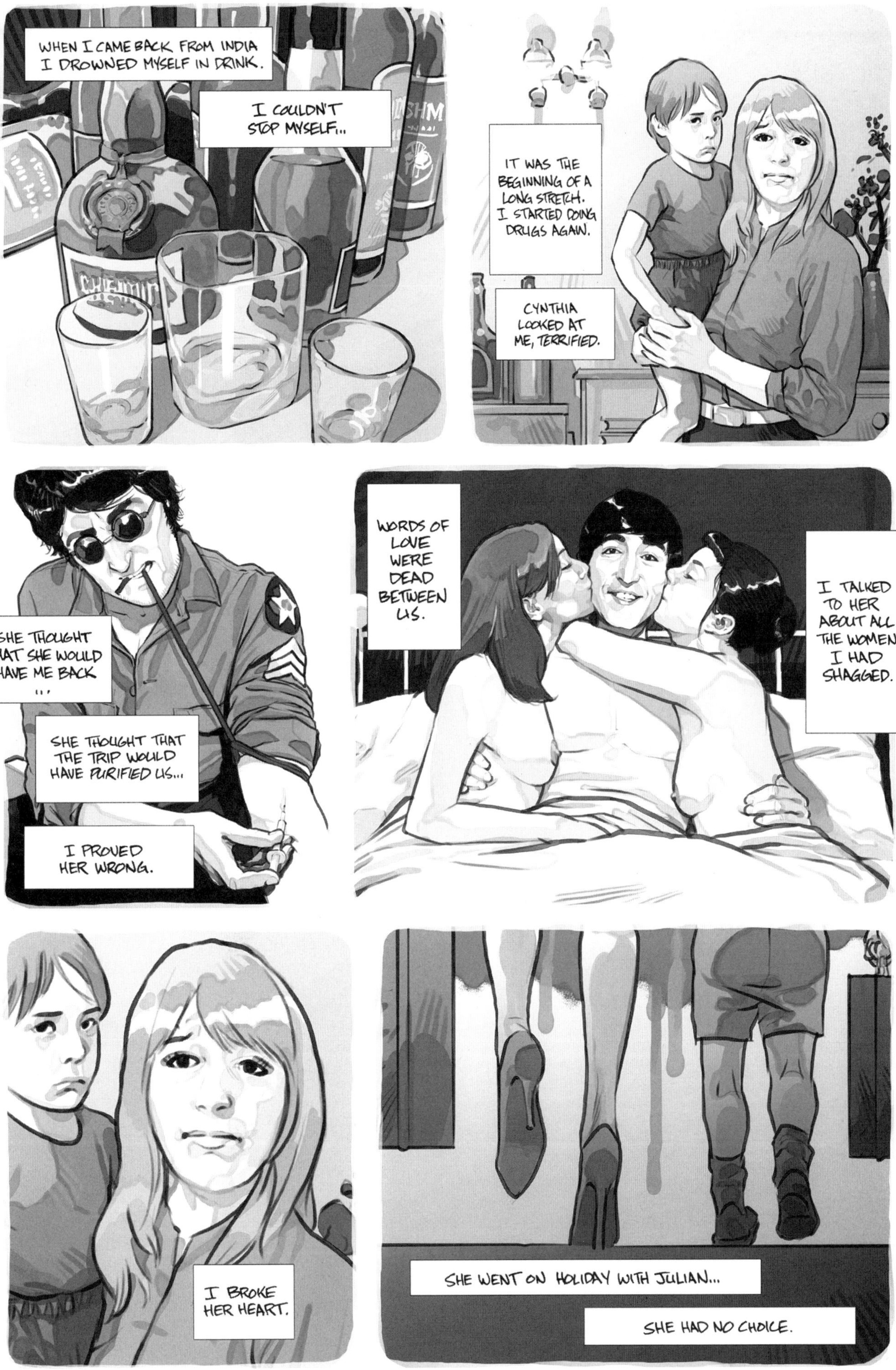
WHEN I CAME BACK FROM INDIA I DROWNED MYSELF IN DRINK.
I COULDN'T STOP MYSELF...
IT WAS THE BEGINNING OF A LONG STRETCH. I STARTED DOING DRUGS AGAIN.
CYNTHIA LOOKED AT ME, TERRIFIED.
SHE THOUGHT THAT SHE WOULD HAVE ME BACK ...
SHE THOUGHT THAT THE TRIP WOULD HAVE PURIFIED US...
I PROVED HER WRONG.
WORDS OF LOVE WERE DEAD BETWEEN US.
I TALKED TO HER ABOUT ALL THE WOMEN I HAD SHAGGED.
I BROKE HER HEART.
SHE WENT ON HOLIDAY WITH JULIAN...
SHE HAD NO CHOICE.

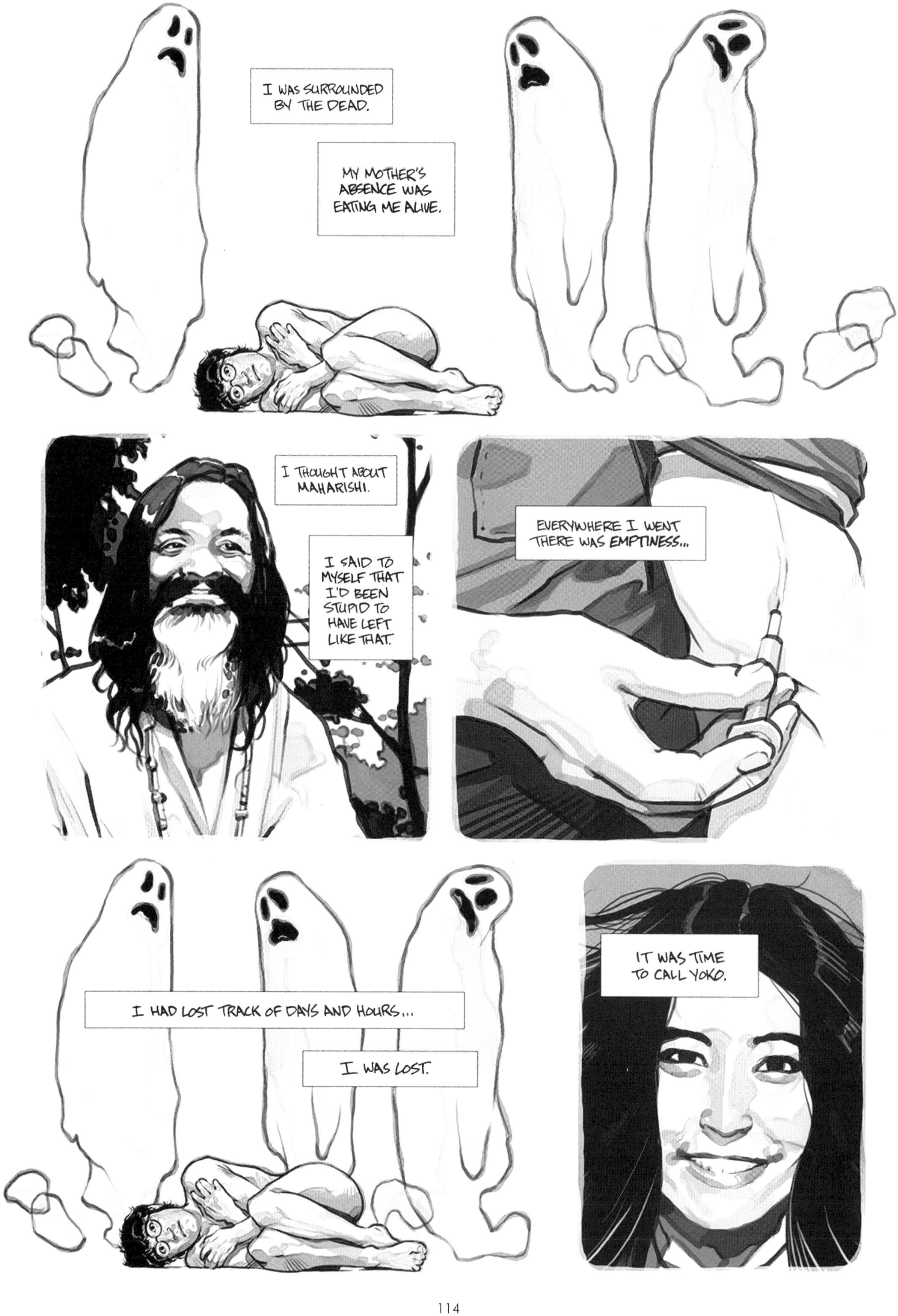

I WAS SURROUNDED BY THE DEAD.
MY MOTHER'S ABSENCE WAS EATING ME ALIVE.
I THOUGHT ABOUT MAHARISHI.
I SAID TO MYSELF THAT I'D BEEN STUPID TO HAVE LEFT LIKE THAT.
EVERYWHERE I WENT THERE WAS EMPTINESS...
I HAD LOST TRACK OF DAYS AND HOURS...
I WAS LOST.
IT WAS TIME TO CALL YOKO.

fifteenth session

I FOUND HER BEAUTIFUL
AND AMAZING

YOKO WAS MARRIED AND HER HUSBAND WAS CONVENIENTLY NOT THERE WHEN I CALLED.

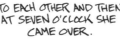

WE HARDLY SAID A WORD TO EACH OTHER AND THEN AT SEVEN O'CLOCK SHE CAME OVER.

I HAD HER LISTEN TO SOME OF THE NEW TRACKS. SHE HAD WORKED WITH JOHN CAGE AND WAS VERY SENSITIVE TO MUSIC...

WE RECORDED OTHER TRACKS THAT NIGHT. OUR FIRST NIGHT TOGETHER WAS EXTREMELY PRODUCTIVE.

I WAS LOOKING AT WHAT I'D BEEN SEARCHING FOR—A WOMAN WHO WOULD ALSO BE A CREATIVE PARTNER.

THE SUN CAME UP AND WE MADE LOVE.

WORDS CANNOT *DESCRIBE* THE *PURE JOY* THAT WAS GROWING INSIDE ME.

I WAS GOING TO BURY MY PAST.

I WAS TELLING MYSELF THAT THINGS WERE GOING TO GET SIMPLER NOW...

I WAS ALMOST SURPRISED TO SEE CYNTHIA COME THROUGH THE DOOR.

I'D FORGOTTEN ABOUT HER.

SHE STOOD THERE FROZEN IN PLACE, STARING AT THE TWO OF US...

SHE OBVIOUSLY UNDERSTOOD THAT IT WAS OVER.

I ACTED LIKE SHE WASN'T THERE. I DIDN'T CARE ABOUT HER...

I DIDN'T CARE ABOUT ANYTHING.

I'D FOUND MY REASON TO LIVE... A REASON TO LEAVE EVERYTHING BEHIND.

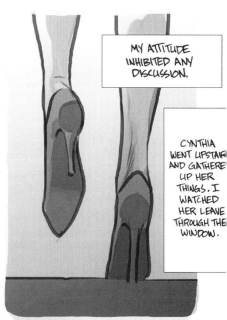

MY ATTITUDE INHIBITED ANY DISCUSSION.

CYNTHIA WENT UPSTAIRS AND GATHERED UP HER THINGS. I WATCHED HER LEAVE THROUGH THE WINDOW.

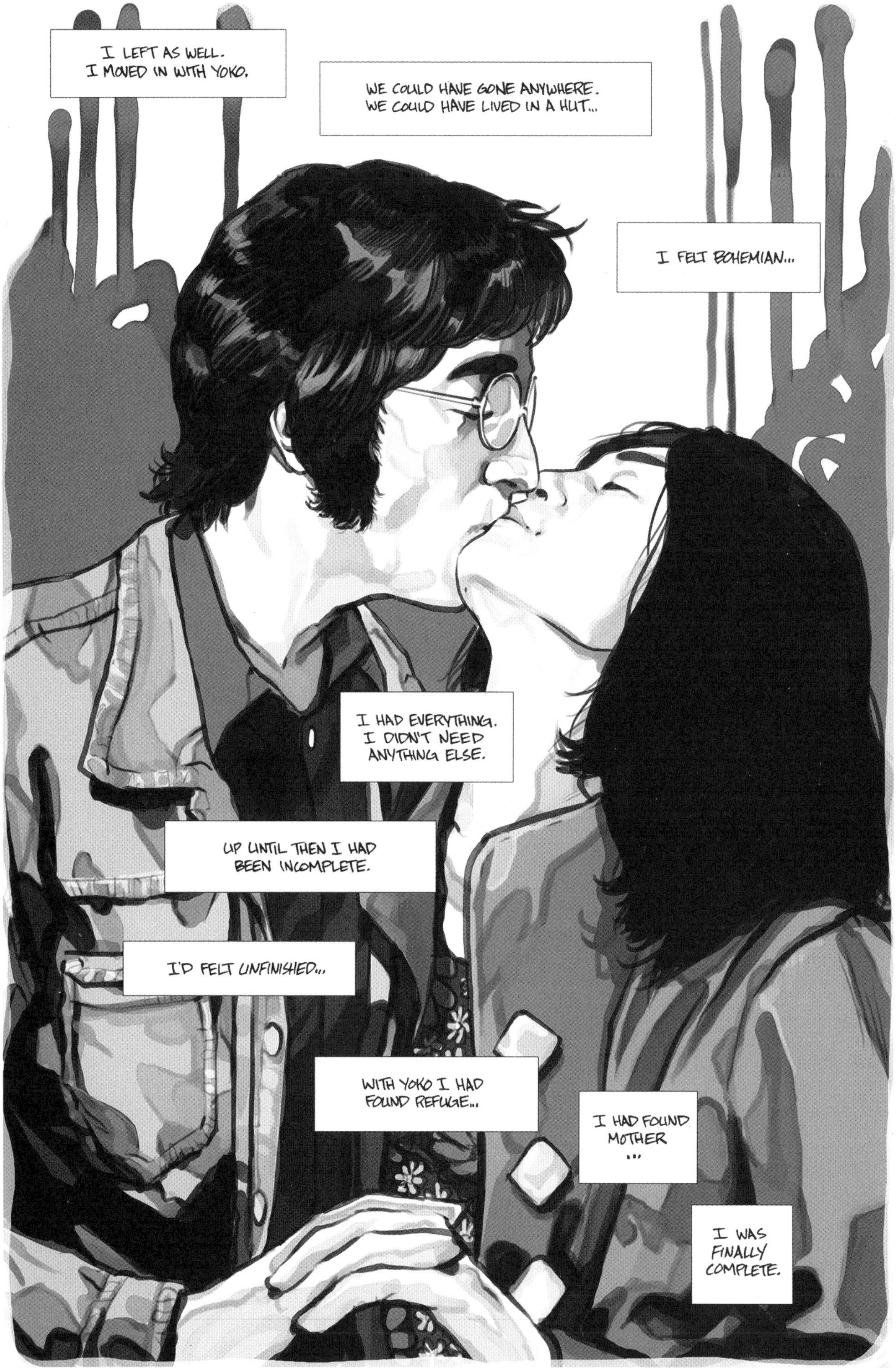
I LEFT AS WELL. I MOVED IN WITH YOKO.
WE COULD HAVE GONE ANYWHERE. WE COULD HAVE LIVED IN A HUT...
I FELT BOHEMIAN...
I HAD EVERYTHING. I DIDN'T NEED ANYTHING ELSE.
UP UNTIL THEN I HAD BEEN INCOMPLETE.
I'D FELT UNFINISHED...
WITH YOKO I HAD FOUND REFUGE...
I HAD FOUND MOTHER ...
I WAS FINALLY COMPLETE.

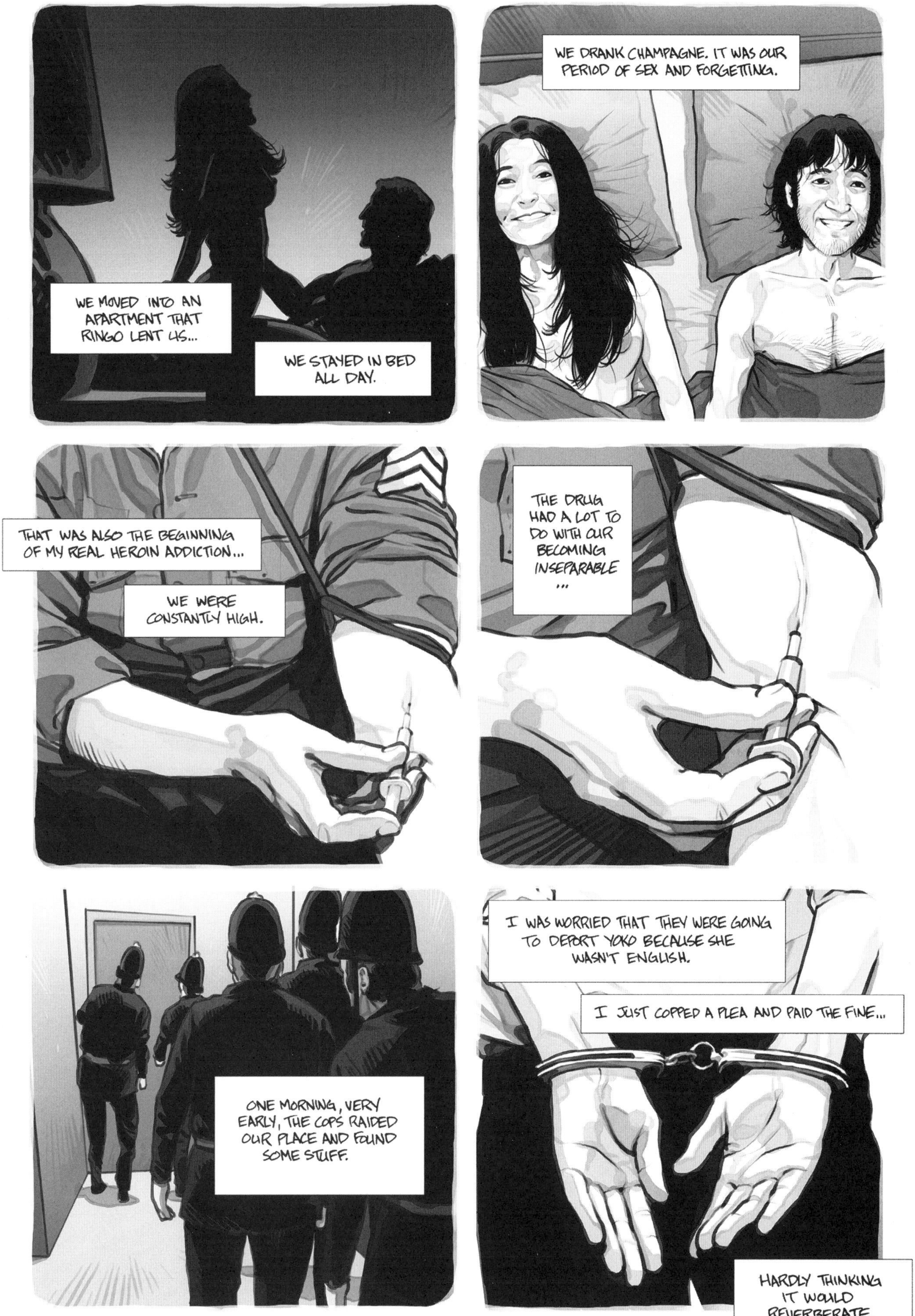
WE MOVED INTO AN APARTMENT THAT RINGO LENT US...
WE STAYED IN BED ALL DAY.
WE DRANK CHAMPAGNE. IT WAS OUR PERIOD OF SEX AND FORGETTING.
THAT WAS ALSO THE BEGINNING OF MY REAL HEROIN ADDICTION...
WE WERE CONSTANTLY HIGH.
THE DRUG HAD A LOT TO DO WITH OUR BECOMING INSEPARABLE ...
ONE MORNING, VERY EARLY, THE COPS RAIDED OUR PLACE AND FOUND SOME STUFF.
I WAS WORRIED THAT THEY WERE GOING TO DEPORT YOKO BECAUSE SHE WASN'T ENGLISH.
I JUST COPPED A PLEA AND PAID THE FINE...
HARDLY THINKING IT WOULD REVERBERATE.

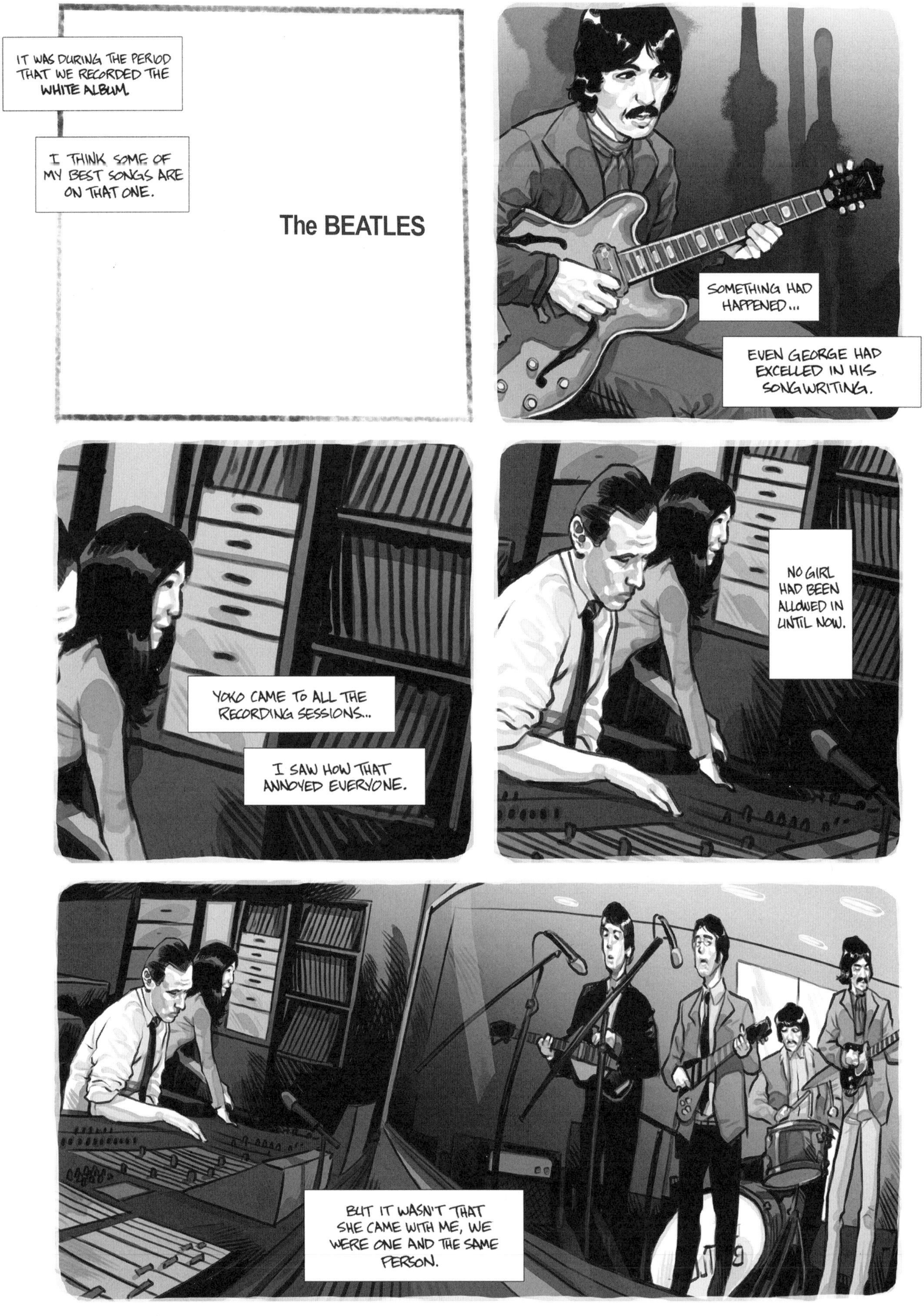
IT WAS DURING THE PERIOD THAT WE RECORDED THE WHITE ALBUM.
I THINK SOME OF MY BEST SONGS ARE ON THAT ONE.
The BEATLES
SOMETHING HAD HAPPENED...
EVEN GEORGE HAD EXCELLED IN HIS SONGWRITING.
YOKO CAME TO ALL THE RECORDING SESSIONS...
I SAW HOW THAT ANNOYED EVERYONE.
NO GIRL HAD BEEN ALLOWED IN UNTIL NOW.
BUT IT WASN'T THAT SHE CAME WITH ME, WE WERE ONE AND THE SAME PERSON.

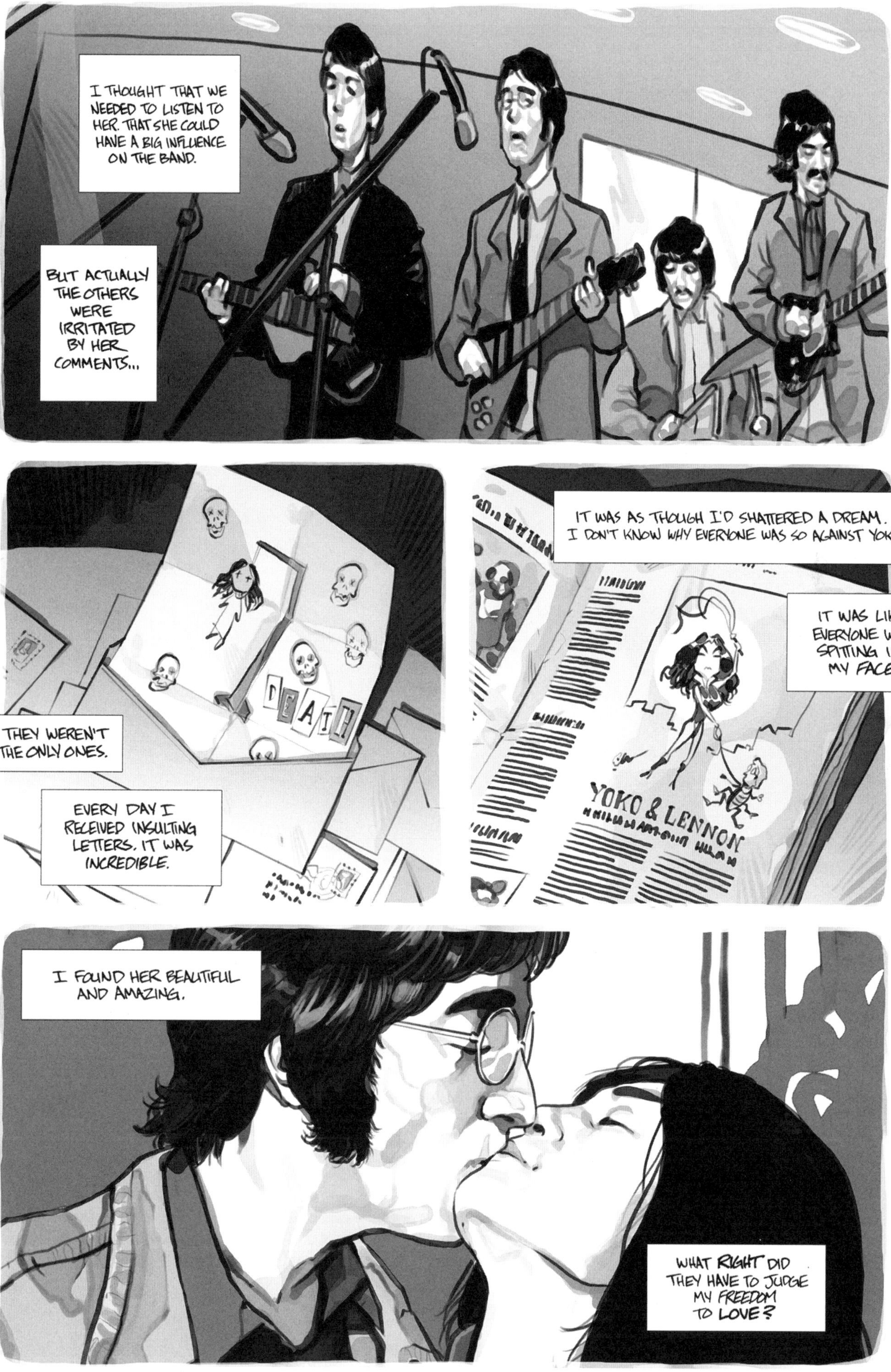
I THOUGHT THAT WE NEEDED TO LISTEN TO HER. THAT SHE COULD HAVE A BIG INFLUENCE ON THE BAND.
BUT ACTUALLY THE OTHERS WERE IRRITATED BY HER COMMENTS...
THEY WEREN'T THE ONLY ONES.
EVERY DAY I RECEIVED INSULTING LETTERS. IT WAS INCREDIBLE.
DEATH
IT WAS AS THOUGH I'D SHATTERED A DREAM. I DON'T KNOW WHY EVERYONE WAS SO AGAINST YOKO.
IT WAS LIKE EVERYONE WAS SPITTING IN MY FACE.
YOKO & LENNON
I FOUND HER BEAUTIFUL AND AMAZING.
WHAT RIGHT DID THEY HAVE TO JUDGE MY FREEDOM TO LOVE?

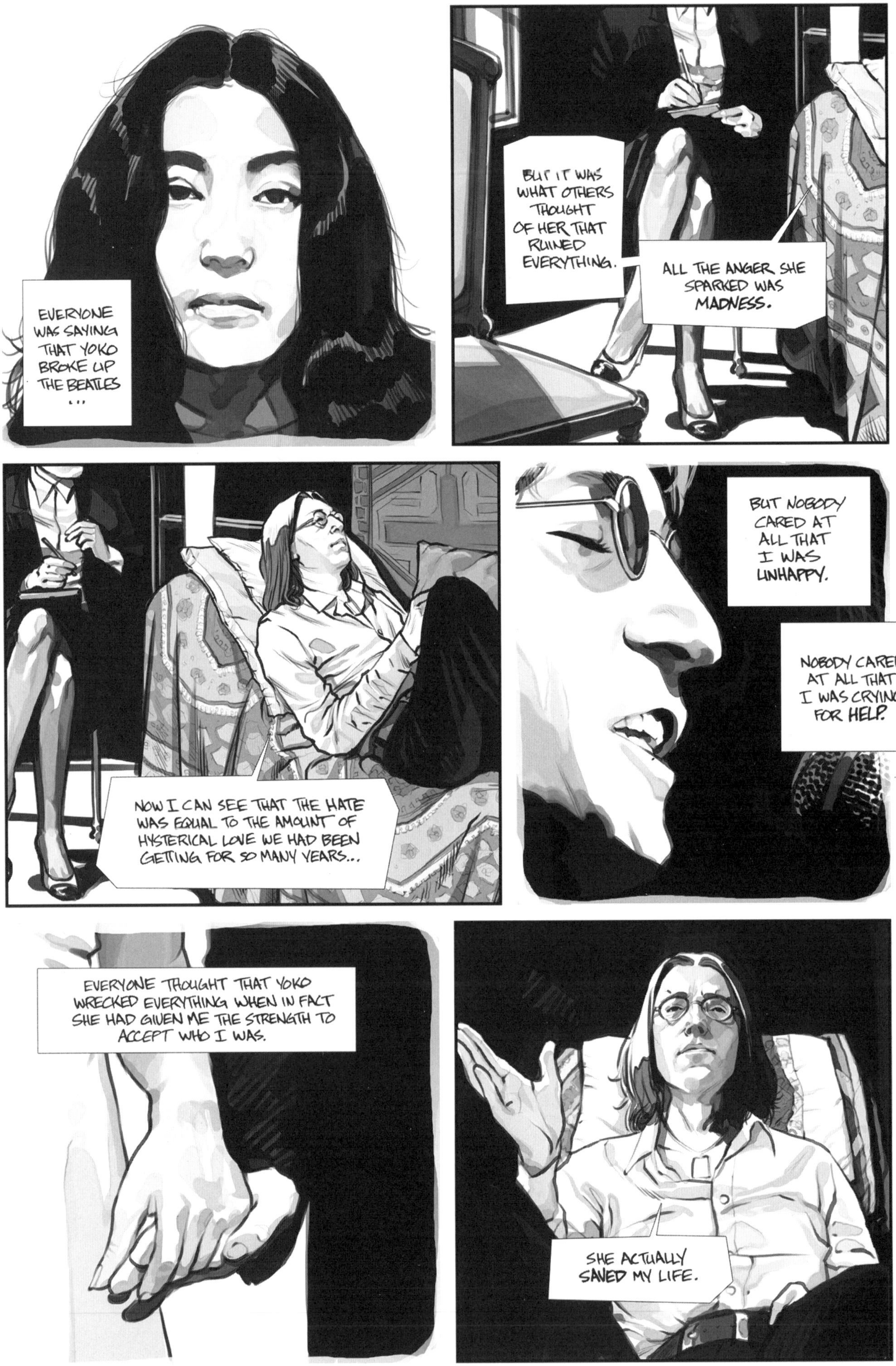
EVERYONE WAS SAYING THAT YOKO BROKE UP THE BEATLES ...
BUT IT WAS WHAT OTHERS THOUGHT OF HER THAT RUINED EVERYTHING.
ALL THE ANGER SHE SPARKED WAS MADNESS.
NOW I CAN SEE THAT THE HATE WAS EQUAL TO THE AMOUNT OF HYSTERICAL LOVE WE HAD BEEN GETTING FOR SO MANY YEARS...
BUT NOBODY CARED AT ALL THAT I WAS UNHAPPY.
NOBODY CARED AT ALL THAT I WAS CRYING FOR HELP.
EVERYONE THOUGHT THAT YOKO WRECKED EVERYTHING WHEN IN FACT SHE HAD GIVEN ME THE STRENGTH TO ACCEPT WHO I WAS.
SHE ACTUALLY SAVED MY LIFE.

sixteenth session

WE WANTED TO BE USEFUL

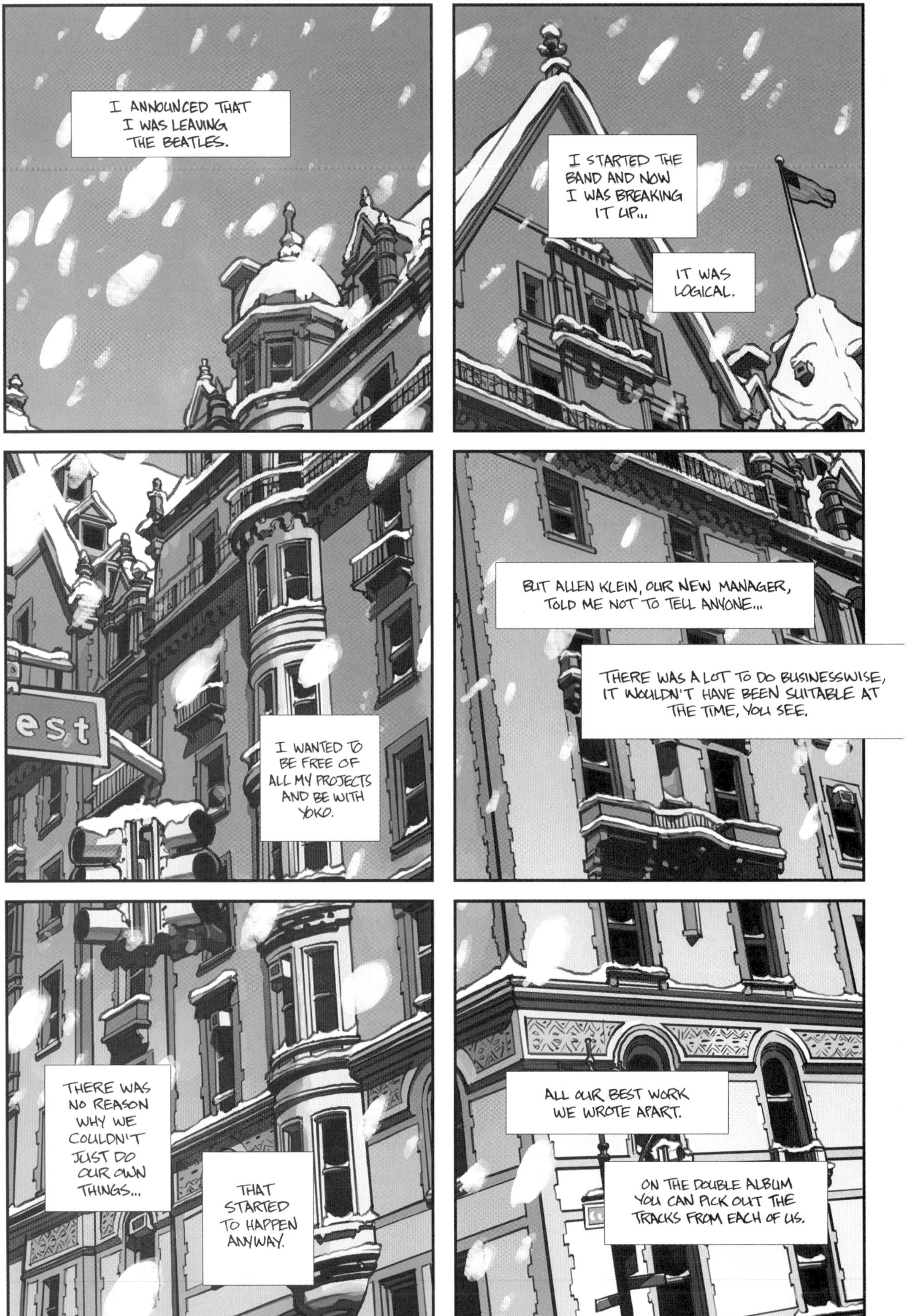
I ANNOUNCED THAT I WAS LEAVING THE BEATLES.
I STARTED THE BAND AND NOW I WAS BREAKING IT UP...
IT WAS LOGICAL.
est
I WANTED TO BE FREE OF ALL MY PROJECTS AND BE WITH YOKO.
BUT ALLEN KLEIN, OUR NEW MANAGER, TOLD ME NOT TO TELL ANYONE...
THERE WAS A LOT TO DO BUSINESSWISE, IT WOULDN'T HAVE BEEN SUITABLE AT THE TIME, YOU SEE.
THERE WAS NO REASON WHY WE COULDN'T JUST DO OUR OWN THINGS...
THAT STARTED TO HAPPEN ANYWAY.
ALL OUR BEST WORK WE WROTE APART.
ON THE DOUBLE ALBUM YOU CAN PICK OUT THE TRACKS FROM EACH OF US.

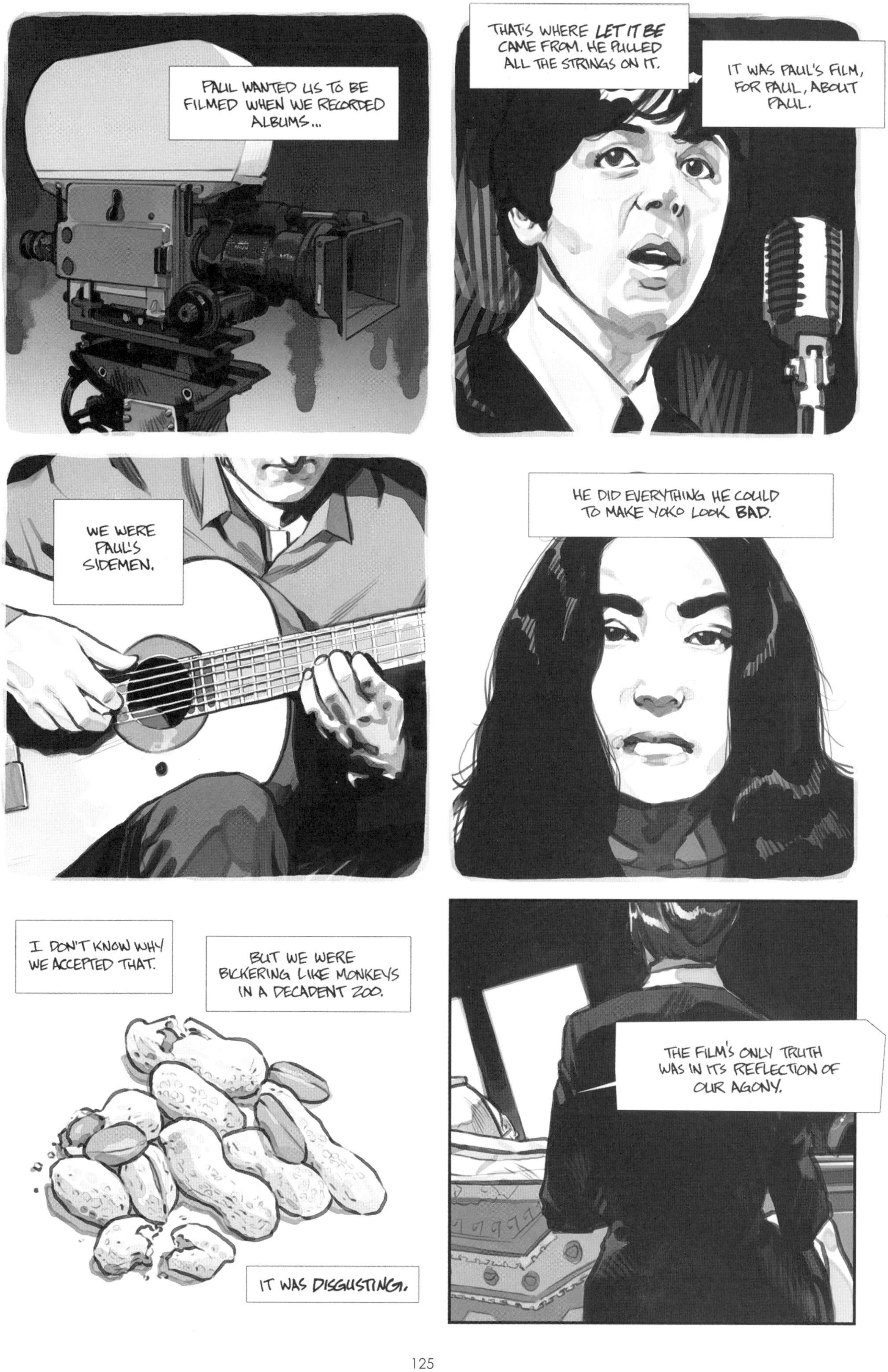

PAUL WANTED US TO BE FILMED WHEN WE RECORDED ALBUMS...
THAT'S WHERE LET IT BE CAME FROM. HE PULLED ALL THE STRINGS ON IT.
IT WAS PAUL'S FILM, FOR PAUL, ABOUT PAUL.
WE WERE PAUL'S SIDEMEN.
HE DID EVERYTHING HE COULD TO MAKE YOKO LOOK BAD.
I DON'T KNOW WHY WE ACCEPTED THAT.
BUT WE WERE BICKERING LIKE MONKEYS IN A DECADENT ZOO.
IT WAS DISGUSTING.
THE FILM'S ONLY TRUTH WAS IN ITS REFLECTION OF OUR AGONY.

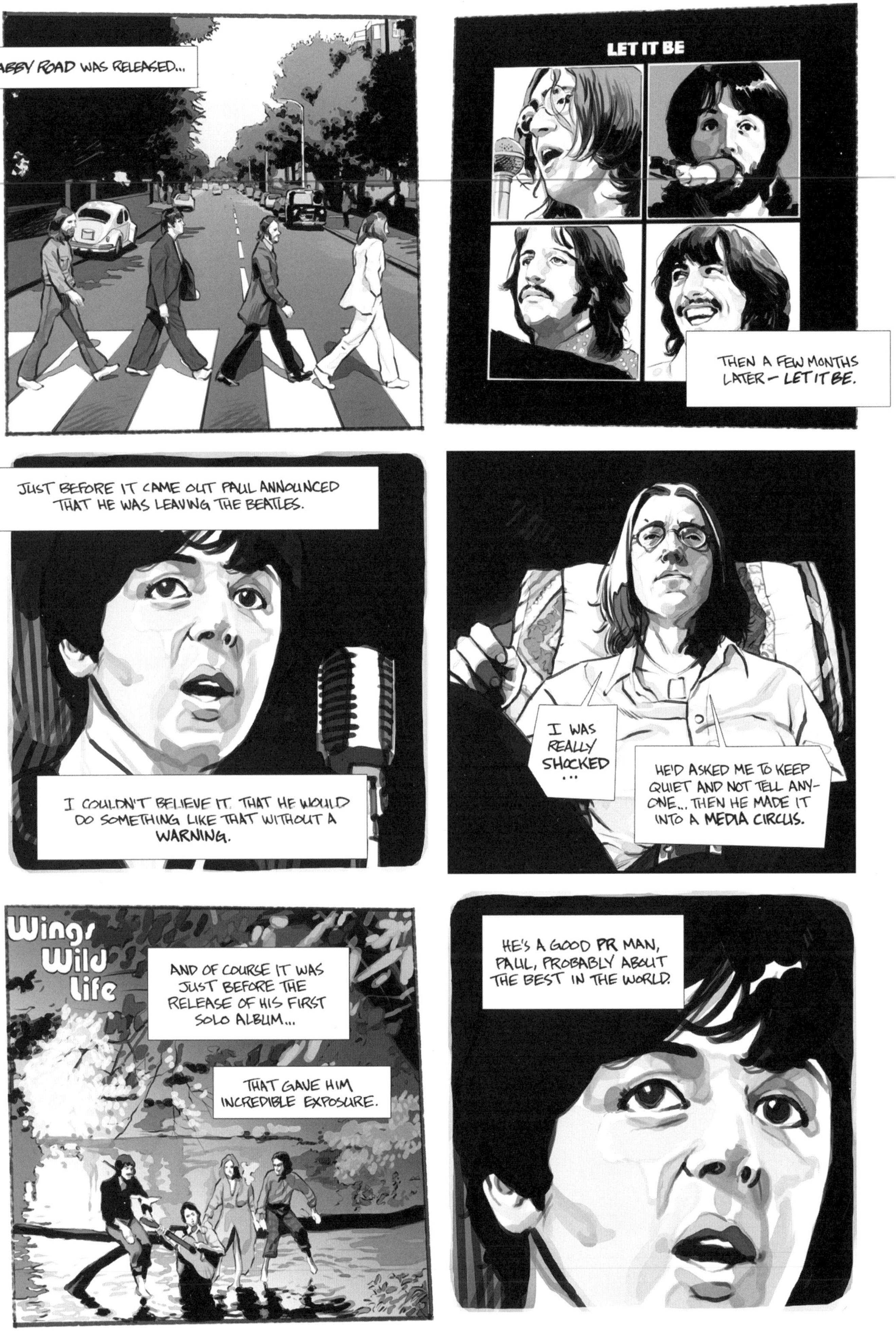
ABBY ROAD WAS RELEASED...
LET IT BE
THEN A FEW MONTHS LATER — LET IT BE.
JUST BEFORE IT CAME OUT PAUL ANNOUNCED THAT HE WAS LEAVING THE BEATLES.
I COULDN'T BELIEVE IT. THAT HE WOULD DO SOMETHING LIKE THAT WITHOUT A WARNING.
I WAS REALLY SHOCKED...
HE'D ASKED ME TO KEEP QUIET AND NOT TELL ANYONE... THEN HE MADE IT INTO A MEDIA CIRCUS.
Wings Wild Life
AND OF COURSE IT WAS JUST BEFORE THE RELEASE OF HIS FIRST SOLO ALBUM...
THAT GAVE HIM INCREDIBLE EXPOSURE.
HE'S A GOOD PR MAN, PAUL, PROBABLY ABOUT THE BEST IN THE WORLD.

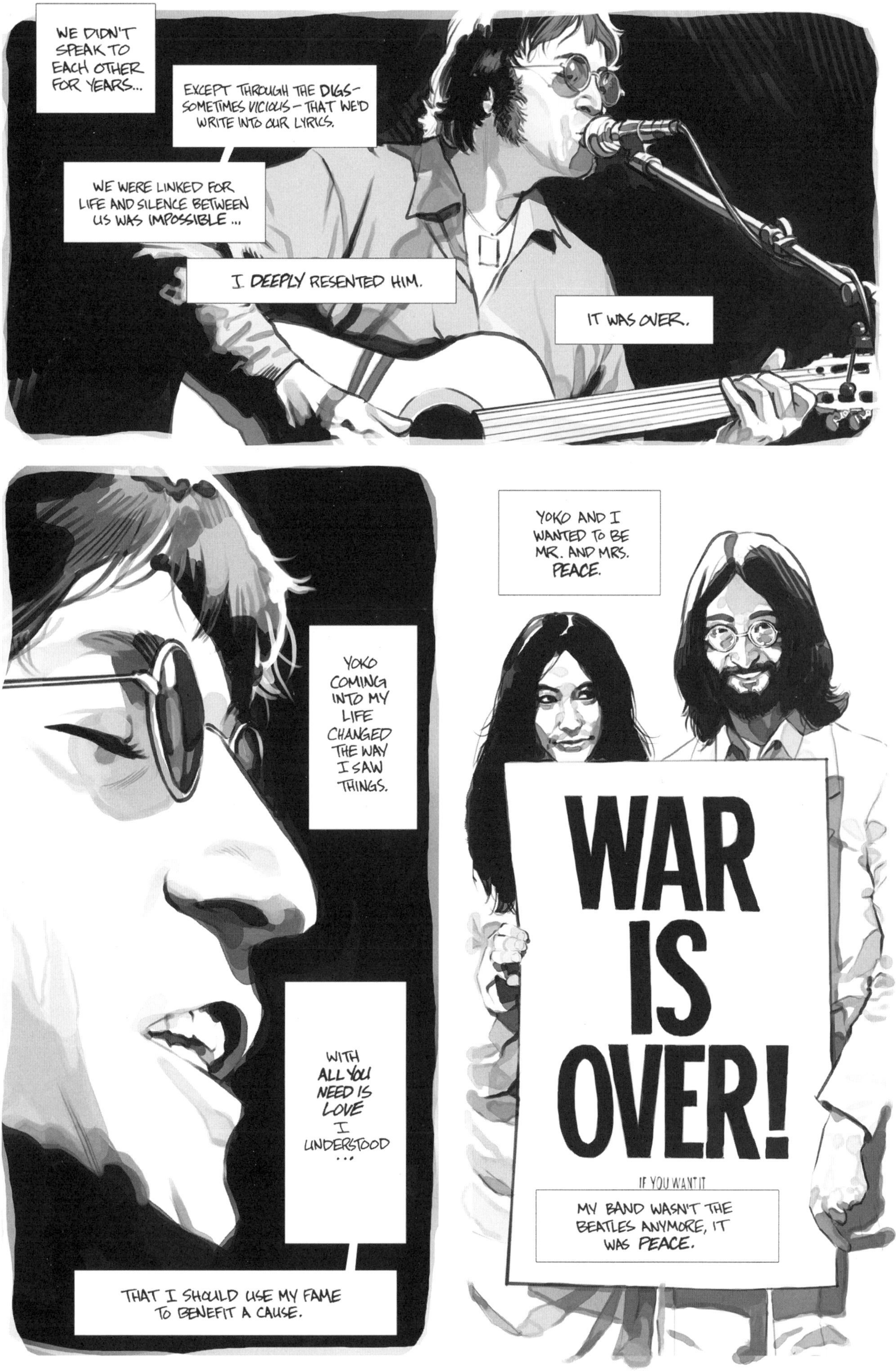
WE DIDN'T SPEAK TO EACH OTHER FOR YEARS...
EXCEPT THROUGH THE DIGS-SOMETIMES VICIOUS-THAT WE'D WRITE INTO OUR LYRICS.
WE WERE LINKED FOR LIFE AND SILENCE BETWEEN US WAS IMPOSSIBLE...
I DEEPLY RESENTED HIM.
IT WAS OVER.
YOKO COMING INTO MY LIFE CHANGED THE WAY I SAW THINGS.
WITH ALL YOU NEED IS LOVE I UNDERSTOOD...
THAT I SHOULD USE MY FAME TO BENEFIT A CAUSE.
YOKO AND I WANTED TO BE MR. AND MRS. PEACE.
WAR IS OVER!
IF YOU WANT IT
MY BAND WASN'T THE BEATLES ANYMORE, IT WAS PEACE.

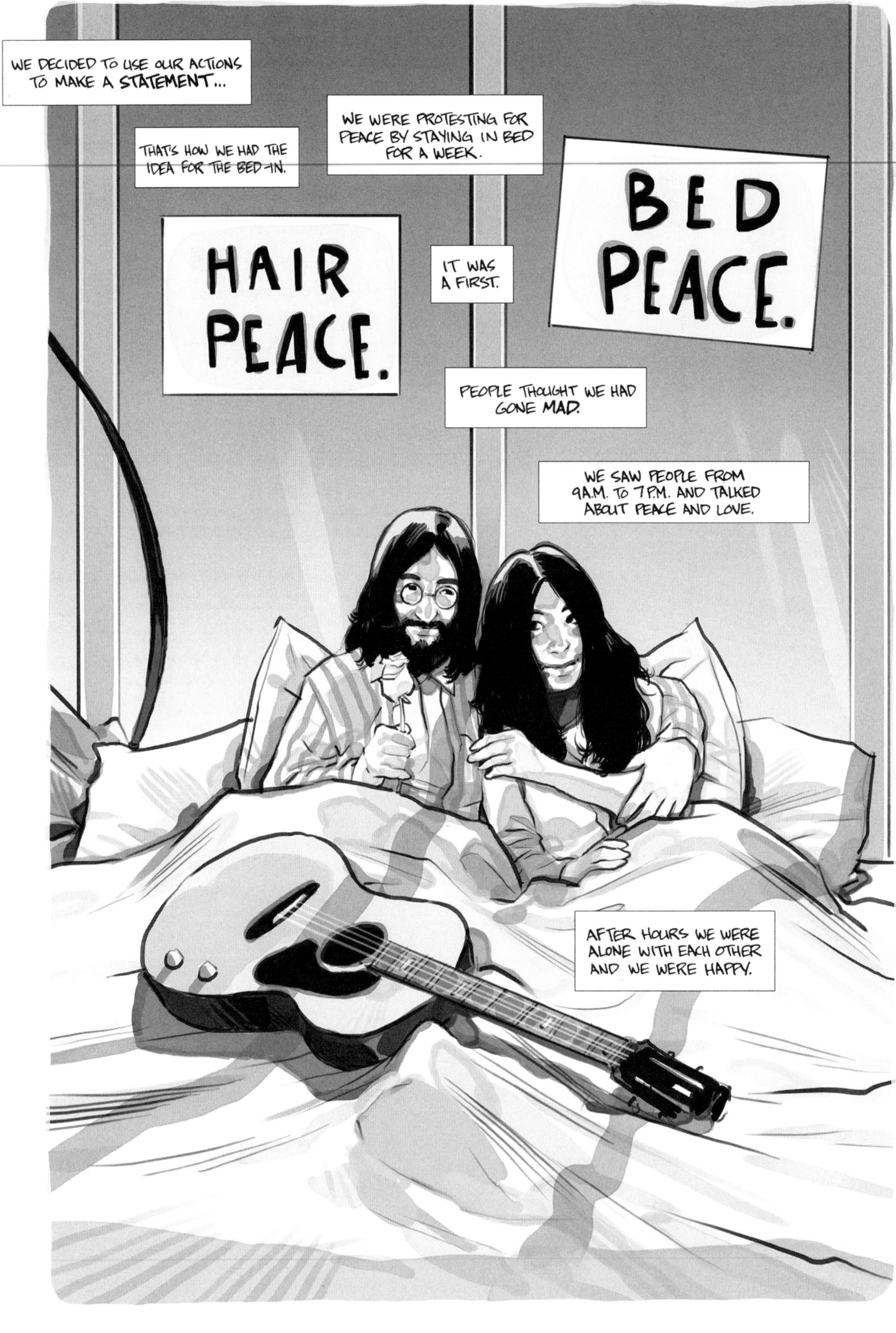
WE DECIDED TO USE OUR ACTIONS TO MAKE A STATEMENT...
THAT'S HOW WE HAD THE IDEA FOR THE BED-IN.
WE WERE PROTESTING FOR PEACE BY STAYING IN BED FOR A WEEK.
BED PEACE.
HAIR PEACE.
IT WAS A FIRST.
PEOPLE THOUGHT WE HAD GONE MAD.
WE SAW PEOPLE FROM 9A.M. TO 7 P.M. AND TALKED ABOUT PEACE AND LOVE.
AFTER HOURS WE WERE ALONE WITH EACH OTHER AND WE WERE HAPPY.

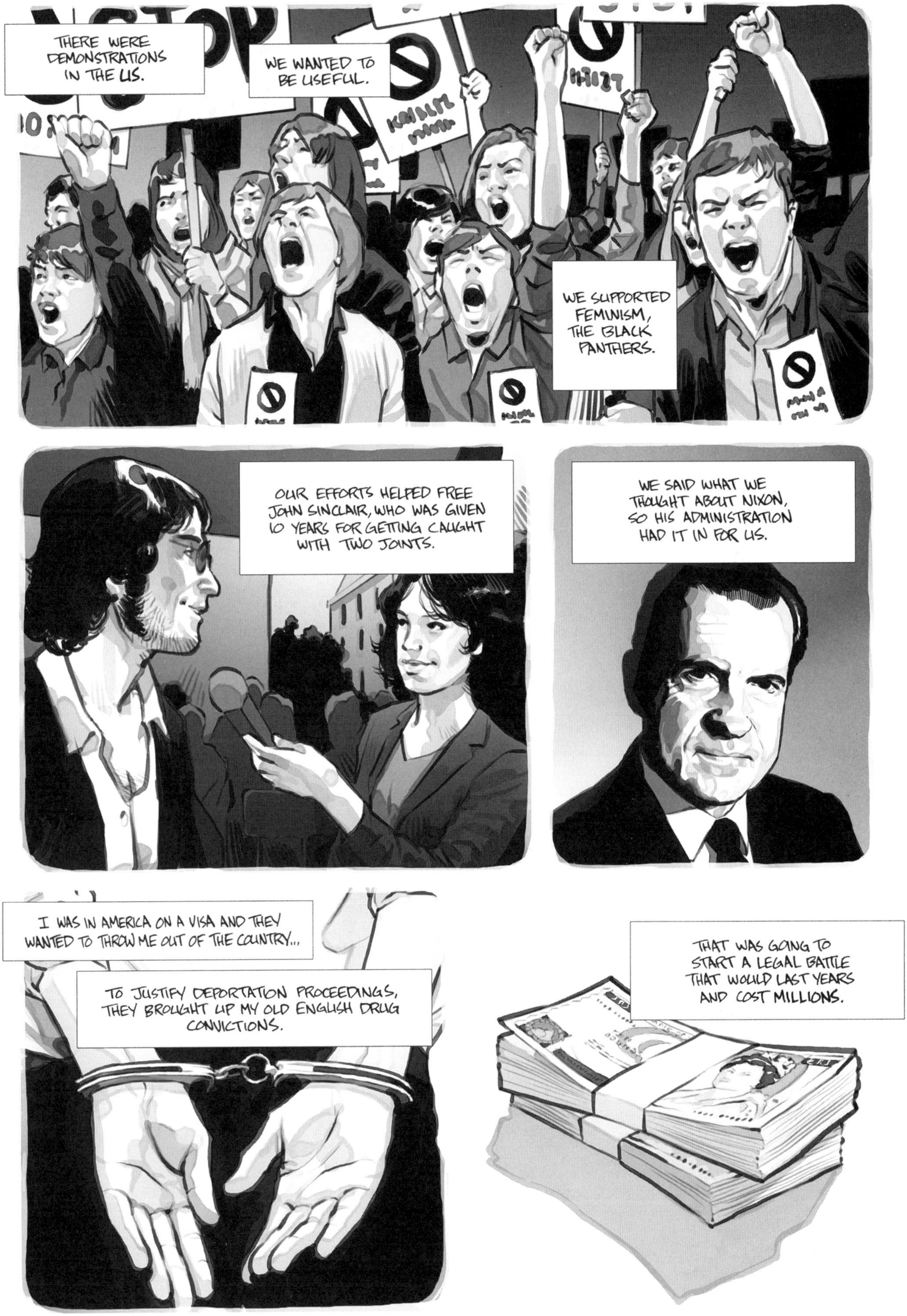
THERE WERE DEMONSTRATIONS IN THE US.
WE WANTED TO BE USEFUL.
WE SUPPORTED FEMINISM, THE BLACK PANTHERS.
OUR EFFORTS HELPED FREE JOHN SINCLAIR, WHO WAS GIVEN 10 YEARS FOR GETTING CAUGHT WITH TWO JOINTS.
WE SAID WHAT WE THOUGHT ABOUT NIXON, SO HIS ADMINISTRATION HAD IT IN FOR US.
I WAS IN AMERICA ON A VISA AND THEY WANTED TO THROW ME OUT OF THE COUNTRY...
TO JUSTIFY DEPORTATION PROCEEDINGS, THEY BROUGHT UP MY OLD ENGLISH DRUG CONVICTIONS.
THAT WAS GOING TO START A LEGAL BATTLE THAT WOULD LAST YEARS AND COST MILLIONS.

seventeenth session

YOU CAN COME BACK, JOHN

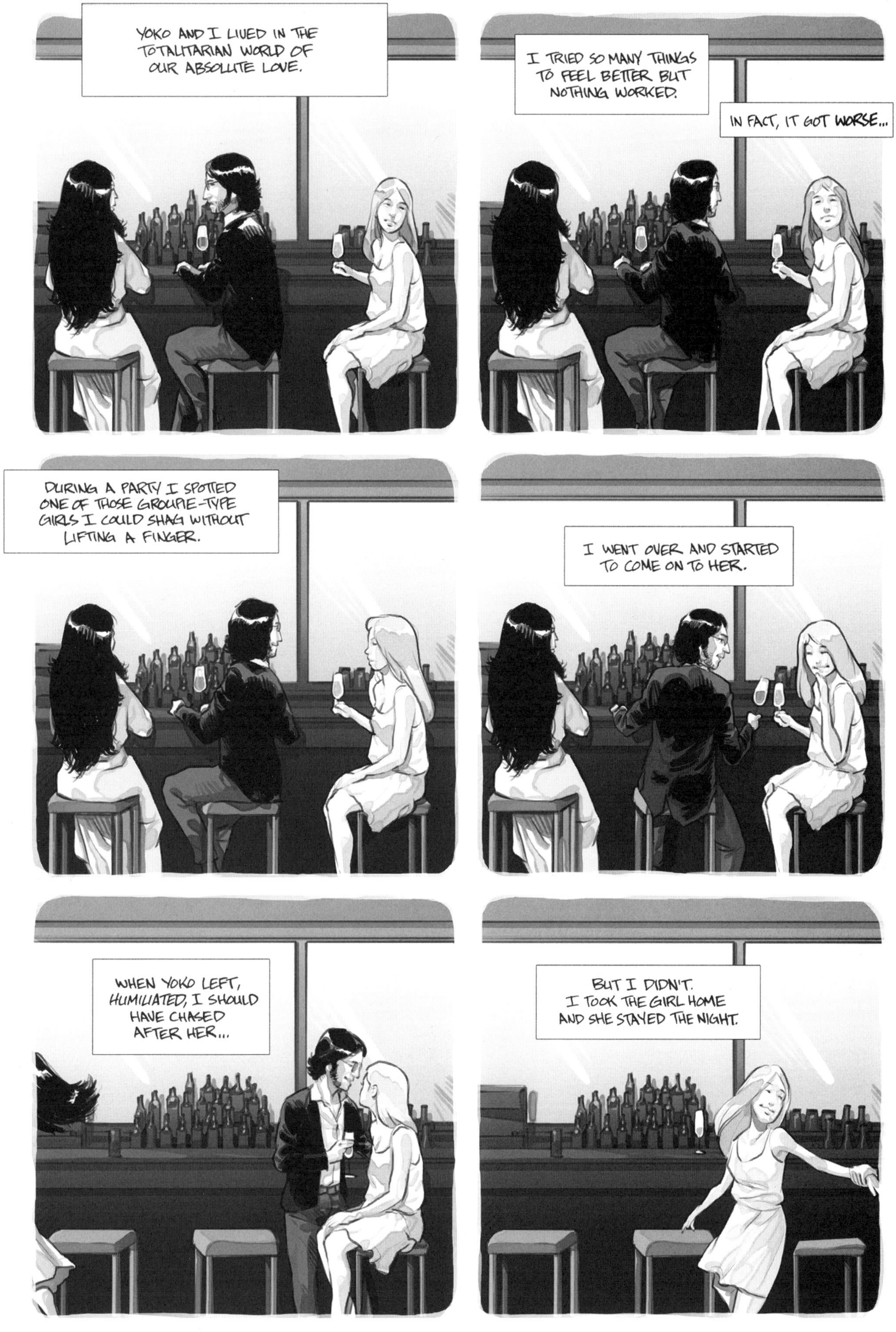
YOKO AND I LIVED IN THE TOTALITARIAN WORLD OF OUR ABSOLUTE LOVE.
I TRIED SO MANY THINGS TO FEEL BETTER BUT NOTHING WORKED.
IN FACT, IT GOT WORSE...
DURING A PARTY I SPOTTED ONE OF THOSE GROUPIE-TYPE GIRLS I COULD SHAG WITHOUT LIFTING A FINGER.
I WENT OVER AND STARTED TO COME ON TO HER.
WHEN YOKO LEFT, HUMILIATED, I SHOULD HAVE CHASED AFTER HER...
BUT I DIDN'T. I TOOK THE GIRL HOME AND SHE STAYED THE NIGHT.

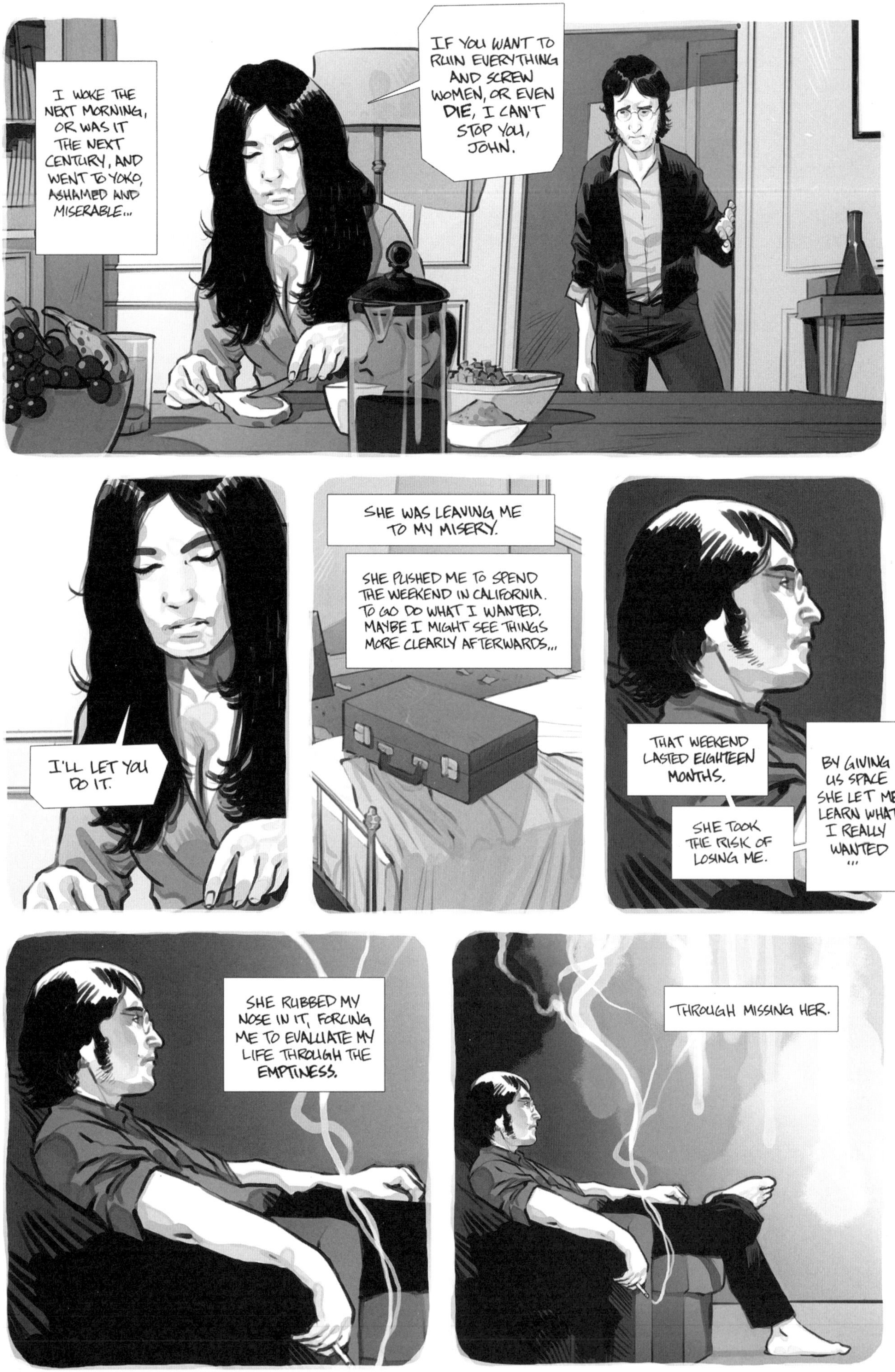
I WOKE THE NEXT MORNING, OR WAS IT THE NEXT CENTURY, AND WENT TO YOKO, ASHAMED AND MISERABLE...
IF YOU WANT TO RUIN EVERYTHING AND SCREW WOMEN, OR EVEN DIE, I CAN'T STOP YOU, JOHN.
I'LL LET YOU DO IT.
SHE WAS LEAVING ME TO MY MISERY.
SHE PUSHED ME TO SPEND THE WEEKEND IN CALIFORNIA. TO GO DO WHAT I WANTED. MAYBE I MIGHT SEE THINGS MORE CLEARLY AFTERWARDS...
THAT WEEKEND LASTED EIGHTEEN MONTHS.
SHE TOOK THE RISK OF LOSING ME.
BY GIVING US SPACE SHE LET ME LEARN WHAT I REALLY WANTED ...
SHE RUBBED MY NOSE IN IT, FORCING ME TO EVALUATE MY LIFE THROUGH THE EMPTINESS.
THROUGH MISSING HER.

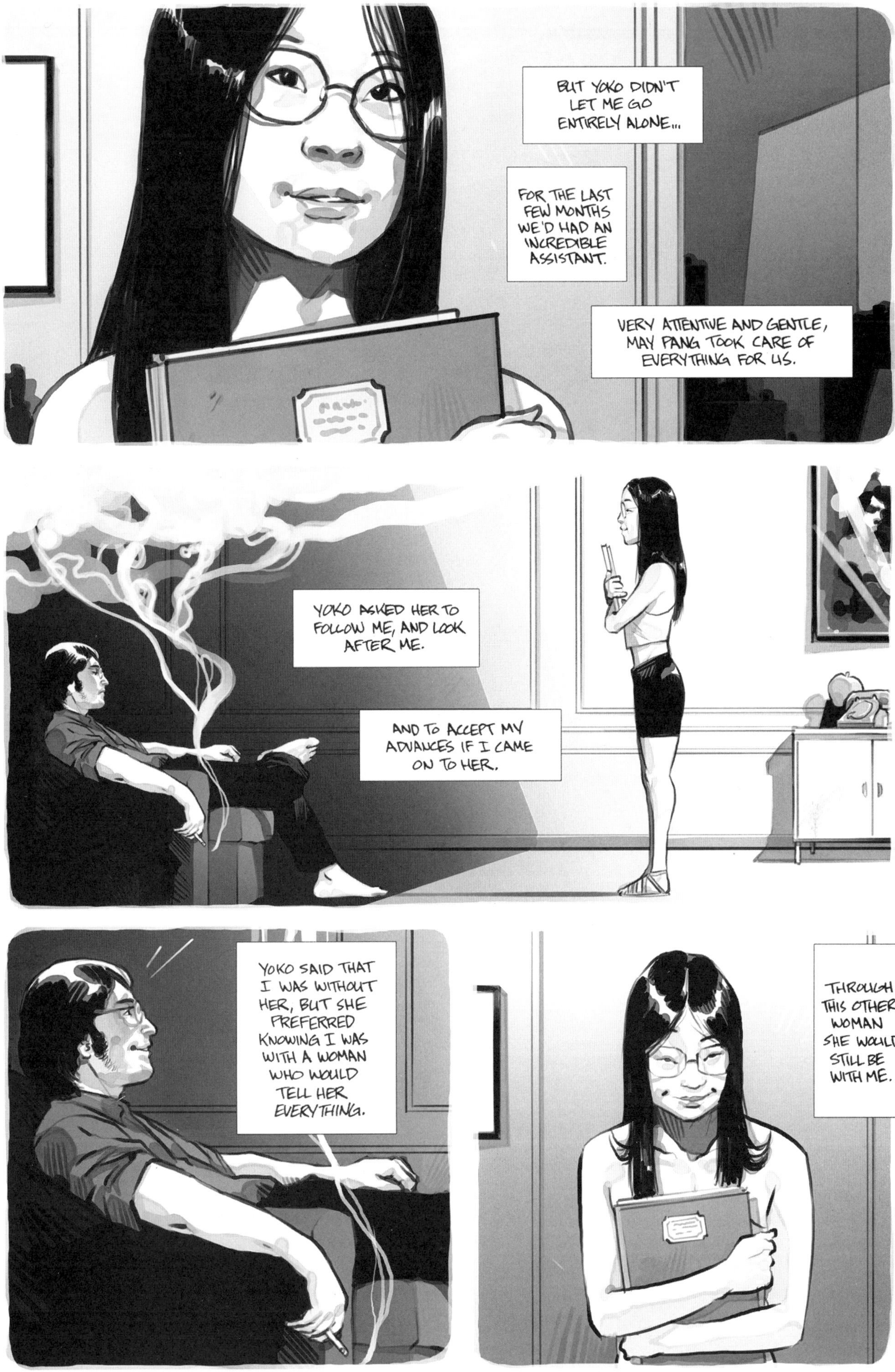
BUT YOKO DIDN'T LET ME GO ENTIRELY ALONE...
FOR THE LAST FEW MONTHS WE'D HAD AN INCREDIBLE ASSISTANT.
VERY ATTENTIVE AND GENTLE, MAY PANG TOOK CARE OF EVERYTHING FOR US.
YOKO ASKED HER TO FOLLOW ME, AND LOOK AFTER ME.
AND TO ACCEPT MY ADVANCES IF I CAME ON TO HER.
YOKO SAID THAT I WAS WITHOUT HER, BUT SHE PREFERRED KNOWING I WAS WITH A WOMAN WHO WOULD TELL HER EVERYTHING.
THROUGH THIS OTHER WOMAN SHE WOULD STILL BE WITH ME.

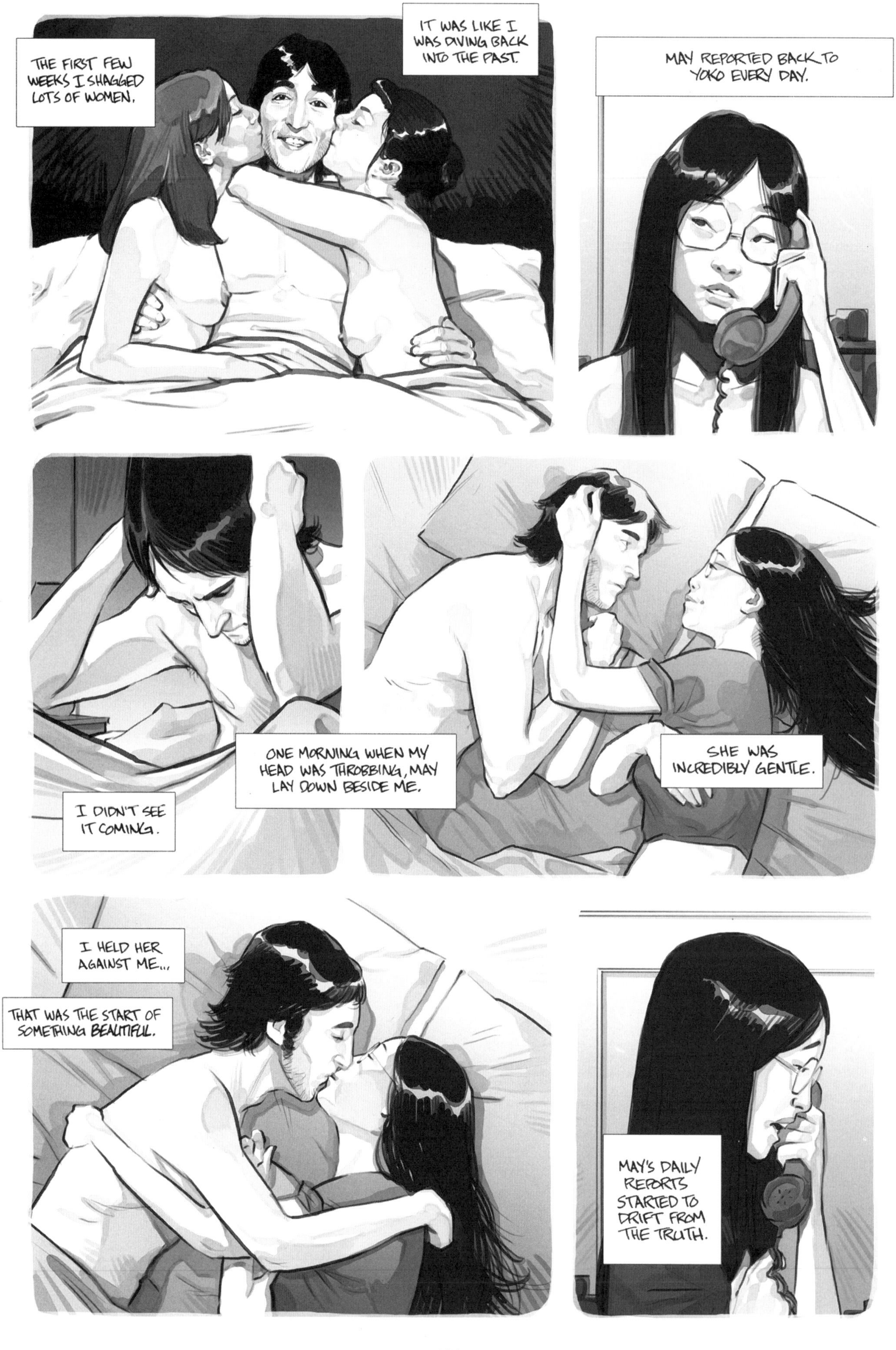
THE FIRST FEW WEEKS I SHAGGED LOTS OF WOMEN.
IT WAS LIKE I WAS DIVING BACK INTO THE PAST.
MAY REPORTED BACK TO YOKO EVERY DAY.
I DIDN'T SEE IT COMING.
ONE MORNING WHEN MY HEAD WAS THROBBING, MAY LAY DOWN BESIDE ME.
SHE WAS INCREDIBLY GENTLE.
I HELD HER AGAINST ME...
THAT WAS THE START OF SOMETHING BEAUTIFUL.
MAY'S DAILY REPORTS STARTED TO DRIFT FROM THE TRUTH.

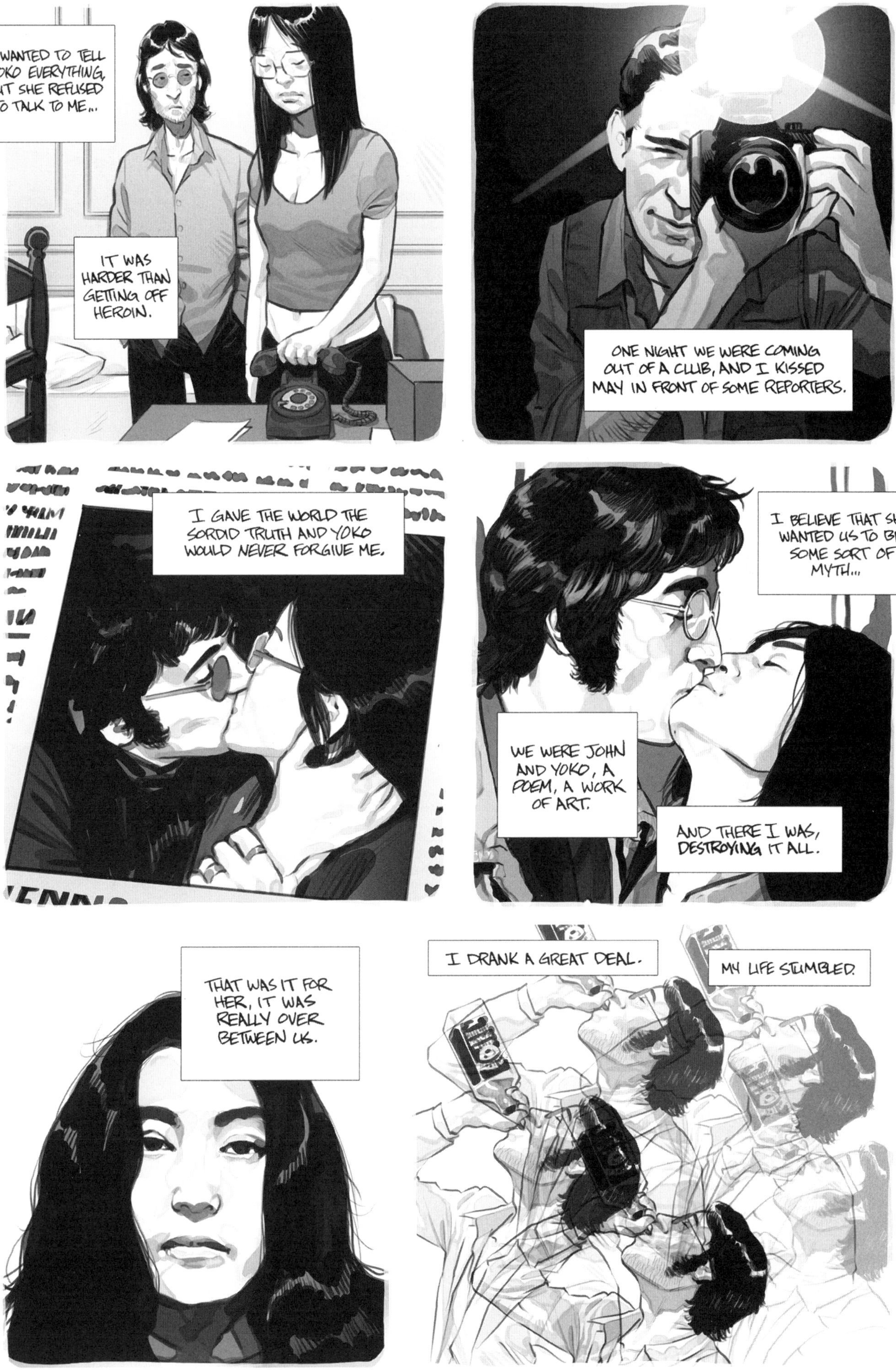
I WANTED TO TELL YOKO EVERYTHING, BUT SHE REFUSED TO TALK TO ME...
IT WAS HARDER THAN GETTING OFF HEROIN.
ONE NIGHT WE WERE COMING OUT OF A CLUB, AND I KISSED MAY IN FRONT OF SOME REPORTERS.
I GAVE THE WORLD THE SORDID TRUTH AND YOKO WOULD NEVER FORGIVE ME.
I BELIEVE THAT SHE WANTED US TO BE SOME SORT OF MYTH...
WE WERE JOHN AND YOKO, A POEM, A WORK OF ART.
AND THERE I WAS, DESTROYING IT ALL.
THAT WAS IT FOR HER, IT WAS REALLY OVER BETWEEN US.
I DRANK A GREAT DEAL.
MY LIFE STUMBLED.

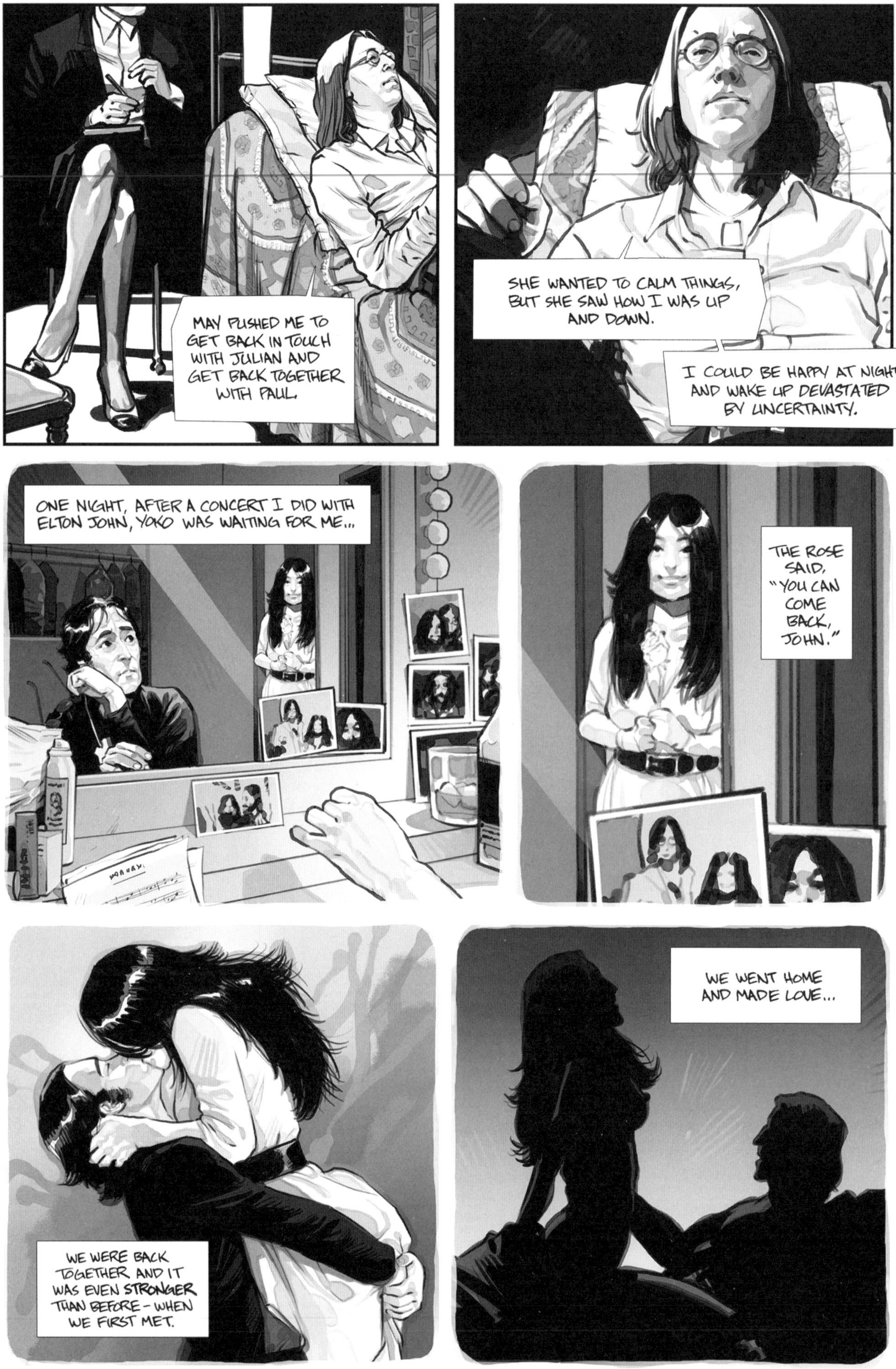
MAY PUSHED ME TO GET BACK IN TOUCH WITH JULIAN AND GET BACK TOGETHER WITH PAUL.
SHE WANTED TO CALM THINGS, BUT SHE SAW HOW I WAS UP AND DOWN.
I COULD BE HAPPY AT NIGHT AND WAKE UP DEVASTATED BY UNCERTAINTY.
ONE NIGHT, AFTER A CONCERT I DID WITH ELTON JOHN, YOKO WAS WAITING FOR ME...
THE ROSE SAID, "YOU CAN COME BACK, JOHN."
WE WERE BACK TOGETHER AND IT WAS EVEN STRONGER THAN BEFORE - WHEN WE FIRST MET.
WE WENT HOME AND MADE LOVE...

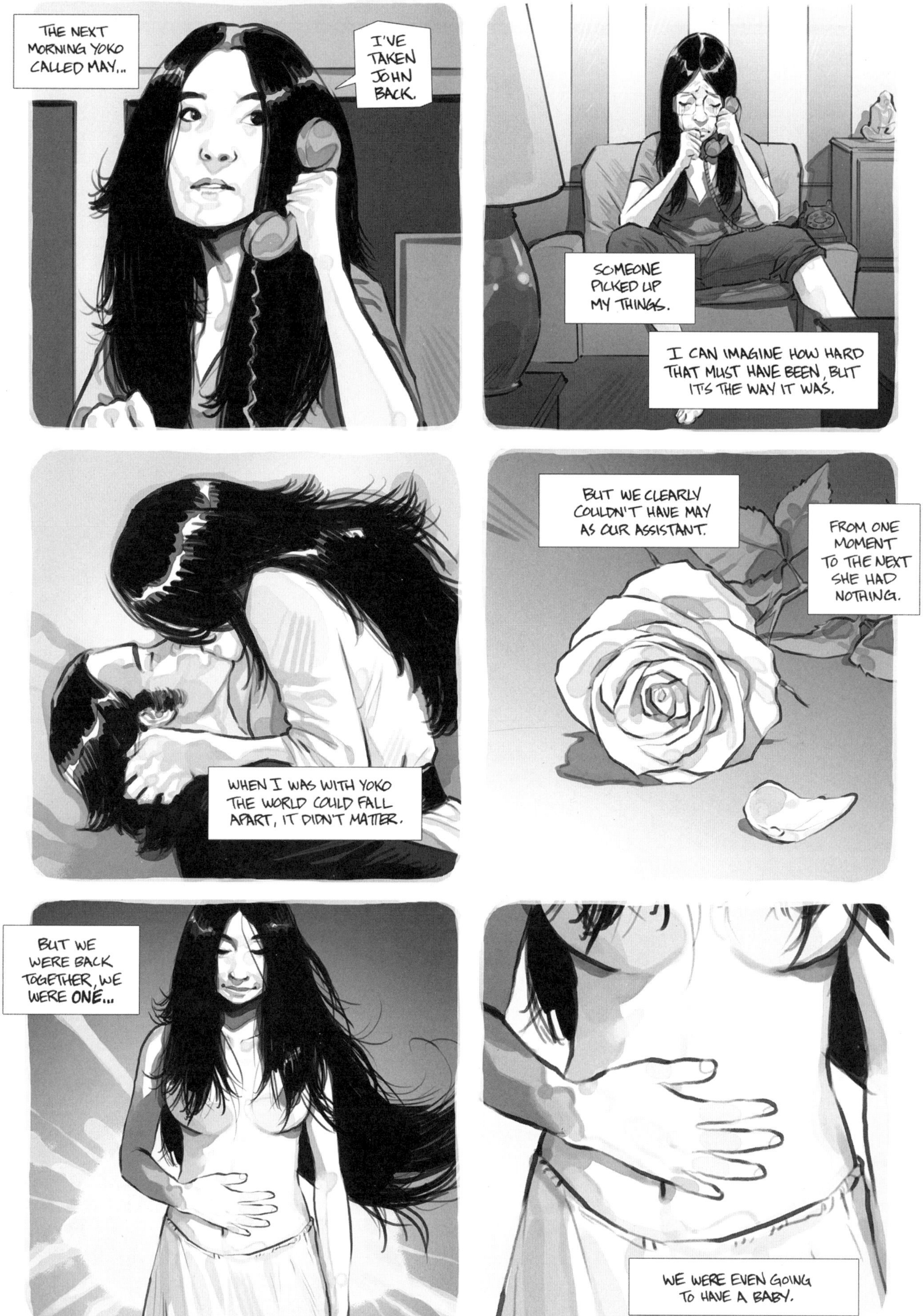
THE NEXT MORNING YOKO CALLED MAY...
I'VE TAKEN JOHN BACK.
SOMEONE PICKED UP MY THINGS.
I CAN IMAGINE HOW HARD THAT MUST HAVE BEEN, BUT IT'S THE WAY IT WAS.
WHEN I WAS WITH YOKO THE WORLD COULD FALL APART, IT DIDN'T MATTER.
BUT WE CLEARLY COULDN'T HAVE MAY AS OUR ASSISTANT.
FROM ONE MOMENT TO THE NEXT SHE HAD NOTHING.
BUT WE WERE BACK TOGETHER, WE WERE ONE...
WE WERE EVEN GOING TO HAVE A BABY.

eighteenth session

THROUGH WORDS,
THE MUSIC CAME BACK

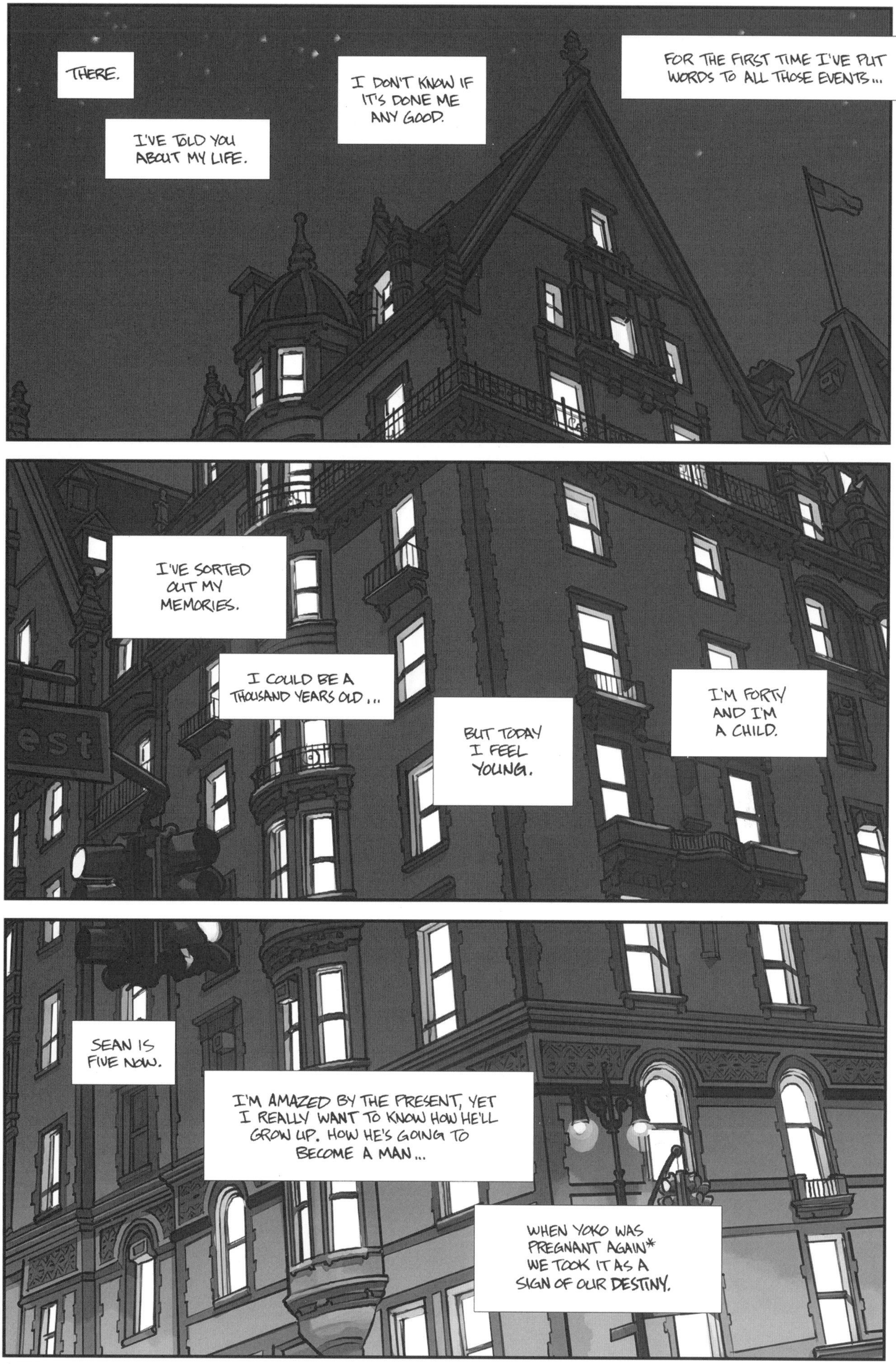
THERE.
I'VE TOLD YOU ABOUT MY LIFE.
I DON'T KNOW IF IT'S DONE ME ANY GOOD.
FOR THE FIRST TIME I'VE PUT WORDS TO ALL THOSE EVENTS...
I'VE SORTED OUT MY MEMORIES.
I COULD BE A THOUSAND YEARS OLD...
BUT TODAY I FEEL YOUNG.
I'M FORTY AND I'M A CHILD.
SEAN IS FIVE NOW.
I'M AMAZED BY THE PRESENT, YET I REALLY WANT TO KNOW HOW HE'LL GROW UP. HOW HE'S GOING TO BECOME A MAN...
WHEN YOKO WAS PREGNANT AGAIN* WE TOOK IT AS A SIGN OF OUR DESTINY.

* YOKO HAD HAD SEVERAL MISCARRIAGES BY THAT TIME.

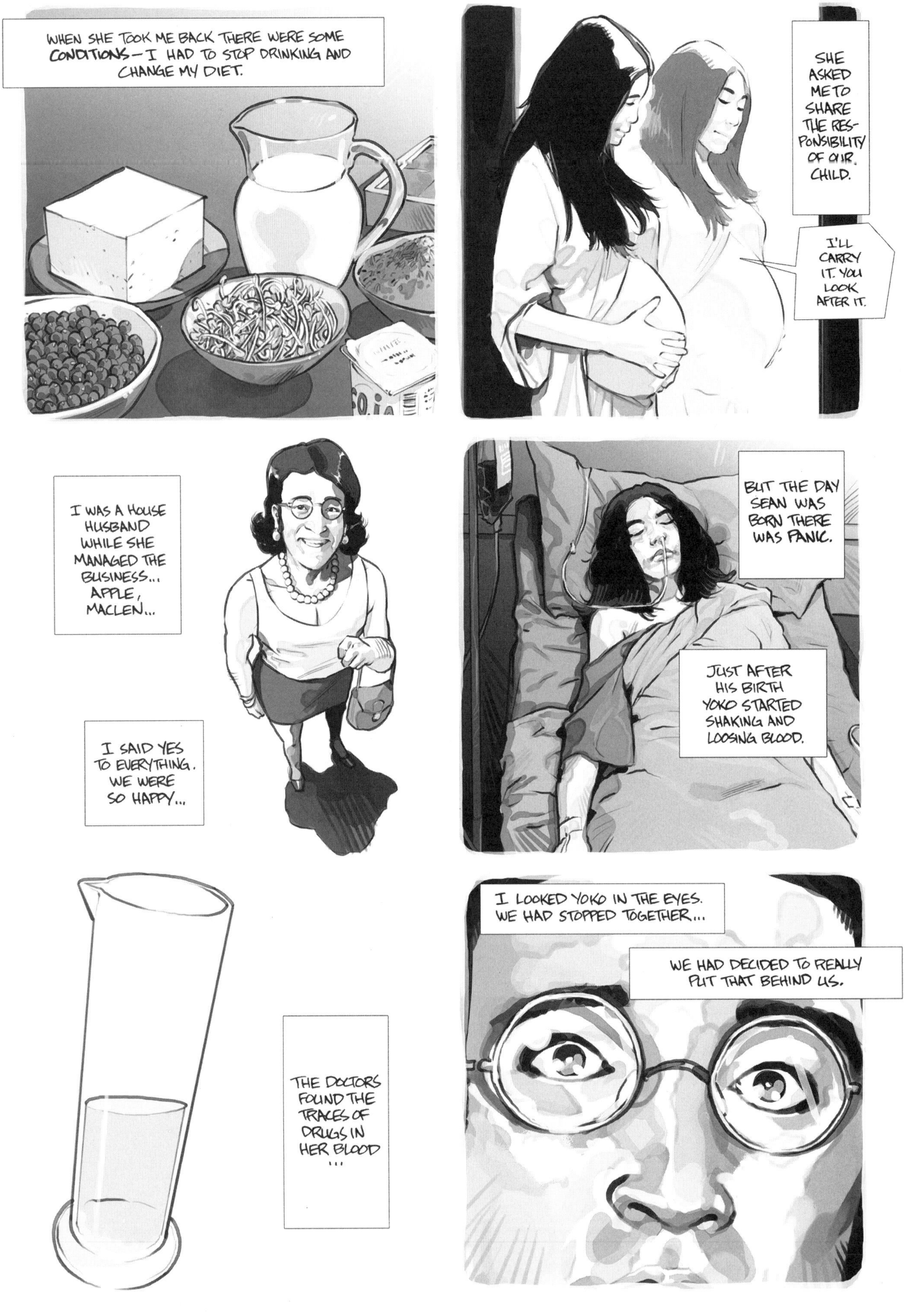
WHEN SHE TOOK ME BACK THERE WERE SOME CONDITIONS — I HAD TO STOP DRINKING AND CHANGE MY DIET.
SHE ASKED ME TO SHARE THE RES-PONSIBILITY OF OUR CHILD.
I'LL CARRY IT. YOU LOOK AFTER IT.
I WAS A HOUSE HUSBAND WHILE SHE MANAGED THE BUSINESS... APPLE, MACLEN...
I SAID YES TO EVERYTHING. WE WERE SO HAPPY...
BUT THE DAY SEAN WAS BORN THERE WAS PANIC.
JUST AFTER HIS BIRTH YOKO STARTED SHAKING AND LOOSING BLOOD.
THE DOCTORS FOUND THE TRACES OF DRUGS IN HER BLOOD ...
I LOOKED YOKO IN THE EYES. WE HAD STOPPED TOGETHER...
WE HAD DECIDED TO REALLY PUT THAT BEHIND US.

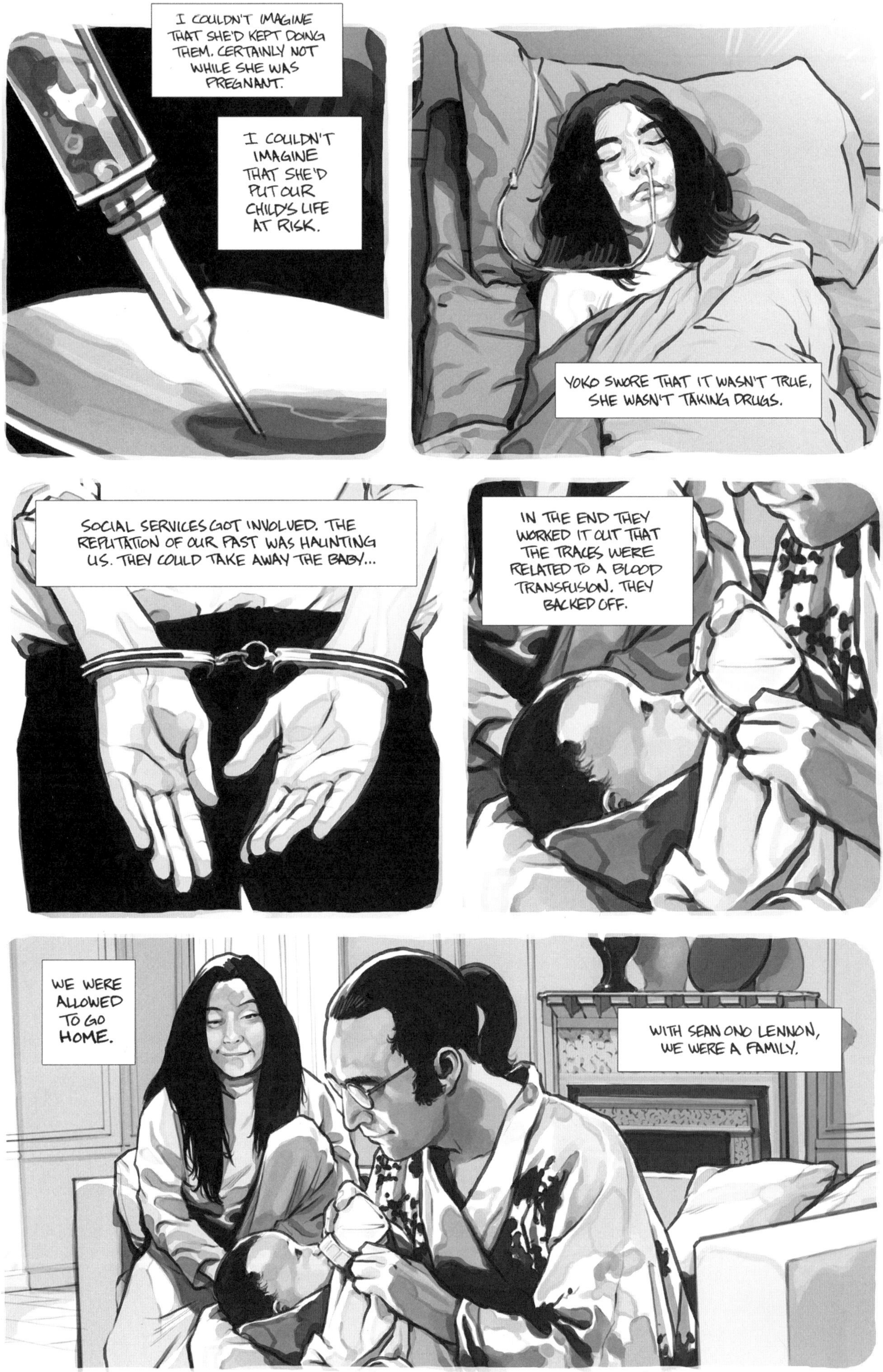
I COULDN'T IMAGINE THAT SHE'D KEPT DOING THEM. CERTAINLY NOT WHILE SHE WAS PREGNANT.
I COULDN'T IMAGINE THAT SHE'D PUT OUR CHILD'S LIFE AT RISK.
YOKO SWORE THAT IT WASN'T TRUE, SHE WASN'T TAKING DRUGS.
SOCIAL SERVICES GOT INVOLVED. THE REPUTATION OF OUR PAST WAS HAUNTING US. THEY COULD TAKE AWAY THE BABY...
IN THE END THEY WORKED IT OUT THAT THE TRACES WERE RELATED TO A BLOOD TRANSFUSION. THEY BACKED OFF.
WE WERE ALLOWED TO GO HOME.
WITH SEAN ONO LENNON, WE WERE A FAMILY.

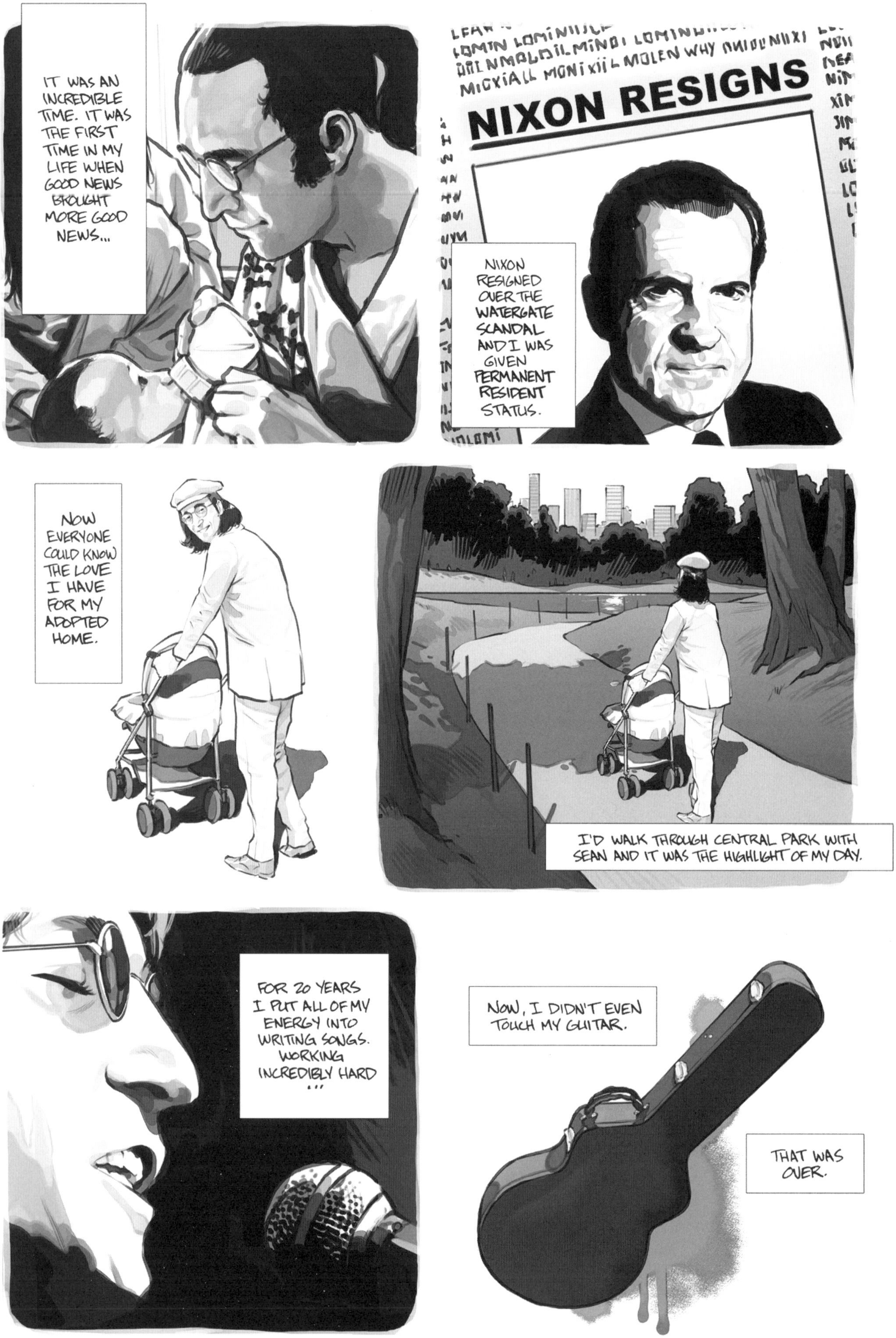
IT WAS AN INCREDIBLE TIME. IT WAS THE FIRST TIME IN MY LIFE WHEN GOOD NEWS BROUGHT MORE GOOD NEWS...
NIXON RESIGNS
NIXON RESIGNED OVER THE WATERGATE SCANDAL AND I WAS GIVEN PERMANENT RESIDENT STATUS.
NOW EVERYONE COULD KNOW THE LOVE I HAVE FOR MY ADOPTED HOME.
I'D WALK THROUGH CENTRAL PARK WITH SEAN AND IT WAS THE HIGHLIGHT OF MY DAY.
FOR 20 YEARS I PUT ALL OF MY ENERGY INTO WRITING SONGS. WORKING INCREDIBLY HARD ...
NOW, I DIDN'T EVEN TOUCH MY GUITAR.
THAT WAS OVER.

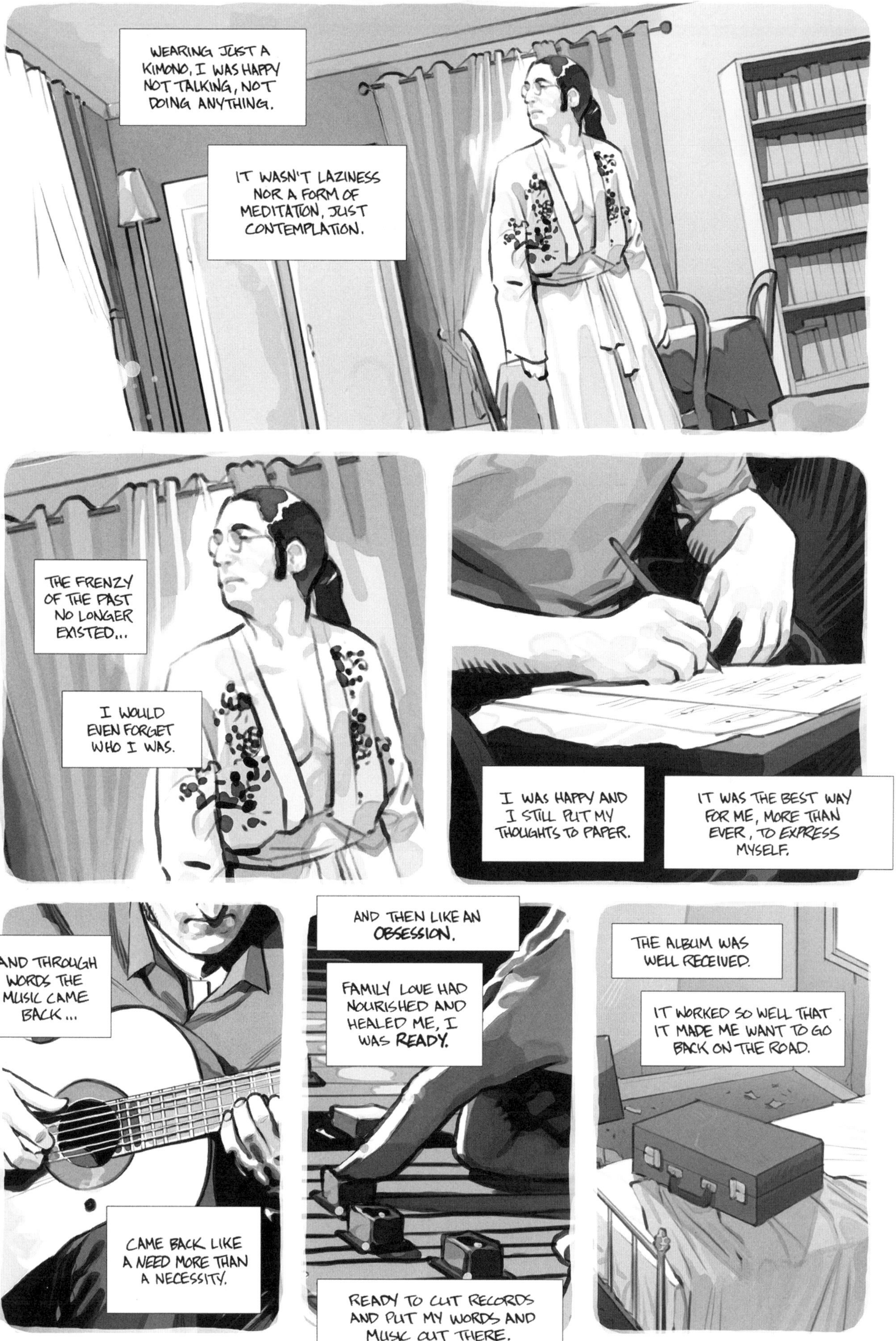
WEARING JUST A KIMONO, I WAS HAPPY NOT TALKING, NOT DOING ANYTHING.
IT WASN'T LAZINESS NOR A FORM OF MEDITATION, JUST CONTEMPLATION.
THE FRENZY OF THE PAST NO LONGER EXISTED...
I WOULD EVEN FORGET WHO I WAS.
I WAS HAPPY AND I STILL PUT MY THOUGHTS TO PAPER.
IT WAS THE BEST WAY FOR ME, MORE THAN EVER, TO *EXPRESS* MYSELF.
AND THROUGH WORDS THE MUSIC CAME BACK...
CAME BACK LIKE A *NEED* MORE THAN A NECESSITY.
AND THEN LIKE AN **OBSESSION**.
FAMILY LOVE HAD NOURISHED AND HEALED ME, I WAS **READY**.
READY TO CUT RECORDS AND PUT MY WORDS AND MUSIC OUT THERE.
THE ALBUM WAS WELL RECEIVED.
IT WORKED SO WELL THAT IT MADE ME WANT TO GO BACK ON THE ROAD.

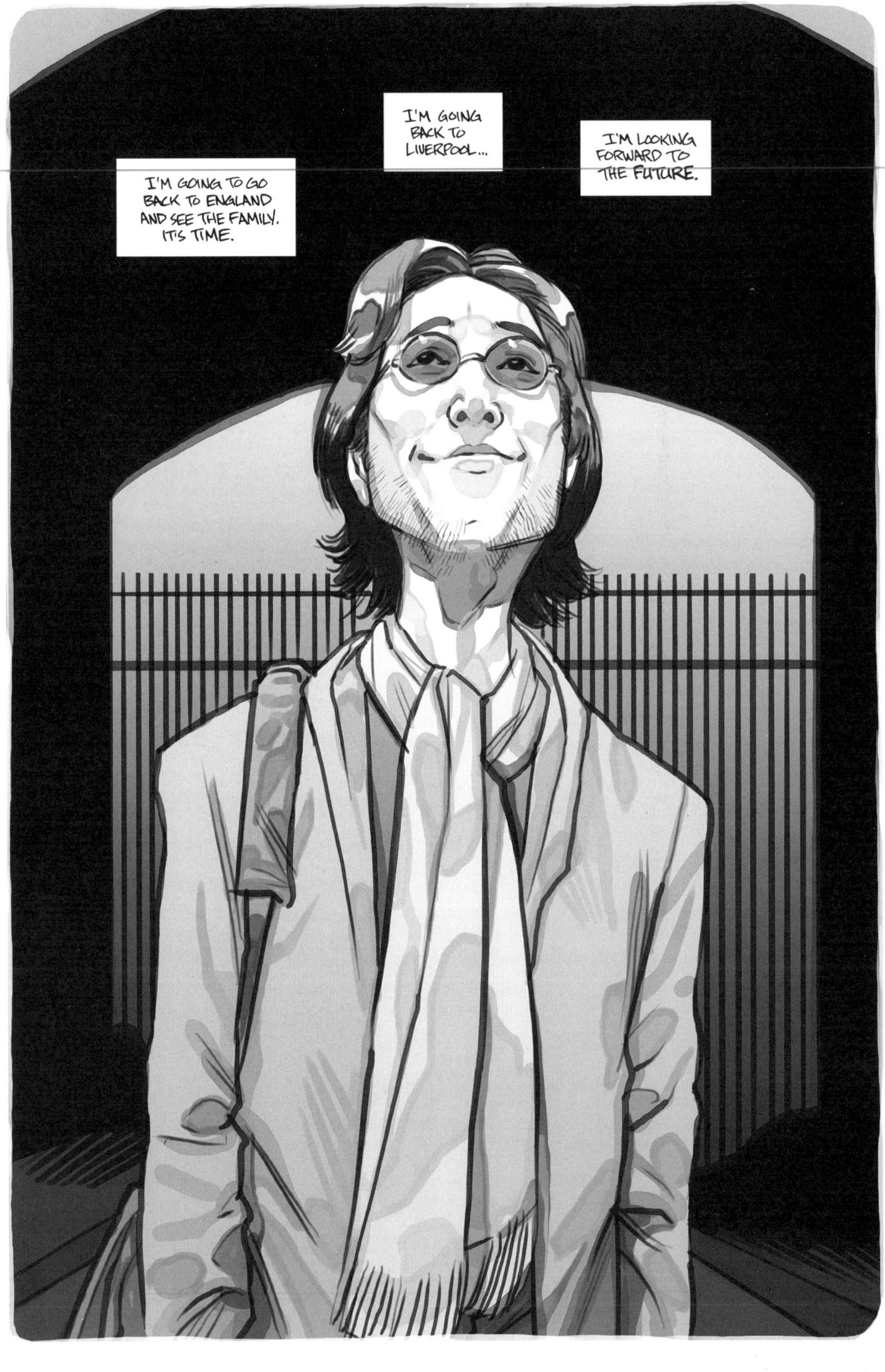
I'M GOING TO GO BACK TO ENGLAND AND SEE THE FAMILY. IT'S TIME.
I'M GOING BACK TO LIVERPOOL...
I'M LOOKING FORWARD TO THE FUTURE.

epilogue
EVEN THOUGH CHAPMAN
WAS A FAN

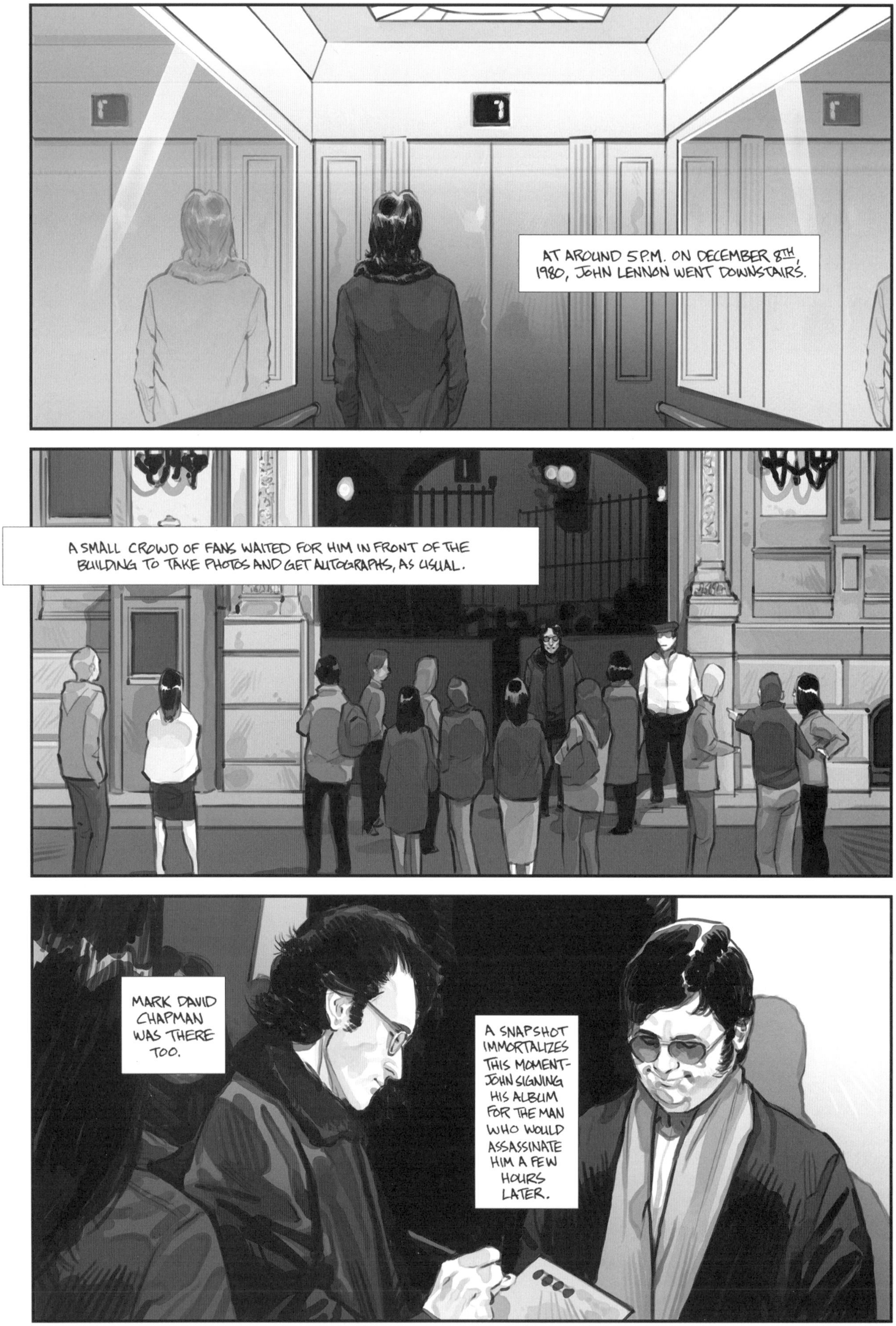
AT AROUND 5 P.M. ON DECEMBER 8TH, 1980, JOHN LENNON WENT DOWNSTAIRS.
A SMALL CROWD OF FANS WAITED FOR HIM IN FRONT OF THE BUILDING TO TAKE PHOTOS AND GET AUTOGRAPHS, AS USUAL.
MARK DAVID CHAPMAN WAS THERE TOO.
A SNAPSHOT IMMORTALIZES THIS MOMENT- JOHN SIGNING HIS ALBUM FOR THE MAN WHO WOULD ASSASSINATE HIM A FEW HOURS LATER.

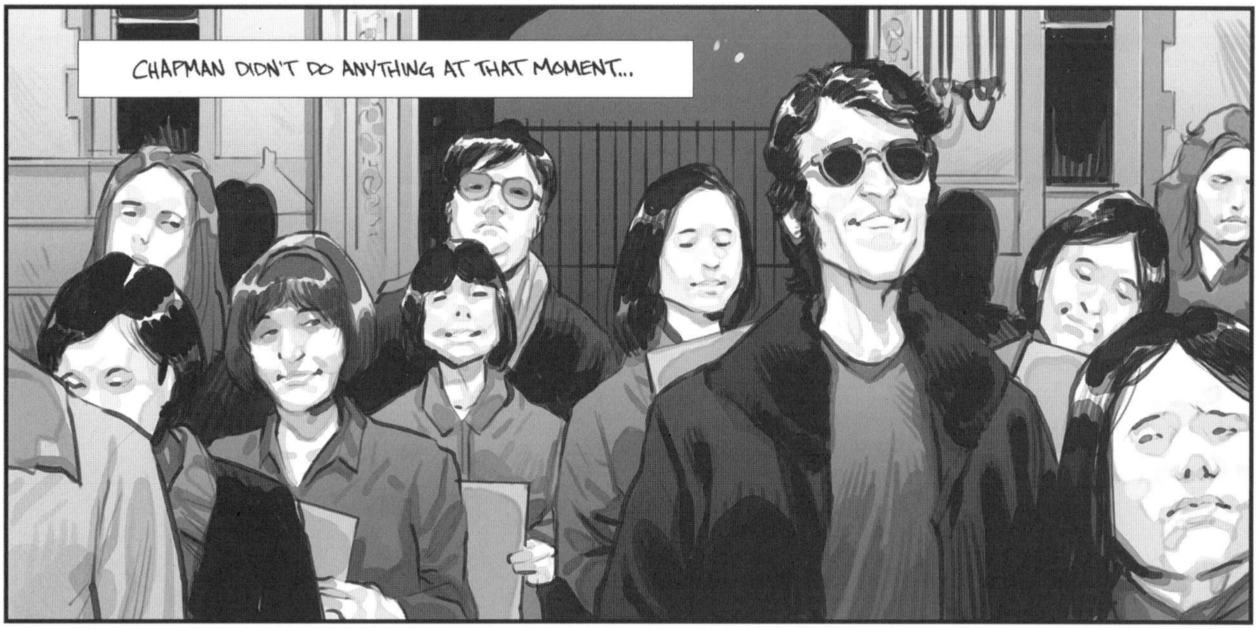
CHAPMAN DIDN'T DO ANYTHING AT THAT MOMENT...

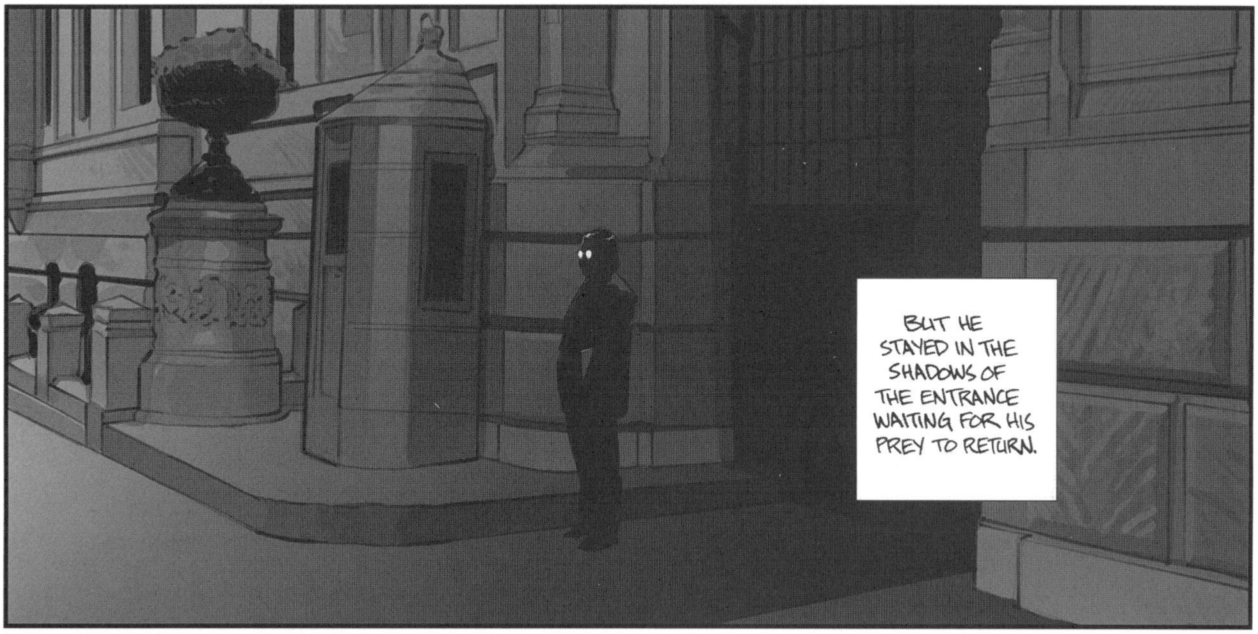
BUT HE STAYED IN THE SHADOWS OF THE ENTRANCE WAITING FOR HIS PREY TO RETURN.

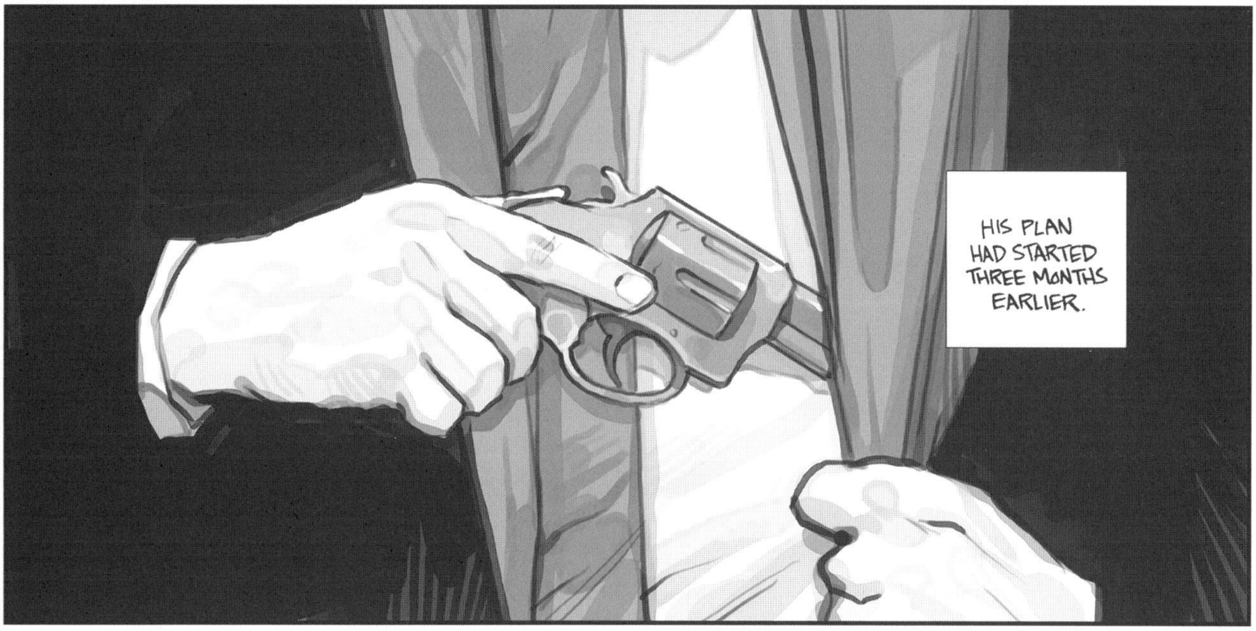
HIS PLAN HAD STARTED THREE MONTHS EARLIER.

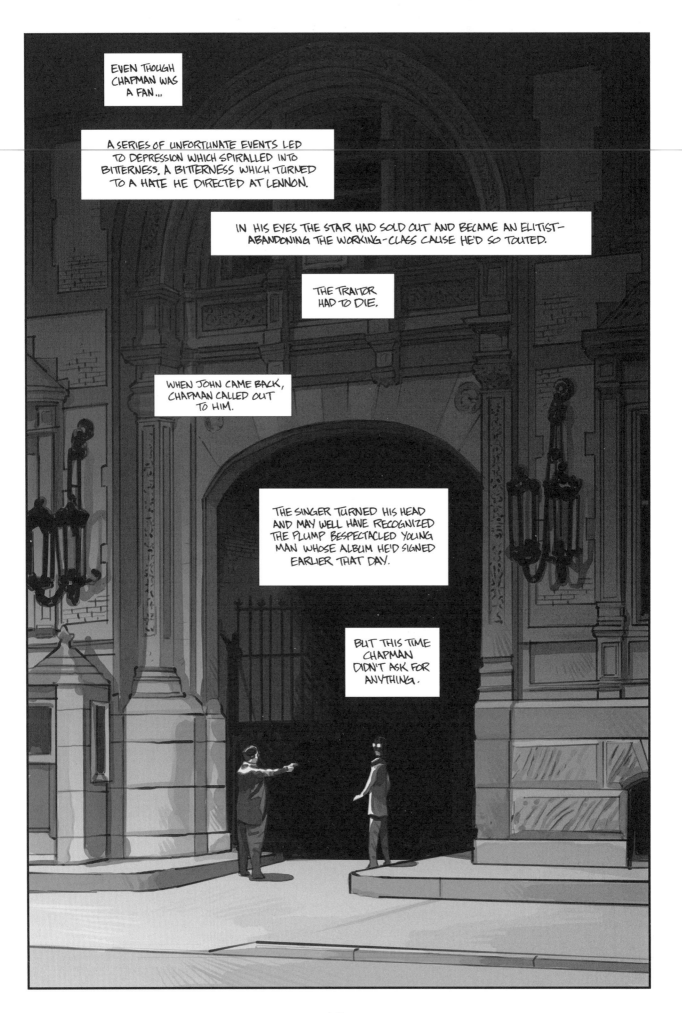

EVEN THOUGH CHAPMAN WAS A FAN...

A SERIES OF UNFORTUNATE EVENTS LED TO DEPRESSION WHICH SPIRALLED INTO BITTERNESS. A BITTERNESS WHICH TURNED TO A HATE HE DIRECTED AT LENNON.

IN HIS EYES THE STAR HAD SOLD OUT AND BECAME AN ELITIST—ABANDONING THE WORKING-CLASS CAUSE HE'D SO TOUTED.

THE TRAITOR HAD TO DIE.

WHEN JOHN CAME BACK, CHAPMAN CALLED OUT TO HIM.

THE SINGER TURNED HIS HEAD AND MAY WELL HAVE RECOGNIZED THE PLUMP BESPECTACLED YOUNG MAN WHOSE ALBUM HE'D SIGNED EARLIER THAT DAY.

BUT THIS TIME CHAPMAN DIDN'T ASK FOR ANYTHING.

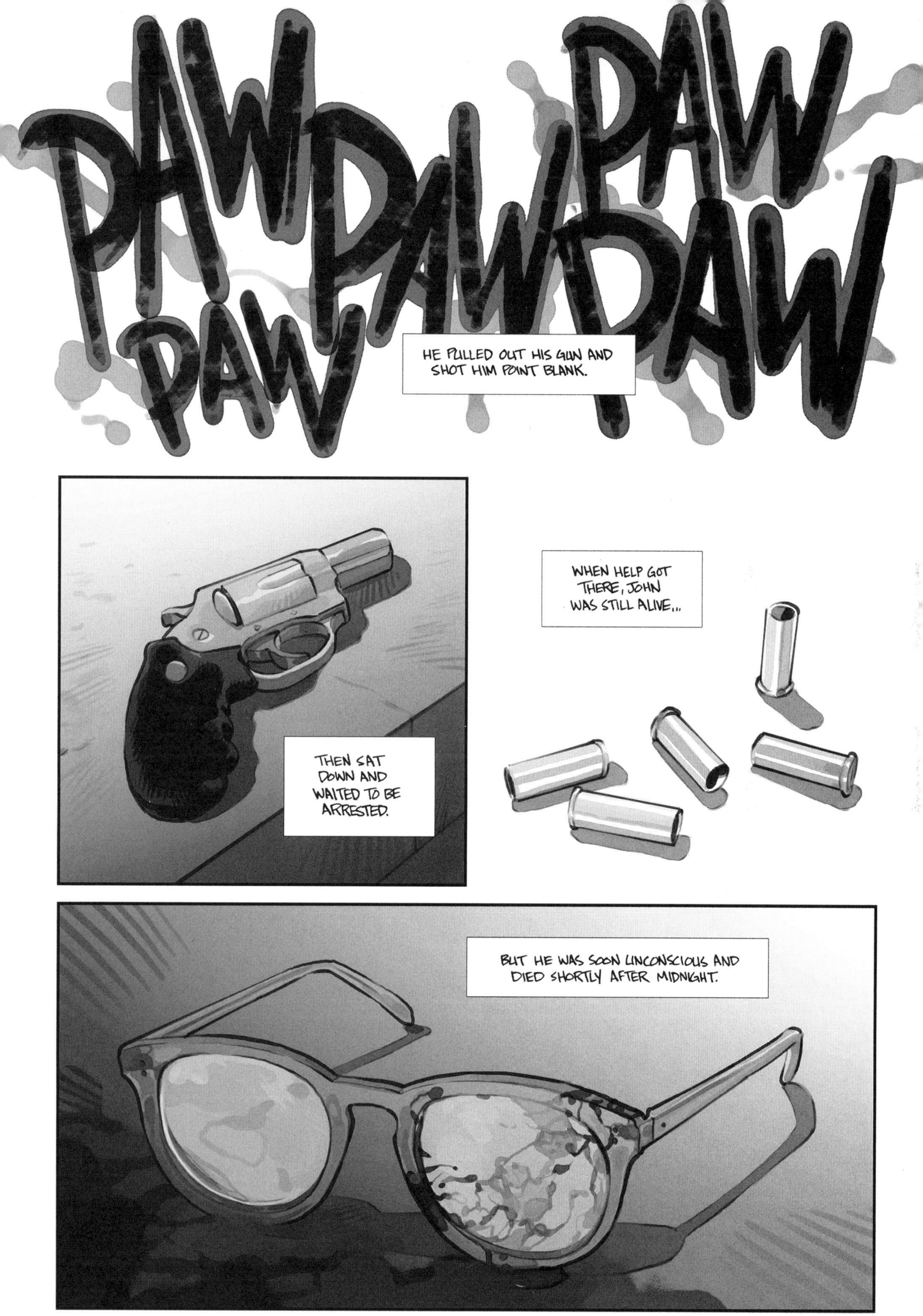
PAW
PAW
PAW
PAW
PAW
HE PULLED OUT HIS GUN AND SHOT HIM POINT BLANK.
THEN SAT DOWN AND WAITED TO BE ARRESTED.
WHEN HELP GOT THERE, JOHN WAS STILL ALIVE...
BUT HE WAS SOON UNCONSCIOUS AND DIED SHORTLY AFTER MIDNIGHT.

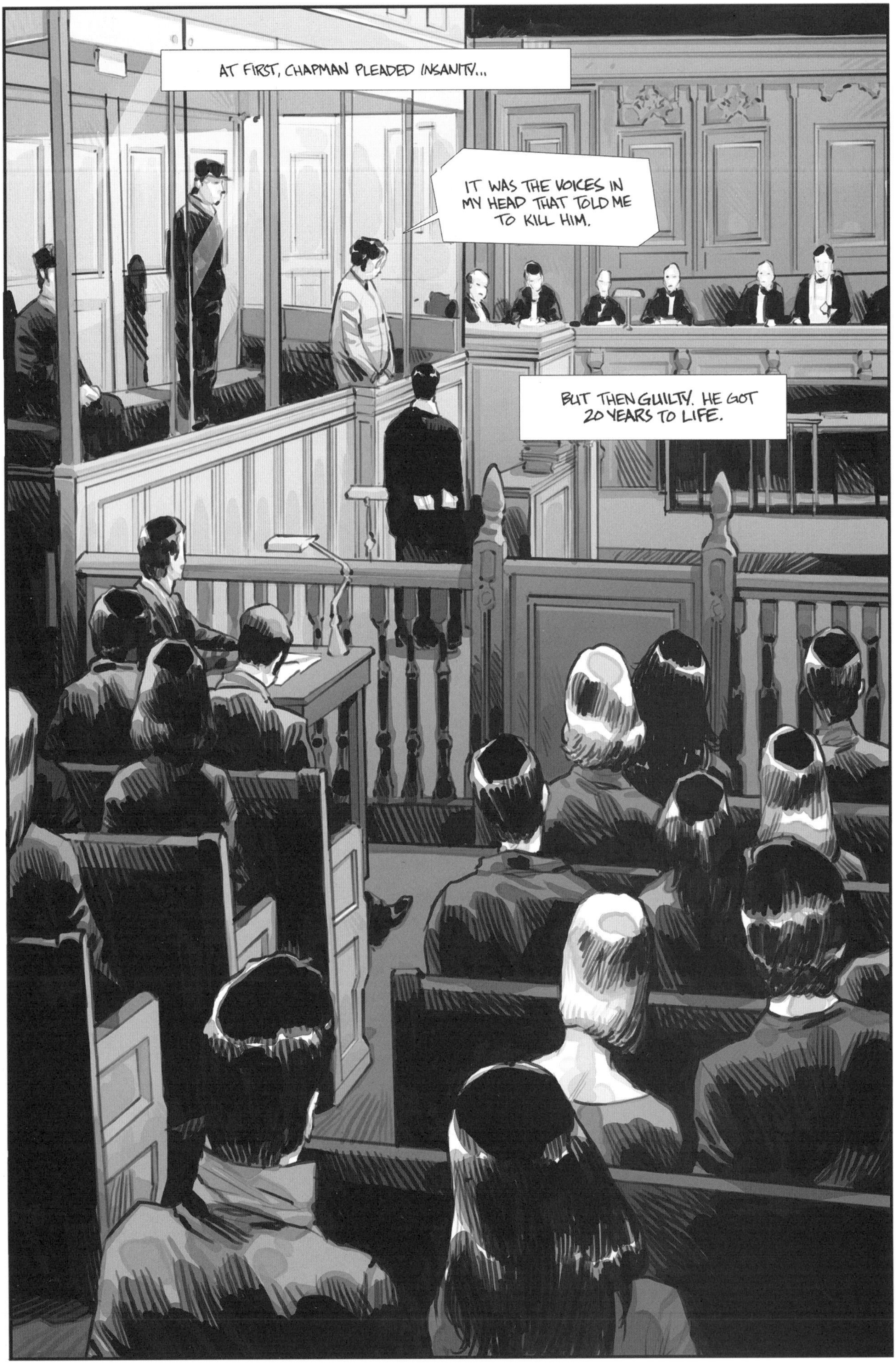
AT FIRST, CHAPMAN PLEADED INSANITY...
IT WAS THE VOICES IN MY HEAD THAT TOLD ME TO KILL HIM.
BUT THEN GUILTY. HE GOT 20 YEARS TO LIFE.

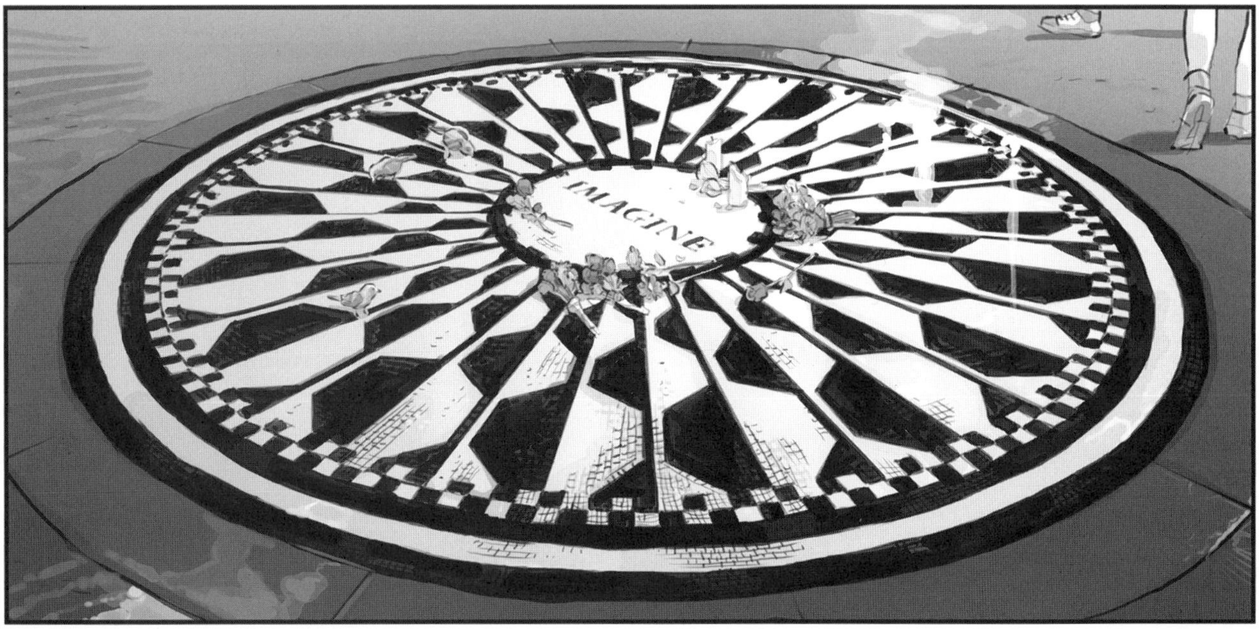
IMAGINE

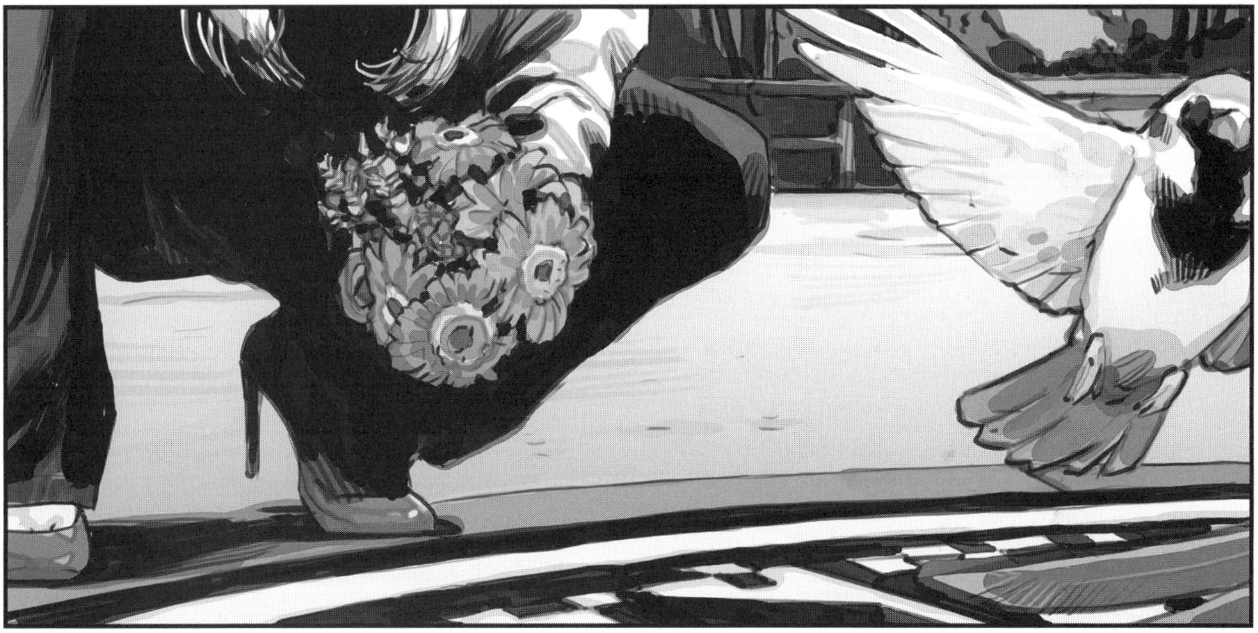

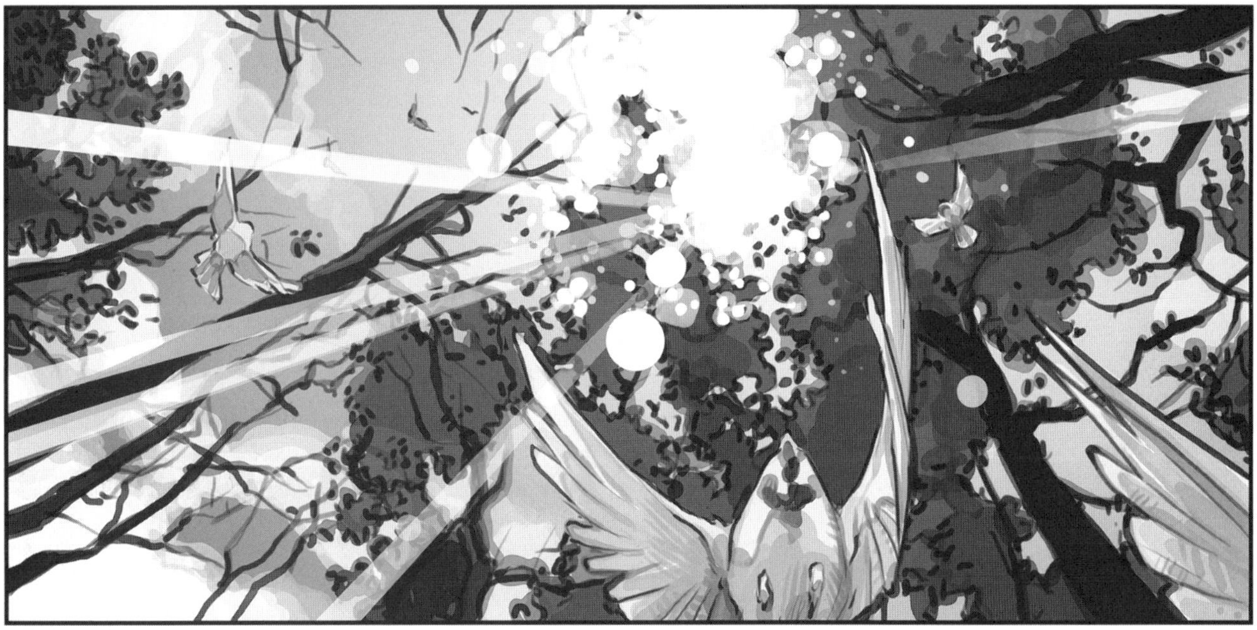

END